W9-AOD-605

Encounters

Encounters

Philosophy of History

after Postmodernism

Ewa Domańska

University Press of Virginia

Charlottesville and London

The University Press of Virginia
© 1998 by the Rector and Visitors of the University of Virginia
All rights reserved
Printed in the United States of America
First published 1998

Library of Congress Cataloging-in-Publication Data

Domańska, Ewa.
    Encounters : philosophy of history after postmodernism / Ewa
Domańska.
        p.   cm.
    Includes bibliographical references and index.
    ISBN 0-8139-1766-2 (cloth : alk. paper). — ISBN 0-8139-1767-0
(pbk. : alk. paper)
    1. History—Philosophy.   I. Title.
D16.8.D635   1998
901—dc21   98-10323
                                                            CIP

Rodzicom
i Marianowi

Contents

Acknowledgments

This book is the result of an intellectual adventure that began in 1993. It would not have come into existence but for the extraordinary support of the professors I interviewed: Hayden White, Hans Kellner, Franklin R. Ankersmit, Georg G. Iggers, Jörn Rüsen, Jerzy Topolski, Arthur C. Danto, Lionel Gossman, Peter Burke, Stephen Bann. They found time to talk with me. I would like to thank each and every one of them not only for their time but also for their tolerance and patience. For me the meetings and interviews were the precious source of unconventional learning. They were also the source of inspiration and unforgettable experiences. I would also like to express my gratitude to Professor Allan Megill and Professor Lynn Hunt for writing the introduction and postscript to my collection of interviews.

I am particularly grateful to my master professor, Jerzy Topolski, and to Professor Ankersmit and Professor Kellner for all their help and advice. It sustained my enthusiasm.

I also want to thank the Institute of History of Adam Mickiewicz University and the Faculty of Arts and Humanities of the University of Groningen for their financial contributions.

Warm thanks are due to Marta Dubrzynska and Bartosz Fasiecki, who carried out my graphical project of the manuscript design. I am also grateful for David Slattery's helpful comments and proofreading and for Paweł Ozdowski's translation. Jonathan Megill helped review the page proofs.

About the Contributors

FRANKLIN R. ANKERSMIT (1945). Professor of
Intellectual History and Historical Theory at the University of Groningen,
The Netherlands

STEPHEN BANN (1942). Professor of Modern Cultural Studies
at the University of Kent, Canterbury, England

PETER BURKE (1937). Reader in Cultural History at the
University of Cambridge and Fellow of Emmanuel College, England

ARTHUR C. DANTO (1924). Professor of Philosophy
at Columbia University, New York, USA

EWA DOMAŃSKA (1963). Assistant Professor of Theory of
History and History of Historiography at Adam Mickiewicz University,
Poznań, Poland

GEORG G. IGGERS (1926). Distinguished Professor
of European Intellectual History at the State University of New York,
Buffalo, USA

LIONEL GOSSMAN (1929). Professor of Romance Languages
and Literature at Princeton University, USA

LYNN HUNT (1945). Annenberg Professor of History at the
University of Pennsylvania, USA

HANS KELLNER (1945). Professor of Rhetoric and Historical
Discourse at the University of Texas, Arlington, USA

ALLAN MEGILL (1947). Professor of History at the University
of Virginia, USA

JÖRN RÜSEN (1938). President, Kulturwissenschaftliches Institut Essen at the Wissenschaftszentrum Nordrhein Westfalen, and Professor for General History and Historical Culture at the University of Witten/Herdecke, Department of Studium Fundamentale

JERZY TOPOLSKI (1928). Professor of Modern History and Methodology of History at Adam Mickiewicz University, Poznań, Poland

HAYDEN WHITE (1928). Professor of the History of Consciousness, the University of California at Santa Cruz, USA

Encounters

Introduction

■ Read *Encounters* for one simple reason: the interviews offer the best meditation that you are likely to find on the state of historiography at the end of the twentieth century. The account does not come in the form of a summary of current research results or a survey of preferred methods, for at the present moment one cannot plausibly claim that a single set of concerns constitutes history's "backbone," nor can one claim that there exists a single, authoritative set of methods for the study of the past. Consequently, those who think seriously about historiography find themselves driven beyond the limits of the historical discipline to a metadisciplinary level. The historians and theorists represented here raise issues that are rooted as much outside the discipline as within it. In so doing they cast light not only on history-writing as it is done today but also on aspects of our cultural condition generally.

It was once plausible to think of historiography as a unified enterprise. In the nineteenth century the belief that particular histories would ultimately aggregate into an account of the totality of human history was endemic in—indeed, largely definitive of—professional historiography. In the twentieth century that belief faded, but its place was taken by belief in the unity of the historical profession itself, held together by a common method. At the end of the twentieth century, belief in a single authorized historical method is also fading. Today, much of the most interesting historical writing investigates areas of life not previously investigated, or approaches the past in new ways, or does both of these things. In short, it breaks out from the confines of a single story or a single method.

As long ago as 1957, Leonard Krieger suggested that the emergence of such fields as African history and intellectual history showed "an awareness of a historical world outside the familiar sphere of the politics of western civilization," and that such fields marked a "burgeoning of history . . . beyond the capacity of the historian to organize it."[1] Since the 1950s it has become even more difficult to "organize" history. Characteristically, surveys of the discipline now take the form of compilations of essays by many authors: each author deals with a particular problem or subfield in relative separation from the whole.[2] The most widely noticed recent study of a national tradition of historiography, Peter Novick's *That Noble Dream: The "Objectivity Question" and the American Historical Profession*, concludes that the discipline is now multicentered and fragmented.[3] The multicenteredness and fragmentation become even more striking when one looks beyond the historical discipline to other fields that deal with the past, such as art history and literary studies.

If one is to make sense of the study of the past today, both history and theory are required. The interviewer, Ewa Domańska, began her university studies in Poznań in 1982; thus, at the same time that she was learning history, she lived through the slow collapse of the Polish Communist state. There was much that needed reinterpretation, in both past and present. Domańska found her way to "postmodern" theory in general and to "postmodern" theory of history in particular. One result is the present book. Domańska's interviewees have a long experience with historiography, and they also have something much rarer—a broad theoretical perspective that gives them an awareness of issues going far beyond particular historical fields. In consequence, they are able to offer us insight into some of the important peculiarities—the disputed questions and paradoxes—of historiography today.

The peculiarities arise in part from developments internal to the discipline. For example, vast numbers of historical books and articles are produced annually. The existence of a huge historical literature makes it ever more difficult for the individual historian to "stand out"—to satisfy the discipline's demand that the historian produce knowledge that is both interesting and new. There is thus an incentive to find significance in topics that most historians previously thought were without significance, or at least without *historical* significance. Thus, whole new fields devoted to such topics as everyday life (*Alltagsgeschichte*) and gender have emerged. But, as the gender topic suggests, the disciplinary drive for originality explains only in part the increasingly variegated character of history. Also important is the wider social and cultural context. We live, it seems, within the "postmodern condition," in which (to use Jean-François Lyotard's formulation) there is no "grand narrative," no single, authoritative, overarching story that would allow us to make sense of the world in which we live.[4] Absence of grand narrative changes the writing of history, by calling into doubt the possibility of its unification.

No one book can hope to give access to the vast territory of historiography today, but this book gives us at least a sense of what lies behind some of the most interesting and challenging work. The interviewees do not all adhere to the same position, but they do agree on a problematic—that is, they agree about which issues are important. Most strikingly, they agree that issues of art and aesthetic theory are important. Beyond that basic agreement, disagreements pile up. Some of the interviewees are themselves strongly inclined to the aesthetic dimension (White, Kellner, Ankersmit, Bann, Danto), while others voice reservations (Iggers, Topolski, Rüsen). For a third group (Gossman, Burke) the aesthetic dimension is not so central a preoccupation, but it is nonetheless present in the background to their work.

The prominent role that aesthetics plays in the interviews results from no *parti pris* on the part of the interviewer. True, Domańska comes to her interlocutors with a particular set of concerns that she wishes to see addressed, but she is well informed about what is going on in historical theory and her concerns are indeed important in that domain. As for the interviewees, their aesthetic concern arises for reasons related both to a certain internal dynamic in the field of historical theory and to the present state of historical research and writing.

Some readers will be tempted to see the interviews as enacting a conflict between "modernist" and "postmodernist" tendencies in present-day historiography. Such a reading does not strike me as entirely satisfactory: among other things, history as a discipline has never been very "modernist," and the term "postmodernist" is highly disputed. The central issue, it seems to me, is not "modernism" versus "postmodernism," but rather the question of the relation between the aesthetic dimension of history-writing and concerns that we might call "scientific" and "philosophical."

By a "scientific" concern, I mean a concern with the *validity* of the historical account—that is, with its truth or falsity. Historians not only describe and explain things in the past; they also engage in arguments intended to establish that the descriptions and explanations that they offer

4   are true. There is some tension between the argumentative or justificatory task and the spirit of aesthetic production: truth and beauty do not always coincide. By a "philosophical" concern, I mean a concern with the *significance* of the historical account—that is, with its meaning for us, now. The historian's interpretive task has a fundamentally moral bent, since the meaning of a historical account for us, now, is really a matter of its implications for present choices and actions.[5]

The interviews are concerned, then, not with the aesthetic dimension as such but with the relations between art, validity, and significance. Or, to put the matter more strikingly, one might say that they are concerned with the relations, in the researching and writing of history, between beauty, truth, and goodness. Some of the interviewees are closer to one concern and some to another, but they all agree that art, validity, and significance are crucial concerns—perhaps *the* crucial concerns—in our understanding of history today.

The person most closely associated with this configuration of concerns is the first of the interviewees, Hayden White. His controversial *Metahistory: The Historical Imagination in Nineteenth-Century Europe* has had an immense impact on current thinking about historiography.[6] Not surprisingly, White is by far the most widely mentioned figure in the interviews (232 mentions), followed by Michel Foucault (80), Richard Rorty (46), Jacques Derrida (36), Frank Ankersmit (36), and Roland Barthes (34). It is not that the interviewees agree with Hayden White on all points, but they do agree that his work is fundamental for current thinking about historiography. The basis of White's impact is that at an early stage—the mid-1960s—he intuited an aesthetic turn in our thinking about historiography that other thoughtful observers took another decade and more to see. White's work has something of the same status in philosophy of history today that Carl Hempel's "The Function of General Laws in History" (1942) had in the period 1945–65; that is, it serves to define the issues that are up for discussion.[7]

Indeed, the present volume might be seen as almost a *Festschrift* for Hayden White: it certainly manifests his overwhelming presence in philosophy of history as it is pursued today. It is thus worth reflecting on how White arrived at the heterodox view of history articulated in *Metahistory* and elsewhere. One thing that needs to be noted is the antithetical relation between the aesthetic turn and most Marxian or neo-Marxian conceptions of history. More broadly: commitment to any "grand narrative" seems antithetical to the aesthetic turn. R. G. Collingwood suggests something of the reason for this when, in *The Idea of History*, he points out that "purely imaginary worlds cannot clash and need not agree; each is a world to itself." Thus different fictions are under little if any pressure to harmonize. Collingwood maintains that, in contrast, "there is only one historical world."[8] As already noted, since Collingwood's time, history has burgeoned. Simultaneously, in its multiplicity it has come to have more in common with the aesthetic project.

One reason for White's being able to latch onto the aesthetic dimension is that he never committed himself to the ready-made Marxian grand narrative or to any substitute for that narrative. He claims in his interview that he always regarded himself as "a kind of Marxist," but he was a peculiar Marxist in that he was other things as well: "I regarded Marx as one of the great philosophers of history, one among many." White's social and geographic origins may have helped to inoculate him against too single-minded an attraction to orthodoxy. He was born in 1928 in Martin, Tennessee, a town of three thousand people in an impoverished part of that state. In 1936, the family went to Detroit, driven out when the local cotton gin burned down. His father found work in the automobile factories, where White also worked as a high-school student. The family moved back and forth between city and country throughout White's childhood, and White in fact graduated from high school in Fulton, Kentucky, not far from Martin. He was thus rooted in both the rural "middle South" and industrial Detroit. Emerging into adulthood in the post–World War II years, he found himself in a world full of exciting possibilities of a sort he could hardly have dreamed of before the war. Was White's refusal of any view of History with a capital *H* an effect of his disjunctive and discontinuous childhood and youth? It is impossible to know; all we can know is that there is an affinity between his experience and his theoretical position.

Another relevant fact about White is that he was exposed early on to the notion that the highest goal of historical study is to give its students a broad grasp of human culture. Like Arthur Danto, White studied at Wayne University, which was Detroit's city university, under a charismatic teacher, William Bossenbrook, a man who evidently made it his calling to educate in the broadest possible way his heavily lower-class and immigrant-offspring students.[9] When White undertook graduate work at the University of Michigan, a few miles away, he chose to study the one institution in European culture that tried to be universal—the medieval papacy. When he turned later to the study of historiography, he focused on the great historians and philosophers of history of the nineteenth century, who aimed to embrace the entire social and political world. White makes it clear why he

6   was attracted to these writers when, at the end of *Metahistory*, he expresses the hope that "historical consciousness will stand open to the reestablishment of its links with the great poetic, scientific, and philosophical concerns which inspired the classic practitioners and theorists of its golden age in the nineteenth century."[10]

One can disagree with White's conclusions at various levels, but one cannot deny the importance of the questions he asks. Although he was committed from the beginning to the idea that history ought to tell stories making *some* claim to universality, he was inherently a pluralist, never committed to any single grand narrative. With his broadly cultural conception of history, he was open, atypically for most historians, to issues of a theoretical sort. In consequence, he came early to an intuition of the aesthetic dimension and the issues that it raises.[11]

Readers should view the rest of the interviews as a set of attempts to come to grips with—to develop and to question—White's reflections. Two of the interviewees, Hans Kellner and Frank Ankersmit, have strong affinities with White. *Hans Kellner* has been connected with White since the 1960s. Like all the interviewees, Kellner denies the notion that specialized studies of history can be "tallied up" into a single History; he identifies that which cannot be tallied up as "an aesthetic object." His most interesting line of thought has to do with the "tacit anxieties" that mark the professional historian. Much of his work has been concerned with unearthing and commenting on historians' anxieties, the better to judge and appreciate the works they have written. As he puts it, "history to me is the books that people write and call histories." The point is not as trivially self-evident as it seems, since people ranging from politicians to the most eminent literary critics are inclined to talk about "history" without having in mind even a single historical work.

Frank Ankersmit came to White's work only in the second half of the 1980s. His first substantial contribution to historical theory, *Narrative Logic*, was not indebted to White; it was in fact inspired by the holistic ontology of Leibniz.[12] Its most striking and controversial claim is its assertion that although particular historical statements can be judged to be referentially either true or false, the same is not true of the historical account as a whole (which he calls the "narrative substance"). Subsequently, Ankersmit suggested that narrative substances are "substitutes or replacements of past reality itself in the way that the work of art according to Gombrich and Danto is a substitute for something in reality." Among other things, Ankersmit's view implies that on the level of historical writing there is "no longer any room for epistemological questions," since historians are not offering representations of the past but substitutes for it, just as a work of art is not a representation of reality but one part of reality that serves as a substitute for another part. In his most recent work, Ankersmit has come to argue for the importance of "historical experience," which in his view is something that cannot be adequately captured in language. At the same time, he is persuaded of the "rational" character of the historical discipline, and is deeply impressed by "the practical intelligence displayed by historians as a research community."

The three interviewees who follow, Georg Iggers, Jerzy Topolski, and Jörn Rüsen, all have reservations about the aesthetic perspective and about "postmodernism." At the same time, they acknowledge the force and topicality of the issues that White raises. *Georg Iggers* sees himself as offering an assessment of White and Ankersmit from a more orthodox point of view, although he is perhaps not so far from them as he thinks. He agrees with them on the matter of grand narrative. While denying that history-writing is in crisis, he contends that "the concept of history as a unified process" is in crisis, and that "we are living in an age which is no longer convinced that history follows a clear course."

Jerzy Topolski was educated in Poland after World War II, under the Communist regime. Not surprisingly, much of his work involved an engagement and confrontation with the Marxian grand narrative, historical materialism. In the wake of Marxism's collapse, he sees "postmodernism" as playing a "revitalizing role." He warns, however, that "the adoption of the most radical requirements of postmodernism" would lead to "the destruction of the kind of historiography which has been dominant for centuries," and he doubts that historians will accept a view that would make it impossible for them to write history as it has been conventionally understood. Moreover, against relativism, he emphasizes the conception of truth, which in his view is also a moral category. Thus he subordinates the aesthetic dimension to the measuring rods of validity and of significance. As for the "new philosophy of history," which he sees as embracing both narrativist and "postmodernist" concerns, Topolski regards it as useful in clarifying to historians what they do and in directing their self-reflection along new paths.

Jörn Rüsen, too, has reservations about a postmodern perspective. A major concern on his part is "to bridge the dichotomy between narrativism on the one hand and scientific rationality on the other." As a progressive German who came to maturity in the 1950s and 1960s, he is deeply aware of the challenge that the Holocaust poses to historical thinking and historical culture. How does one make sense of a history that includes the Holocaust? What meaning does such a history have? Historians, Rüsen suggests, do not make meaning but only translate it, and he calls for more investigation of the religious life of people as a way of getting at the sources of meaning. He is also deeply concerned with the question of validity. He regrets the "schizophrenia" that he finds in present-day theory of history, where there is a gulf between, on the one hand, an intense awareness of language, rhetoric, and narrative and, on the other, a recognition of the techniques of historical research. He calls for more investigation into the relationships between the cognitive, the political, and the aesthetic dimensions of historiography.

The last four interviewees, Arthur Danto, Lionel Gossman, Peter Burke, and Stephen Bann, come to history from perspectives strongly marked by art and art criticism—or, in Gossman's case, by literature and literary criticism. *Arthur Danto* wanted to be a professional artist. Even as a young professor of philosophy at Columbia University he continued to exhibit his work in the galleries, until finally deciding that he could do art or philosophy, but not both. His experience of the art world, especially the shock of Andy Warhol's Brillo boxes (1962), made him sensitive to historical change in art and to the question of what makes a work of art a work of art. He regards the present era as one of "deep pluralism," which postmodern art "internalizes into itself." In philosophy he remains a modernist. He is a narrative realist, contending against White that "there really are objective organizations of events in history." He maintains that "aesthetics is really inseparable from science," so that the old notion of a "scientific history" purged of all aesthetic considerations amounts, in his view, to a history void of human interest.

As a student at the University of Glasgow just after World War II, the literary and cultural historian *Lionel Gossman* was eager to find "meaning" in history, but he did not find it in the history he was taught, which "seemed void of any philosophical self-consciousness." Instead, he studied French and German literature, fell under the spell of Lukács, and as a result became connected to the German classicist and neohumanist tradition of *Bildung*. He admits to "no consistent theoretical position," and has instead found himself acknowledging the illuminating capacity of such incompatible philosophical positions as existentialism and positivism. Not surprisingly, with his pluralist perspective he is not interested in "the study of History with a capital H"; rather, he is attracted by the enriching discipline "of researching specific historical questions and weighing evidence and arguments." Thus he is heavily concerned with validity as well as with significance—with *Wissenschaft* as well as with *Bildung*. As I noted earlier, an aesthetic concern is less central to him: his attitude toward history, he suggests, is more political and ethical than aesthetic.

The cultural historian *Peter Burke* perhaps least fits the mold of the present collection. True, as a student at Oxford, Burke took as his special subject the art of the Italian Renaissance. But he quickly got beyond any specific concern with art and aesthetics, and he has little interest in the theoretical problem of the relations between art, validity, and significance. Instead, he comes across in his interview as an immensely well-informed practitioner of cultural history. He comments on the relations among cultural history, history from below, historical anthropology, intellectual history, and social history generally. He is fascinated by "postmodernism" but feels "somewhat detached" from it, in large measure because he wants to be able to talk not only about "imaginative freedom" but also about "social constraints."

With the critic *Stephen Bann* we return to a primarily aesthetic focus. Bann has long been involved with the artistic avant-garde. He finds that there is a close relationship between art and history, although "what is happening in the two domains is not identical." Breaching disciplinary boundaries, Bann has become interested in historical representation as it is carried out in historical painting, historical novels, and museums, as well as in history books, and in his interview he has much to say about divergent ways of representing the past.

One of the demands of an academic discipline is the push to "make it new." The search for knowledge is a search for new knowledge, as distinguished from treading water or burnishing pieties. The work that most often strikes the writer of this introduction as interesting is work that goes beyond, or at least pushes against the boundaries of, accepted modes: work that introduces subject matters and approaches not seen before; that contributes to another discipline or field of learning; that acknowledges its own fictive dimension; that succeeds in being historical and theoretical at the same time.

Encounters addresses at least some of these possibilities. It does so because the people whom Domańska has chosen to question are deeply aware both of the historiographical tradition and of the wider intellectual and practical world within which the tradition exists. Present in their thoughts is a sense of the excitement and interest of experimentation. Present, too, is a sense of the continuing importance of the issues of validity and significance. Collingwood's claim that there is "only one historical world" is largely correct as an observation on an earlier, more restricted historiography, in which historians agreed fundamentally about what was important in the world and what was not. When that is not the case, we tend to become much more aware of how deeply suppositional history-writing is. In this sense it becomes more like art, but it is an art put forward with claims to factual truth.

In his essay "On the Lame," Michel de Montaigne writes that "I love terms which soften and tone down the rashness of what we put forward, terms such as "perhaps," "somewhat," "they say," "I think.". . . Anyone who wishes to be cured of ignorance must first admit to it . . . amazement is the foundation of all philosophy; inquiry, its way of advancing; and ignorance is its end."[13] But the ignorance that is the end of inquiry is not a simple "I do not know and cannot hope to know." It is not a breaking off from thought. Rather, in its consciousness of how much cannot be known precisely, it ends up knowing more. The skeptical undertone that one detects in parts of this book ought to be seen, I suggest, as a moment in knowledge-seeking.

The interviews give us some sense of what to look for in current historiography. Of course, a compelling reason to read history is the obvious one of curiosity about some particular part of the past. But the interviews offer a deeper set of reasons, directed to the project of history-writing in general. They identify issues more than they do answers—concerning the relation of history to its modes of presentation, concerning the relation (or not) of particular works of history to some larger notion of History in general, and concerning the personal and civic function of history. The identifying of such issues is not a negligible thing, and will perhaps help us to think more clearly about history as a contribution to knowledge and to life.

NOTES

1. Leonard Krieger, "The Horizons of History," *American Historical Review* 63 (1957): 62–74, at 62, 63; repr. in Krieger, *Ideas and Events: Professing History*, edited by M. L. Brick, with an introduction by Michael Ermarth. Chicago: Univ. of Chicago Press, 1992, 145–58.

2. For example, see *Historical Studies Today*, edited by Felix Gilbert and Stephen R. Graubard. New York: Norton, 1972, and *The Past Before Us: Contemporary Historical Writing in the United States*, edited by Michael Kammen. Ithaca: Cornell Univ. Press, 1980.

3. Peter Novick, *That Noble Dream: The "Objectivity Question" and the American Historical Profession*. New York: Cambridge Univ. Press, 1988, 413–629.

4. Jean-François Lyotard, *The Postmodern Condition: A Report on Knowledge*, translated by Geoff Bennington and Brian Massumi, foreword by Fredric Jameson. Minneapolis: Univ. of Minnesota Press, 1984.

5. I imply, here, four historiographical tasks: "description," explanation, justification, and interpretation. See Allan Megill, "Recounting the Past: 'Description,' Explanation, and Narrative in Historiography." *American Historical Review* 94 (1989): 627–53.

6. Hayden V. White, *Metahistory: The Historical Imagination in Nineteenth-Century Europe*. Baltimore: Johns Hopkins Univ. Press, 1973.

7. Carl G. Hempel, "The Function of General Laws in History," in *Theories of History*, edited by Patrick Gardiner. New York: The Free Press, 1959, 344–56.

8. R. G. Collingwood, *The Idea of History*. Oxford: Oxford Univ. Press, 1994: 246 [original edition, 1946].

9. White edited a *Festschrift* for Bossenbrook: *The Uses of History: Essays in Intellectual and Social History*. Detroit: Wayne State Univ. Press, 1968. See also Danto's acknowledgement of Bossenbrook's impact on him in the preface to his *Analytical Philosophy of History*. Cambridge: Cambridge Univ. Press, 1965, xvi, and in his interview here. It is an interesting and little noted fact that the two most original American philosophers of history both studied under the same obscure scholar.

10. White, *Metahistory*, 434.

11. In this regard, Carlo Ginzburg's attempt to interpret White's intellectual development as a consequence of his exposure "to Italian philosophical neoidealism," and to show affinities between White's development and the work of the fascist philosopher Giovanni Gentile, seems to me mistaken, for, among other things, Ginzburg entirely omits the American context within which White developed his ideas (Carlo Ginzburg, "Just One Witness," in *Probing the Limits of Representation: Nazism and the "Final Solution,"* edited by Saul Friedlander. Cambridge: Harvard Univ. Press, 1992, 82–96, especially 89–92).

12. Franklin R. Ankersmit, *Narrative Logic: A Semantic Analysis of the Historian's Language*. The Hague: Nijhoff, 1983.

13. Michel de Montaigne, *The Complete Essays*, translated by M. A. Screech. London: Penguin, 1991, bk. 3, essay 2, "On the Lame," 1165.

SELECTED WRITINGS

Prophets of Extremity: Nietzsche, Heidegger, Foucault, Derrida. Berkeley: Univ. of California Press, 1985.
The Rhetoric of the Human Sciences: Language and Argument in Scholarship and

12

Public Affairs, co-editor, with John S. Nelson and Donald N. McCloskey. Madison: Univ. of Wisconsin Press, 1987.

Rethinking Objectivity, editor, Durham: Duke Univ. Press, 1994.

"Aesthetic Theory and Historical Consciousness in the Eighteenth Century." *History and Theory* 17 (1978): 29–62.

"The Reception of Foucault by Historians." *Journal of the History of Ideas* 48 (1987): 117–41.

"Recounting the Past: 'Description,' Explanation, and Narrative in Historiography." *American Historical Review* 94 (1989): 627–53.

"Jörn Rüsen's Theory of Historiography between Modernism and Rhetoric of Inquiry." *History and Theory* 33 (1994): 39–60.

"'Grand Narrative' and the Discipline of History," in *A New Philosophy of History*, ed. Frank Ankersmit and Hans Kellner, 151–73, 262–71. Chicago: Univ. of Chicago Press, 1995.

"Historicizing Nietzsche? Paradoxes and Lessons of a Hard Case." *Journal of Modern History* 68 (1996): 114–52.

"Why Was There a Crisis of Historicism?" *History and Theory* 36 (1997): 416–29.

Hayden White

The past is a place of fantasy.

First, I would like to ask you what were your main interests when you were studying?

■ I was born in 1928, so I am 65, in the South of the United States. My parents were working-class people who during the Great Depression made their way to Detroit, Michigan, for work and I went to school there. I went to the local city public university—Wayne State University in Detroit, Michigan. I graduated in 1951. I was in the U.S. Navy in the late 1940s. Later, I went to the University of Michigan, which is the state university. I studied medieval history. I received my doctorate from the University of Michigan in 1955. My thesis was on Saint Bernard of Clairvaux and the papal schism of 1130. I studied twelfth-century church history and the relationship between bureaucratic reorganization of the papacy in Rome and reform of the church led by figures like Saint Bernard of Clairvaux and the mystic reformers of the twelfth century. Then I taught at Wayne State University, the University of Rochester in New York, University of California, Los Angeles, Wesleyan University, Connecticut, and then I went to the University of California at Santa Cruz, where I have been for the last fifteen years. My first publications in philosophy of history were published in Italy. I published materials from my thesis—medieval history—and taught medieval history and cultural history as a young professor.

The 1960s were a time of great expansion of universities in the

I studied medieval history.

United States, and I was very fortunate to enter the profession of scholarship at that time because they were very exciting years. There were student protests and reform of the curriculum in which I participated. I found it a very exciting time, because it seems to me that there are very few times when educational institutions can be reformed; they tend to be very conservative, and you can only introduce new topics during times of instability and crisis. I have always been interested in why people study the past, rather than studying the past myself. That is to say, it struck me as very strange, looked at from a kind of anthropological standpoint. It is very strange that a society would have professional people studying the past. Why should the state, the society, or community pay people to study the past? What can you learn from your study of the past? Why are people fascinated by it? Many cultures do not have that. Why does the West produce such professions?

History was not taught at the universities until the early nineteenth century. History was not a subject for study in the university. There was no history faculty. They had faculties of antiquities who studied the ancient, biblical world, but they did not have historians. History was something that anyone could write. You did not have to write a thesis and get a license to do it.

So, this raises the question for me: what is the social function of the study of the past? What is the function of ideology and propaganda? Here you have a teaching based upon and claiming it is an authority because it knows something about the past. That strikes me as a very strange thing. So I began increasingly to write on these matters.

About 1965 I was asked by the editors of the journal *History and Theory* to write a piece on the social or cultural function of history so I wrote an essay called "The Burden of History." I gave it as a lecture first at Wesleyan University. It did not seem to me to be an especially original piece, but a lot of people liked it and many people take it as my first important piece. But for me it is just another survey of attitudes toward history. That article, "The Burden of History," was what led me also to write *Metahistory*, because someone read the article and wrote to me: "Would you like to write a small book on this topic, on historical thought in the nineteenth century?" and I wrote this small book no one liked. The editor said: "Make it longer because they did not want a survey." So I wrote *Metahistory*. *Metahistory* is something his-

> I have always been interested in why people study the past, rather than studying the past myself.

torians don't like. But some people in other disciplines do, philosophers and literary critics. Because what it does, or pretends to do, is to deconstruct a mythology, the so-called science of history.

Was *Metahistory* a kind of rebellion against positivism?

Yes, that is right, exactly, it is against positivism, against a positivistic notion of history. The discipline of history is systemically antitheoretical. Historians think of themselves as being empirical, and they are, but they are not philosophically empirical. They are empirical in a commonsense way—in an ordinary, everyday way. That is why Marxism in the United States was always regarded as something that was not really genuinely historical because it had theory. And Marxism, of course, was always criticizing bourgeois historians because they had no theory.

We can speak about the narrativist philosophy of history, but it is very hard to speak about the applications of this theory. We can imagine that, for example, Foucault or some historians connected with the *mentalité* paradigm as represented by Le Roy Ladurie, Ginzburg, they are in this trend, but no one writes historical books using the directives that arose from the narrativist philosophy of history.

That is true, but the thesis about the narrative conception of history is an analytical finding, it's not a prescription. It is not something that lays down rules about how to write, any more than a literary critic who studies the novel tells one how to write a novel. The theory of history as a narrative is not prescribing rules; I mean, it is reflective and analytical; it is a reflection on practice. It contemplates practice. The most important thing about narrative is that it is a mode of organizing one's perception of the world, one's experiences. And I think it is an anti-, a nontheoretically informed mode. Narrative is something that you do not have to be trained to do. You surely have to learn to narrate, but it is like learning your own language. People do not need to have a theory of speech in order to speak. They do have to have some internalized conception of grammar and morphology and so on, but unlike—let me say—scientific or algorithmic thinking, that is not subconsciously applying a theory. Narrative is, I would say, something that comes

15

What *Metahistory* does, or pretends to do, is to deconstruct a mythology, the so-called science of history.

Narrative is a mode of organizing one's perception of the world, one's experiences.

Natural history
was the narrative
account of the
evolution of the
world.

with social life, intrinsic to social and group identification. That is what makes it continuous with myth and what makes it suspect for scientists. When Darwin transformed natural history into biology, he got rid of narrative. Natural history was the narrative account of the evolution of the world. But on the other hand, the theory of narrative history gives a license to people who try to experiment with different kinds of narrative writing. Ginzburg, for example, hates *Metahistory*. He thinks I am a fascist. He is also naive in many respects. He thinks that my conception of history is like that of Croce, that it is subjectivist, and that I think you can manipulate the facts for an aesthetic effect. I think that one can do so, and although Ginzburg thinks you ought not do that, in my view, he himself does it quite often.

There are many different ways of studying history, and we study it for different reasons. There is no possibility of legislating an orthodoxy about the way history is to be studied. It is not like the study of physics. One can improvise different techniques of representation for the past, and that is why the writing of history has a different kind of history from the study of physics. We have only to look at the history of historical writing to recognize that there are different stylistic variations. And what is really naive about historians is that they always think that the current way of doing history is finally the best way.

If we look back at someone like Michelet, we say: "Well, too bad, we are superior to him. He was naive." Modern historians look back on Voltaire, or Ranke, or Burckhardt and they presume: "Yes, they were experimenting with different ways of writing history. They were interesting as writers, but we have a superior way of doing history." And I think that is always an illusion. It is impossible to legislate the way people are going to relate to the past because, above all, the past is a place of fantasy. It does not exist anymore. One can only study it by way of things that have been left. The events of history by definition are not replicable. We can't repeat it as you can repeat physical events in a laboratory. You can't replicate—by definition—historical events. They are no longer perceivable. So they cannot be studied empirically. They can be studied by other, nonempirical kinds of methods; but there is no way of finally determining what is the best theory for studying and guiding research in history. That is my view.

The past is a place
of fantasy.

Most historians, I think, would agree that there can be no ultimate theory of history. But you can have a theory of historical writing. I mean, you can step back and look at historical writing in the same way that you have philosophy of science. Philosophers of science do not tell physicists how to do science. They reflect on what the physicists are doing in order to make some statements about the epistemological presuppositions of physics.

Let me come back to the general question about the philosophy of history. You think that the purpose of the philosophy of history is not to give some directives or to show how to apply those directives to historical writing but rather that philosophy of history can help us to understand how historians in the past wrote history.

Not really that. It reflects on the question of the relationship between the discipline of history and other disciplines. For example, what is the relationship between the writing of history and the novel—literary writing? What is the relationship between historical research and sociological research? Those are philosophical questions. Historians are doing their work. They do not necessarily think about the relation. Historians do not often think about the cultural function of their work. They enter the discipline. They do their work. When you point out to them, that "Well, the kind of work you do, presupposes or is based upon a number of implicit assumptions," they say "Well, I am not concerned with that. I must continue to do my work."

Knowledge is organized into various disciplines. Historians, for example, in the United States at least, suddenly decide that one can use anthropology; that they can make use of some theory about kinship systems; and they come back and they apply it to history. Then someone else decides not anthropology, but rather psychoanalysis, or sociology, or some theory of social classes. They are continually borrowing. What interests me is the principle by which it is decided to practice this kind of history, rather than some other one.

Who was your first source of inspiration?

18

I was fascinated by Collingwood and Croce from the beginning.

I do not believe you study the past just because you are interested in the past.

Collingwood and Croce. I was fascinated by Collingwood and Croce from the beginning because they raise questions about why we study history. You see, in many respects most historians do not even ask these questions. They think it is obvious why we study history. But they are always surprised when people do not like the history they write.

When I was a graduate student at the University of Michigan, I worked with Maurice Mandelbaum, who was the only person in the United States at that time who worked in the philosophy of history.

The other inspirations were the great reflective historians, like Huizinga. I mean, he was someone who not only did history but reflected on how you do history. I think that all of the great historians do both history and philosophy of history. They always asked the question, how do you do history? what is the best way of doing it? what are the grounds for thinking that one way is better than another? what are the purposes, the social purposes of studying the past?

I was interested in proper history. Well, I was interested in writing history, but I am not an antiquarian. I mean, I do not believe you study the past just because you are interested in the past. If you are interested in the past, there must be some psychological motivation. *Metahistory* is a result of a historical investigation; it's just a study of nineteenth-century historical writing. I mean, I was studying the nineteenth-century writing of history. That is a historical project. But I thought, I need some principles for organizing and characterizing the different ways the nineteenth century did history, wrote about history. That is why I started with the historian's text. It seemed to me that the way most people had written the history of history writing was to listen to what the historians had said they did, rather than analyzing what they actually wrote. Ranke, for example, pointed out: we go to the archives, we study this, we study that, we come out, we arrange the things, then we write it up. There is the research phase and there is the writing phase. I found that if we start not with that kind of information but look at the text itself, you can see that a lot of times they have said things that cannot be justified on the basis of their reports about the research. The composition of the historian's text, just on the basis of compositional considerations themselves, transforms the materials that they have worked up from the archives. So I

needed a way of characterizing different styles of representation.
That is why I started studying literary theory, people like Northrop
Frye, but not only Frye, Kenneth Burke and others. Basically my
book, *Metahistory*, is structuralist. It also has the limitations of
structuralism.

I always regarded myself as a kind of Marxist. And I am politically a socialist, I always have been. I regarded Marx as one of
the great philosophers of history, one among many. Not better
than Hegel, different from Hegel, but giving profound insights.
The Marxists in my own country and abroad, for example Mogil-
nitsky in Russia, say: "This is formalism." I say: "Yes, it is formalist!" In my introduction, I said: "My method is formalist!" Why?
Because, I think, no one had ever done a formalist analysis of the
historian's text.

**Could you tell me about your interest in Vico and in Re-
naissance humanism. Was it because the humanists tried to
replace logic by rhetoric or tried to reduce logic to rhetoric?**

Well, that is true. Why did I use this tropology, this theory of
tropes? Because narrative writing is not informed by logic. There
is no narrative that ever displays the consistency of a logical deduction. And anyone who ever wrote a story that could provide
rules of deducing one phase of the story from another would be
a very unsuccessful storyteller. I thought that you needed either
an alternative logic or a logic of narrative composition, which you
can find in modern rhetoric. You do not find it, I think, in ancient
rhetoric.

I believed that Hegel's dialectic, that Hegel's logic, is an attempt to formalize practical thinking. When people relate to one
another in politics and love, they do not relate syllogistically.
It is not a syllogism. That's something else. It's an enthymeme.
And most compositions, most of everyday speech, are enthyme-
mic. They do not follow rules of logical deduction; they are not
syllogistic.

So, as both J. S. Mill and Hegel realized, you need another
kind of logic to talk about practical affairs—a logic of praxis. The
logic of praxis cannot follow the logic of identity and noncontra-
diction. Society creates situations in which you must act in contradiction. That is what "vulgar" Marxists never understood when

The logic of praxis
cannot follow
the logic of
identity and non-
contradiction.

20

Lives are made up
of contradictions.
So you need a the-
ory of the repre-
sentation of life
lived in contra-
diction.

I turned to rhetor-
ical theories be-
cause I believed
that rhetoric pro-
vides the theory of
improvisational
discourse.

Rhetoric is the
theory of the poli-
tics of discourse.

Truth is produced,
not found.

they kept saying that when you have discovered a contradiction in an argument then you have destroyed the argument. But it does not. People live in contradictions. Lives are made up of contradictions. So you need a theory of the representation of life lived in contradiction. That would allow you to account for the syntax of real lives. In the study of narrative, people who try to provide a logic of narrative fail. They try to provide a grammar of narrative, and they fail. Because the point and fact is that a narrative is not a large sentence. And grammar can tell you only about sentences, not about discourses. In the same way, syllogistic logic can tell you only about propositions. But although there are propositions in narratives, narrative itself is not an extended set of propositions. The components of narrative are not propositions only. There are extrapropositional components and they have to do with syntax. But it is not a grammatical syntax. It is a syntax of language use, beyond the sentence. It is putting sentences together. You can link sentences together by logic, or you can do it by tropologic. Tropology because you need a theory of swerve, of systematic deviation, from logical expectation. That is what is fascinating about narrative. It cannot be governed by strict rules of logical deduction. So I turned to rhetorical theories because I believed that rhetoric provides the theory of improvisational discourse.

Since Plato, the philosophers claimed that rhetoric is suspect, duplicitous, artificial, and that logic is natural. That is ridiculous! Plato was prejudiced against the Sophists because he was an idealist who believed in absolute truths. And rhetoric is based upon a genuinely materialistic conception of life; it is skeptical. Gorgias and Protagoras recognized that there is no such thing as one correct way of speaking and representing the world, because language is arbitrary in its relationship to the world that it speaks about. And what was proper speech, correct or truthful speech, depended on who had the power to determine it. So rhetoric is the theory of the politics of discourse, in my estimation. It says that discourse is worked out in conflicts between people. Those who determine who will have the right, the power and authority, to say what correct speech is and those who attempt to name correct speech—in other words, to legislate it—are always authoritarian, from Plato on. What the rhetorician knows is that meaning is always being produced; that truth is produced, not found. That is why I think that a rhetorical conception of forms of discourse like history, which cannot be formalized, provides some kind of equivalent to what poetics tries to do with its analysis of poetic diction and speech.

Poetics does not predict how the poem should be written. It does not give rules. But after the poems are written, you can reflect on them and see different structures. Lotman's way of thinking about the artistic text is, I think, consistent with that way of thinking about poetics. Lotman tries to determine how the artistic text differs from the practical text, the utilitarian text. The question is: is history a utilitarian knowledge or is it more like an artistic knowledge? Because no one would deny, no one would say, that poetry does not give us insight into the world; at least it gives us insight into language. So I think that is true, but also about all sorts of discourses like history that are not sciences. History is not a science. What is it, then?

History is not a science.

History has a double face: a scientific and an artistic one.

Sure—that is what makes it interesting. You are always facing in two directions. But the historians do not know that, because since the nineteenth century they have been taught that they must keep literary effects and poetic effects out of their writing. So what they say is: "You do your research as a scientist, but then, when it comes to writing, it is okay, make it pretty so that people can read it easily; but your writing does not add anything except cosmetics to your truth." And that is wrong. Any modern linguist knows that the form of the representation is a part of the content itself. That is why I call my most recent book *The Content of the Form*. It is consistent with ideas developed since Lukács and critics like Fredric Jameson stressed that ideology has to do with the form of the thing as much as with the content of the given representation. To choose the form is already to choose a semantic domain. What do you think?

I think that if we can say that history has a double face, we can also say that when a historian does his research— it is a scientific face. I mean, he has to analyze sources and

22 examine archives using scientific tools. But when he writes about history and presents in this way the results of research, there is only one way of doing it—by narrative, and this is an artistic face. We cannot divide these two sides. They are always connected with one another. Recall Plato's famous metaphor of the double sides of a human being. According to it, at the beginning, woman and man were connected in one body. Dividing it into parts was a punishment.

Sure—I agree. That is why in my book I used Lodvik Hjelmslev's conception of levels. I said, there is one level at which you have the constitution of facts, the chronicle; and then next you have a plot, you emplot these facts. Then historians typically will have an argument, in the form of an explanation. Oftentimes they will even try to draw morals, which I call the ideological dimension. My question is: how do these different aspects relate to one another? Many historians think that there is ideology in what they do. I think that ideology is already there, in the form.

But by the way, when you talk about doing your research scientifically, what kind of science are you talking about? Certainly, it is not experimental science; that is, laboratory science. Beyond that, when you do your research, if you have already explicitly chosen the form you are going to use to write up your representation, then your research is governed by the necessity of the genre, the generic considerations of your form itself. So, it is not as if you can go into archives and study the documents without any ideas of how you are going to write it up. You carry that in there with you, too.

We know the attitude of historians of the last generation in my country was: "We are not going to write narratives. We are not interested in writing narratives." In the *Annales* school, Braudel said: "I do not like narratives. Narrative is childish, delusory." He makes the decision before he even goes into the archives. I do not think you can separate easily, as you would agree, the scientific side and the artistic side. But I do not think that the nineteenth-century way of conceptualizing that relationship is fully convincing. These historians, I know, still say that the form of the writing has nothing to do with the content. They may decide to tell the story, or they may not, and this has nothing to do with the validity of the facts they produced in research. But Braudel and

the *Annales* school said that to write narrative is in itself ideological distortion.

So, taking this into consideration, from the perspective of the narrativist philosophy of history, can we speak about truth in history in terms of "the point of view"?

Well, but "point of view" is an epistemological concept. By the way, "point of view" is a question dealt with in literary theory, namely the conception of point of view inside the novel. Bakhtin is the theoretician of this. So, when you say "point of view," that is a complex idea. It is a very complicated thing. You do not *have* to make it complicated. You can say: "Look, I have been a Nazi. From my point of view the Third Reich was a very good thing. It is from my point of view." No one can accept that because there are certain points of view that are ruled out. But if you accept "point of view" theory, you cannot really rule out any given one.

I would like to clarify my position and say that truth ceased to be a relation and has become a judgment. I am thinking all the time about the narrativist philosophy of history, of course.

Judgment is deliberative. Yes, I know, but for the last one hundred and fifty years they have been talking about truth as a relation. I try to argue that theory of judgment has much more in common with a rhetorical conception of discourse, about how you arrived at a decision, than it does with logical conceptions.

It is possible to say that *Metahistory* was an attempt to leave history and that by using rhetoric you try to avoid the problem of truth in history?

You cannot avoid the problem of truth, to be sure. Because that is one of the conventions that establishes the possibility of writing history. History defines itself and its nature in contrast to fiction (poetry), on the one side, and against philosophy, on the other side. In many respects the practice of history is defined by what it does not do as much as by what it does. So, the problem of truth cannot be avoided. The problem of the relationships of truth to

24 representation, however, cannot be avoided either. One of the things that twentieth-century linguistic philosophy has taught us is that it is not a matter of truth being there and being detachable from the representation or the form of the representation of the truth. If truth presents itself to us as statements, as utterances, the form of the utterance is as important as the content. You cannot distinguish.

One thing on which contemporary philosophy of many different kinds agrees is that the language in which the truth is represented is very important for determining the force of the truth statements contained implicitly and explicitly on the surface of the utterance.

Do you not think that, from the point of view of the narrativist theory, it seems very useful to apply a metaphorical theory of truth?

Yes, but you see, that is what finally the analytical philosophers in the West have come around to. From Descartes on, metaphor is regarded as error. Metaphor is always regarded as what Ryle called a "category mistake." Some mistake in cross-sorting. That is absurd. You would think that anyone who had read any poetry would know that that is not the case. You need metaphorical expression to characterize the most complicated and difficult aspects of your experience of the world. Nothing can be stated in simple declarative sentences without metaphor. There is no such thing as nonmetaphorical language. But—let us say—there are some statements that can be treated as if they were literal, and not metaphorical, language. However, those aspects of life that one can represent in literal language are really unproblematical. So, we have in the United States people like Davidson and Rorty who have decided finally, what Nietzsche already told us a long time ago, that of course it is all metaphor.

Kant begins his logic, his last book, by saying that "the source of all error is metaphor." Well, too bad. He is wrong. Metaphor is maybe the source of all error but it is also the source of all truth, too. And the relationship therefore between truth and error is not this "either-or" relationship. Most truth statements, most truthful statements about the things important in life, have this kind of dialectical relationship between truth and error, between good and

There is no such thing as nonmetaphorical language.

evil. One of the things that psychoanalysis teaches us, whatever its limitations, is that most human relationships are shot through with ambivalence, not with love, on the one side, and hate on another.

Treating the historical text as a whole is quite new. In previous decades philosophers analyzed the problem of the truth-value of historical statements, examined sentence by sentence. In this way, if we think about a historical statement we can apply the classical theory of truth. But if we analyze the historical text as a whole, we can use a metaphorical theory of truth.

Well, I think we have to. Louis O. Mink wrote a very fine piece in which he pointed out that, if you took each of the sentences of a history and you ask about the truth-value of each one, you might come out with—say—fifteen true, fifteen false. But, he says, it is not the same thing as asking about the truth-value of the whole. And I think that is quite right. *Metahistory* does not give an adequate account of the "whole" work. It tried to, but of course it failed. But it was written twenty years ago. That is interesting. Young people now come and read it and they think that it is something helpful to them. They sometimes act as if it had been written yesterday. And then they write me letters and say: "You say so and so. What did you mean?" I reply: "I do not know. I was writing in a different milieu at that time and by the way, for different purposes, than I would write for today and for a different audience." I mean, I certainly would not like to write this book again. So, too, when people say to me: "I love *Metahistory*. I am applying its principles to my own work," I say: "It is not meant to be applied. It is analytical. It does not tell you how to do something." Psychologists write to me and say that they use the theory of tropes that I developed to treat their patients. So they will talk about the metaphoric mind or consciousness, or metonymic; and I say "That's being very literal-minded. I only used the concept of tropes metaphorically. It's not supposed to be taken literally."

So, do you not think that *Metahistory* became "a new science," as Kuzminski called it in his review?

26   No. I do not think so. There is another thing about writing in this way. You never convince your own contemporaries. Many people said that *Metahistory* had some virtues, but many more said that it was wrong. But the next generation of young people came along, and they were working against the inherited authorities; they looked for a deviant, an alternative way. Young historians who were not satisfied with the ways in which they had been taught to think about historical research found something useful in my book; and it still sells a lot. It has had eight printings. I do not think people really want to read it; it's an intimidatingly long book. It's very tiresome and repetitive. Most people who read it read some of the introduction and maybe read around a bit. But no one reads it through. By the way, I don't think that in order to have an effect, you must produce books that people want to read. It is the project that interests people and not so much a particular way of doing it. I think the gesture of the project is toward innovation and changing the way we think about history. And I think in the 1960s it was everywhere and that was my intention. So if the historical establishment is offended, I do not mind. They were supposed to be shocked.

In an essay written by Professor Gertrude Himmelfarb in the 18 October 1992 *Times Literary Supplement*, she attacks me, among others, because she thinks I represent a postmodernist conception of history.

But you do not?

No!

I always thought I could connect you with postmodernism.

I see my own project as modernist.

My conception of history has much more in common with the kind of aesthetic of the sublime than with postmodernism.

People do. But Linda Hutcheon who works on it, always insists that I am a modernist—that I am stuck in modernism. And I agree. I see my own project as modernist. My whole intellectual formation, my own development took place within modernism. By that I mean a specifically Western—or, in Russia, the equivalent will be something like the futurist, or symbolist—cultural movement. In the West, the great modernist experiments of Joyce, Virginia Woolf, Eliot, Pound, and also a number of people who wrote history, like Spengler and Theodor Lessing. My con-

ception of history has much more in common with the kind of
aesthetic of the sublime that derives from romanticism than with
postmodernism, which is much more hip.

How do you consider yourself?

I am structuralist. I said—I am formalist and structuralist.

But that was twenty years ago.

And that has changed now. People have gone beyond and submitted structuralism to criticism. Most of which I have sympathy
with. I have a great deal of admiration for people like Derrida,
and above all Roland Barthes, whom I regard as the greatest and
most inventive critic of the postwar period of the last forty years
in the West.

**And by the way, what can I call you: a critic, a philosopher,
a historian, a representative of intellectual history?**

Well, I do not know, because I am not a philosopher. Philosophers recognize that. People like Rorty claimed to like *Metahistory*
but they do not think of it as philosophy. I thought at the time
that I was doing intellectual history. I call myself a cultural histo-   I call myself a cul-
rian. I am interested in culture, in philosophy of culture. But I am   tural historian.
not trained as a philosopher and I do not do the kind of rigorous
philosophical analysis that my friend Arthur Danto does. I do not
participate in the philosophers' world, but I would say the same
thing about people like Vico and Croce. Croce and Nietzsche did
not have a degree in philosophy.

**What would you call your theory: poetics of history, rhe-
torical theory of history, aesthetic historism, new rhetorical
relativism, poetic logic of historical writing?**

It is hard to do but I am really trying to work now on the development of the notion of tropic as a continuum of logic, dialectic,
and poetics. And I would say, instead of rhetoric, tropic—tropics being a theory very much like that of Jakobson. Jakobson's

thesis was this: you cannot distinguish between poetic language and nonpoetic language. There is a poetic function, and in some discourses the poetic function is dominant; in others it is not, but it is still there.

My question is this, if the old nineteenth-century, easy distinction between fact and fiction can no longer be maintained, and if we instead see them as a continuum in discourse, then I would ask: What is the "fictional function" in nonfictional discourse, or in discourse that tries to be nonfictional? Because anyone who writes a narrative is fictionalizing. I use the term *poetic*, I use *rhetoric*. The problem with both of those terms is that already their connotations are so connected with romanticism and Sophism that they turn people off; they are not helpful. One needs a different set of terms; and I am increasingly thinking that I have got to work out a theory of tropics. That is why I come back to the study of Vico again.

And by the way, tropology—when I was writing *Metahistory*—was just because I was teaching a seminar on Vico. I needed some way of thinking about how you coordinate levels of argument and connections between different parts of the narrative that were not those of logical connections. I was teaching Vico, and he suggested to me the new way of thinking about the different aspects of complicated discourses, like history. It's not a matter of being logical. It's tropical. It's put very crudely in *Metahistory* because I did not know anything about rhetoric then. I had been taught that rhetoric is a bad thing. It is immoral, it is not interested in the truth, it is interested only in persuasion. So, I was completely brainwashed by my teachers who taught that rhetoric is a bad thing. Poetry is OK, I was taught. It is hard to be poetic, and that is good. Science and logic are OK but rhetoric is always bad. Well, it all depends on what you mean by rhetoric. Vico represented two conceptions of rhetoric: you can see rhetoric as the art of persuasion, or you can see rhetoric as the science of discourse. It was tropology as a basis for a science of discourse that I found in Vico.

I was much inspired by Jakobson. He had a major impact on all the human sciences of the twentieth century, from linguistics and anthropology to psychology. Less so in sociology, but that is because sociology is dead. For discourse analysis you can do a lot worse than to study Jakobson and contemplate his way of thinking about discourse.

So tropics. That is why I called this second book, a collection

Anyone who writes a narrative is fictionalizing.

Sociology is dead.

of essays, *Tropics of Discourse*. The publishers did not want to use
this title because they said tropics are about geography and this
book will be put in the geography section of the library if you use
that title.

**If I can come back to the problem of rhetoric. I think
that rhetoric is no longer what it was in classical times but
is simply some kind of philosophy. Could you please tell
me what do you think, for example, about Nelson et al's
The Rhetoric of the Human Sciences, where the authors
pointed out that there is no one rhetoric but several kinds
of rhetoric, such as the rhetoric of history, the rhetoric
of economics, and so on.**

You see, I do not agree with these people because they have a very
old-fashioned notion of rhetoric. They believe that rhetoric is
about form. Their notion of rhetoric is more like that of Cicero
and Quintilian. My notion of rhetoric, which comes from Vico,
is more like that of Gorgias and Protagoras and is a philosophy.
Cicero's rhetoric is not philosophy. He says there is philosophy
here and then there is rhetoric. Quintilian says: "No, there is philosophy and then you use rhetoric to teach schoolboys." But the
inventors of rhetoric, Gorgias and Protagoras and all the people
who were attacked by both Plato and Aristotle, really were philosophers of language. So, I think you are quite right that rhetoric is philosophy; it is a materialist philosophy and presumes an
entire ontology. What the Sophists taught is that metaphysics is
impossible (I learned that from Paolo Valesio): the very thing that
Nietzsche finally tried to teach in the nineteenth century. And
rhetoric is conceived as a theory of how meaning is produced, of
how meaning is constructed, not how meaning is found. Plato
believes that you can find meaning; it is in things.

> My notion of
> rhetoric, which
> comes from Vico,
> is more like that of
> Gorgias and Pro-
> tagoras and is a
> philosophy.

    There are a lot of applications of rhetoric to contemporary
historical writing. But the historians do not like it because they
think that, in what they are doing, there is not any rhetoric. They
always resist. They resist anyone who tries to tell them something
about what they are doing.

**And what about your evolution from *Metahistory* to *The Con-
tent of the Form*? Quite a big change can be observed there.**

30 I respond to poststructuralism positively. I think it is full of new brilliant insights, into techniques of reading especially. Roland Barthes had a structuralist phase. But Barthes never stayed dogmatically locked into the same position.

My critics said to me: "Well, *Metahistory* is too formalist. It doesn't say anything about the author, about the audience, about praxis." And I said: "Yes, OK, let's start thinking about the author." And I started to ask questions about intentionality. But I'm inclined to follow people like Foucault and Barthes. So I say the text in some sense is detached from the author. When the text is actually published, the author is not the best interpreter of it any longer. And that is a poststructuralist way of thinking.

Beyond that, poststructuralism depends upon semiotic conceptions of the sign. I think that texts, novels, poems, histories have a certain instability, just on the basis of the inner dynamics of the process of discourse formation that deconstruction tells us about. Textualism is an interesting ideology. It is an ideology, but it yields some insights that I find helpful.

Textualism is
an interesting
ideology.

Poststructuralism has very sophisticated things to say about cultural production, about how ideology works, about ideology as a production of subjectivities, about culturally produced subjects. I think poststructuralism tells an awful lot about processes of maturation in the individual. It has added a lot to psychoanalysis. So, I do not see myself as having to be committed to a given doctrine. I don't mind what anyone calls me. I don't think labels are important. My view is this: Don't worry about labels or schools. Here is a book. Read it. If it helps you in your own work—good; if it doesn't—forget it.

I have a list with names of several philosophers. Could you please tell me what is the most important point of these persons' theories and what point of these theories most influences your theory of history. The first is Vico.

Poetic logic. The whole section in the *New Science* on what he calls poetic logic and poetic metaphysics.

Collingwood and Croce.

Collingwood had a notion that the whole of history is the history of thought. It appealed to me early on. I admired also Hegel, of

course. And both Croce and Collingwood were Hegelians.
Croce's reworking of Hegelian aesthetics to bring it into accord
with modern art, that influenced me.

Nietzsche.

Well, *The Genealogy of Morals*. Nietzsche says: "How is it possible
to breed an animal capable of promising. How is it possible to remember forward." Beautiful idea. That is what ethics is. That is
what morality is. Nietzsche was the philosopher for me who said:
"I study ethics from the aesthetic point of view."

Frye.

He is the archetypal critic. Frye was influenced, inspired to a very
large degree by Spengler. Spengler himself said in the introduction to *The Decline of the West* that Nietzsche had inspired him; that
he is writing from the aesthetic point of view. So, too, for Frye's
archetypal theory of myth. He is reworking the notion of myth as
the repressed content of fiction, much as Nietzsche reworked aesthetics as the repressed content of ethics.

Burke.

Burke is the philosopher of negation. He says that man is the only
animal that can say "no." Negation is unique to human speech. Animals may refuse things, but they do not say "no." Burke builds a
whole theory of language on that. In many respects, you can say
that Burke is the philosopher of the negation of the negation.
Hegel's conception of positivity is negation of negation. Burke
brings that over not only into the study of literature but into philosophy as well. For him there is no philosophy over here, social
sciences here, and literature there. It is a continuum. He is the
theoretician of discourse.

Foucault.

I think that what he does is "counterhistory." His conception of
archeology and genealogy asks us to reverse the traditional, conventional presuppositions of historical inquiry. One of the things

32 that he teaches us in his *Histoire de la folie* is that you cannot conceptualize sanity without conceptualizing madness at the same time. And Freud teaches us that there is a little madness in every sanity and a little sanity in every madness. So, again it is a continuum rather than an opposition. The one thing I am uncomfortable with in Foucault is what makes him closest to Nietzsche; that is, the way he generalizes the concept of power. I do not quite understand that. Power is such a comprehensive term that it seems to be another form of metaphysics, like Schopenhauer's will, Foucault's will to know is a metaphysical idea.

Ricoeur.

Ricoeur is a very old-fashioned philosopher in a nineteenth-century, hermeneutic mode. What is inspiring about Ricoeur is the amplitude of his mind. He is capable of entertaining the widest range of positions. So, whenever he picks up any philosopher or any theorist, he reads them sympathetically. He is always trying to sort out what can be saved. So, I like the catholicity of his taste. Ricoeur has also a very important thing to say about the symbol. He is the philosopher of symbolic form, very much in the tradition of Cassirer. But I think it is passé. That tradition, it is a very nineteenth-century, aristocratic, European tradition.

Barthes.

Barthes was the most inventive critic of his time. When I heard the news of Barthes's death, I was profoundly saddened because I realized that I always looked forward to anything new that he had written. I could always be sure that it would be original—that it would be inventive. Every time I read anything by him it showed me something about reading. His book about photography. He was not a professional photographer. I have talked to photographers, and they say they learn more from Barthes about photography than they learned from their own teachers of photography.

Derrida.

I mentioned Derrida in an essay once and I called him "an absurdist critic," and people thought that was critical. But I meant that

he was a philosopher of the absurd. I did not mean that he was
absurd. You know what I mean? I was using an existentialist term,
absurdism. And I characterized him as the philosopher of paradox, or of the absurd. But people thought that I meant that I was
hostile to him, but I did not see it that way. Derrida's readings are
very hard, of course, to follow. I see Derrida as the philosopher
who finally shows us how to analyze all of the kinds of binary op-
positions that we take for granted in the conceptualization of relationships. And I think that is his principal function. Also I like
Derrida because he is consciously an outsider to the French intellectual scene.

And what about Rorty?

What I like about Rorty is that he finally revived a version of
American pragmatism. The only original philosophy, the only philosophy America produced, is pragmatism: James, Dewey, Peirce.
And Rorty is the one who really revived that because it virtually
disappeared after Dewey died. He is very smart. And I think his
book about Cartesianism, *Philosophy and the Mirror of Nature*, is
very brilliant and it has had a major impact in introducing anti-
idealistic thinking. I think Rorty is too ethnocentric. He is too focused on America. And within America there is a class bias to his
philosophy that idealizes upper-middle-class, eastern, Ivy League
culture. He projects American academic life out onto society and
takes that as the standard. I have certainly enjoyed academic life
and it has rewarded me. And one of the things I like about the
American educational system is that it does provide access to
people of all classes; but on the other hand, the professors tend
to be apes of the English ideal gentleman, very masculinist, male
chauvinist. And I think Rorty has some of that in him.

Could you tell me which of these people/theories are re-
lated most to yours: Barthes, LaCapra, Foucault, Mink?

LaCapra's project is like mine but he is much more psychoana-
lytically oriented than I am. I do not believe his notion of transference for a minute. I do not think there is any transference going on between the past and present. The person with whom I
had the closest affinity was Louis O. Mink among philosophers

34 certainly, and Foucault. Foucault was a great egomaniac. A very
difficult person, but I really thought—the one time I met him—
that we talked the same language. Almost all of these people are
critics of mine. I take it as a compliment that people spend enough
time reading one's work, even to criticize it. So, I see us as all engaged in a project of rethinking history and we are doing it from
different perspectives. But the thinker dearest to me is Barthes,
definitely.

Who is the most influential philosopher in contemporary philosophy of history?

I think that Arthur Danto in the United States commands the
most respect among philosophers. Ricoeur, among the philosophers of history, is someone who summarizes rather than someone who offers new insights, quite honestly. The late Michel de
Certeau is having profound influences in France and in the
United States on historical thinking. There are a lot of people in
literary studies who write interestingly on questions of historical
representation, like Ann Rigney and Stephen Bann. The field of
history is differently defined now from what it was from the time
of Hegel through Collingwood. I do not think any philosopher
of history has much of an effect upon historians. The last who did
was Marx, and historians try to apply his principles of philosophy
of history. I think that the people who are thinking about history
in the most interesting way are Heideggerians. Heidegger's *Sein
und Zeit* is after all a book about temporality and history, about
historicality. Someone like Barthes, when he writes a little essay,
"The Discourse of History," suddenly shows you things that my
whole book could not convincingly display. I think that one cannot any longer easily say that the debate is between philosophers
and philosophers of history, historians and theorists of history. I
think the problem now, at the end of the twentieth century, is
how we reimagine history outside of the categories that we inherited from the nineteenth century. The reimagination of history: That is one of the things that psychoanalysis points to. What
is our relationship to our personal past? It cannot be a purely conscious relationship. It is a relationship of the imagination as well
as reason.

Let me tell you, Ewa, personally, I don't believe in interviews.
What are you getting from me? You are not getting any definitive

> I think that the people who are thinking about history in the most interesting way are Heideggerians.

statement. You're getting another version. I would say that what
I do stems from the fact that, as with most historians, the past has
always been a problem for me. Growing up as a working-class person, who had no sense of tradition and for whom high culture
was a kind of mystery, that I came to know through education, I
found it fascinating to think there were whole classes and groups
of people who oriented themselves in terms of the memory of the
provided tradition. That seems to be a mystery for me. And history was the same to me: to be a place you can examine, that relationship of the individual to the past. It seemed to me evident,
the more I studied, that what historians produce are imaginative
images of the past that have a function rather like the recall of the
past events in one's own individual imagination. That is why I
sometimes stressed the subtitle in my book, *Historical Imagination*. Because to imagine something is to construct an image of
it. You do not just construct the past and then relate it in an image.
The philosophers of history of the older school try to suggest that
philosophy of history would deal with history from the epistemological standpoint. That is legitimate enough. It is much more
interesting to me to think of a psychology of historical being.
What does it mean to think that you live *in history*? Frank Ankersmit examined this question. What does it mean to experience
history? What is the historical experience? When you ask about it,
it is a very strange idea, that you can experience history. You do
not experience history. You experience floods, battles, wars. The
Yugoslavians—you think that they are experiencing history? No!
They are experiencing tyranny, death, and terrorism. So, what is
this "history" that people experience? It has to be an imaginative
creation. But real.

> 35

> What historians produce are imagi-native images of the past that have a function rather like the recall of the past events in one's own individ-ual imagination.

> What is the histor-ical experience?

**There is no contradiction between the imagination and
the real?**

No, because what would be meant by the real is always something
that is imagined. Because the real is not directly accessible. It is
accessible only by way of the image. That is why the theory of
metaphor is so important.

> The real is . . . something imagined.

**What is the main focus of discussions in current scientific
periodicals in the United States?**

36   In the kind of periodicals that interest me, it is cultural studies and multiculturalism. Those are the topics even in the conservative and antipostmodernist journals. They spend their time criticizing what they regard as the irresponsibility of the postmodernist. Postmodernism in the United States is thought to be a repudiation of history, a mixture of fact and fiction, relativism, being able to say everything you want to say about anything. We are creating in the United States a new discipline, called cultural studies. And cultural studies is a kind of postmarxist study of consciousness, cultural modes of production, of which discourse is one and in which history would be treated, not as a scientific discipline, but as a discourse in which you have many different voices. And by the way, I think one thinker who goes across all the disciplines and is used by both, by Left and Right, is Bakhtin. It is interesting to think of why Bakhtin would have this appeal among marxists, postmarxists, neomarxists, antimarxists, conservatives, liberals, and so on in the West. The historical profession in the United States recently had a meeting in which they asked whether *The American Historical Review* should review historical movies. For years they tried to get *The American Historical Review* to review historical films, but they said: "No. You cannot represent history on film." It is very interesting to see it put down as a dogma that history has to be written, cannot be shown. Especially inasmuch as the kind of historical writing that comes out as narrative is an attempt to create something like a visual image. So I think that the debate over the relationship between visual media and verbal media is a big and important topic debated across many disciplines.

When I read your books I noticed that you pay very little attention to the German tradition. What about Gadamer, Habermas, and hermeneutics?

I regarded myself as having come out of a German tradition. Kant, Hegel, Marx, Dilthey, people like that, were very influential for me in my own philosophical formation. But you are quite right. I regarded Habermas as having a very naive theory of communication and therefore of discourse. And I think I understand why he has it, and the situation in which he writes. I find him always interesting as a commentator on political questions and on the re-

lationship between philosophy and politics. I am suspicious of
hermeneutics, however, because I think hermeneutics is the last
gasp of metaphysics. Hermeneutics is philosophy done as if metaphysics were still possible but with awareness that there is no real
possibility of doing it. It is like "pretend." It produces what
Barthes would call "the metaphysics effect." So, I found that in
Gadamer usually his arguments boiled down to a defense of the
nineteenth-century positions of Dilthey and Hegel. It is very well
done and interests me, but there is a kind of heaviness to it that I
think does not go well in translation.

I am suspicious of
hermeneutics.

Groningen, The Netherlands
5 February 1993

SELECTED WRITINGS

Metahistory: The Historical Imagination in Nineteenth-Century Europe.
    Baltimore: Johns Hopkins Univ. Press, 1973.
Tropics of Discourse: Essays in Cultural Criticism. Baltimore: Johns Hop-
    kins Univ. Press, 1978.
*The Content of the Form: Narrative Discourse and Historical Representa-
    tion.* Baltimore: Johns Hopkins Univ. Press, 1987.

"Historical Pluralism." *Critical Inquiry* 12, no. 3 (1985): 480–93.
"The Rhetoric of Interpretation." *Poetics Today* 9, no. 2 (1988): 254–74.
"Figuring the Nature of the Times Deceased: Literary Theory and His-
    torical Writing." In *The Future of Literary Theory*, ed. Ralph Cohen,
    19–43. New York: Routledge, 1989.
"Historical Emplotment and the Problem of Truth." In *Probing the Lim-
    its of Representation: Nazism and the "Final Solution,"* ed. Saul Fried-
    lander, 37–53. Cambridge: Harvard Univ. Press, 1992.
"Rancière's Revisionism." Foreword to Jacques Rancière, *The Names of
    History: On the Poetics of Knowledge*, vii–xix. Minneapolis: Univ. of
    Minnesota Press, 1994.
"Bodies and Their Plots." In *Choreographing History*, ed. Susan Leigh
    Foster, 229–34. Bloomington: Univ. of Indiana Press, 1995.
"Response to Arthur Marwick." *Journal of Contemporary History* 30,
    no. 2 (April 1995): 233–46 [a response to Arthur Marwick, "Two
    Approaches to Historical Study: The Metaphysical (Including 'Post-
    modernism') and the Historical." *Journal of Contemporary History*

38   30, no. 1 (Jan. 1995): 5–35]. See a continuation of the discussion: Christopher Lloyd, "For Realism and Against the Inadequacies of Common Sense: A Response to Arthur Marwick." *Journal of Contemporary History* 31, no. 1 (Jan. 1996): 191–207; Beverley Southgate, "History and Metahistory: Marwick versus White." Ibid. 209–13; Wulf Kansteiner, "Searching for an Audience: The Historical Profession in the Media Age—A Comment on Arthur Marwick and Hayden White." Ibid. 215–19.

"A Rejoinder: A Response to Professor Chartier's Four Questions." *Storia della Storiografia* 27 (1995): 63–70 [a response to Roger Chartier, "Quatre Questions à Hayden White." *Storia della Storiografia* 24 (1993): 133–42].

"Auerbach's Literary History: Figural Causation and Modernist Historicism." In *Literary History and the Challenge of Philology.* Stanford: Stanford Univ. Press, 1996, 123–43.

"Commentary" to "Identity, Memory, History," a special issue of *History of the Human Sciences* 9, no. 4 (Nov. 1996): 123–38.

"The Modernist Event." In *The Persistence of History: Cinema, Television, and the Modern Event*, ed. Vivian Sobchack, 17–38. New York: Routledge, 1996.

"Storytelling: Historical and Ideological." In *Centuries' Ends, Narrative Means*, ed. Robert Newman, 58–78. Stanford: Stanford Univ. Press, 1996.

*History is the books that people write
and call histories.*

"Postmodern" philosophy questioned the fundamental categories of modern culture. The category of truth was the most "shaken," it had never been violated in this way before. Could you please tell me what your opinion about truth is? How do you consider the problem of truth in historical writing and the problem of the relative comprehension of the truth?

■ The sensitivity to rhetoric suggests that a truth is always a truth for a particular moment, a particular audience, a particular problem and situation. So a particular configuration of arguments, evidence, facts will appear true rhetorically in a particular time and place. Truth would be what is plausible or convincing to a universal audience. I am skeptical about the existence of a universal audience within any human experience. The universal audience is a kind of ideal concept, like the idea of truth. What we have are stories that are true for a time and a place. As I have recently written in an essay on the problem of historical representations of the Holocaust, it is our ethical responsibility as people who live in history and who reflect on the past to create and maintain a present world in which the visions of history that we deem true and important remain immediate and credible. There is no easy way.

I feel that any theoretical consideration of history at the present time must take a strong interest in how historical truths are validated, from age to age, nation to nation, group to group, person to person. For one thing, such a study would make us a lot less likely to be blinded by current standards (as Foucault might say, "what goes without saying"), and perhaps more open to pondering how the supposed errors of the past worked their effects. Innovations are rediscoveries, after all. I am dismayed that so

What we have are stories that are true for a time and a place.

Any theoretical consideration of history at the present time must take a strong interest in how historical truths are validated.

40   many current attacks on the Enlightenment come from people who have not spent as much as a week, or even a day, reading in sixteenth- and seventeenth-century sources, pondering how things became true for those people, what things went "without saying." If any sort of understanding is the goal of historical study, this should be the central issue. We want to ask not just how people believed what they did, but how it was impossible for them to believe otherwise. The "how" of beliefs is more attainable than the "why." I think I understand why things happen less and less, the more fully they are studied and articulated. For instance, I feel that the French Revolution was never more mysterious than it is now, in spite of the fact that the discourse explaining it was never more plentiful and sophisticated.

Those who attack the idea of progress always seem to be certain of their own progressiveness. Perhaps the great validation of a truth is its existence in the present as an unspoken credo. There are two basic stances regarding the past as an object of the imagination: one is that we, now, have control of it, and can make it do our will and accept our judgments of it. We are its master. This view was an Enlightenment vision. The past was the great Other, both constituting the "good" present by providing a bad, superstitious, irrational background for it, and undermining the "bad" present by showing models of virtue, tolerance, and other desirable things. Eighteenth-century historians seem to have felt that they could make the past *do* things for them. Ironically, this has become the vision again, but the Enlightenment, reason, and tolerance seem to be targets now. What counts, however, is the identical relation of past and present. The second view of the past, however, presumes as an ethical base that it has a certain independence and doesn't need us to give it meaning, although whatever meaning it can have *for us* must be created here and now. This past is still Other, but in a different way. There is a mystery to it, similar to the mystery of other human beings, or even oneself. This view has late-Enlightenment roots, in that it emphasizes the imperfection of our ways of knowing, and perhaps shows some humility before the enormity of human experience. Both visions are useful, of course. Professional historical thought in general has little place for mystery. Nevertheless, academic history, written by professionals, seems more willing to grant limits to the historian's powers than the more popular versions of the past, which must have the truth.

> Those who attack the idea of progress always seem to be certain of their own progressiveness.

Do you see yourself as a philosopher of history?

I do not consider myself a philosopher of history because I have
never been privileged to have those kinds of sensibilities that I believe are characteristic of philosophers. My own way of thinking is
highly associative—basically a metonymic thinking that my philosopher friends just do not engage in. I make connections that
they do not recognize, but which I think of as essentially *historical*
connections. And in the United States, philosophers are less interested in historical discourse than are those in Europe. What used
to be safely called philosophy of history is less and less the preserve of philosophers.

> I do not consider myself a philosopher of history.

**What do you think of the condition of contemporary phi-
losophy of history? Have you noticed the double-track
development that Franklin Ankersmit pointed out, which
refers to the analytical philosophy of history on the one
hand and to the narrativist on the other?**

I don't think I can locate contemporary philosophy of history at
all. Much discussion of history today is based on poststructuralist
assumptions (often Heideggerian in origin) that lead you far, far
away from any practical writing of history or consideration of actual historical texts. On the other hand, the discourse of history
itself is changing, developing, flourishing. The first thing we want
to recognize is the separability of intellectual awareness and rules.
Historians operate on the basis of "tacit knowledge" that they
rarely make explicit to themselves, and that they pass along to
their students in the form of transmitted anxieties.

> Much discussion of history today is based on post-structuralist assumptions that lead you far away from any practical writing of history or consideration of actual historical texts.

In my opinion, what professionalization means in a given
field like history, or philosophy, or chemistry, or sociology, or literary theory, is to imprint a specific set of anxieties on the profes-
sionalizing student, the graduate student. I tried to sketch some
of these anxieties in *Language and Historical Representation*.
What does it mean to be trained as a historian? Two different historians might have never even read the same book, or know the
same names, or think about anything the same way. What do they
all have in common? Little more, I think, than a particular set of
tacit anxieties that shape the boundaries of what may or may not
be done. Literary theory, for example, has a totally different set of

42

anxieties. There the fear is always of being held to the ground, being weighed down by the stuff of literality; this is very different from what one fears in history.

The philosophy of history has always been troubled in my opinion by an ambiguity concerning which anxieties are in play in any given situation. Philosophy of history today increasingly looks like historical practice as literary theory. The links there to the normal practice of historical writing become increasingly tenuous.

Philosophy of history today increasingly looks like historical practice as literary theory.

I would say that philosophy of history has no particular discourse of its own. Perhaps Ankersmit will disagree. History has become a subject that belongs to everyone right now. And everyone will project upon it his own needs and anxieties. I find that suddenly everyone was talking about history; books of literary theory were being written about "history this, history that." "Always historicize . . ."—that sort of thing. And I used to respond: "Why, you haven't even mentioned one single practicing historian, not a single historical work has been written about." They talk about history the way Kant or Heidegger talks about history. Let's talk about Burckhardt or Lucien Febvre, or somebody, because history to me is the books that people write and call histories. Who talks about poetry without mentioning poems? I was very puzzled by Ricoeur's idea that history as event and history as discourse reflect each other. That disturbed me and struck me as being in bad taste. But now, in retrospect, I think that you can never limit discussions about history because almost any situation can be dissolved into some historical terms.

History is the books that people write and call histories.

Karl Popper once wrote that philosophy of history involves "three big questions": (1) What is the plot of history? (2) What is the use of history? and (3) How are we to write history, or what is the method of history? I would like to ask you a question that relates to Popper's first question: Why is the plot so fascinating in the present debate on historical writing?

Plot creates meaning.

Plot creates meaning. Henry James said in one of his essays about literature that characters do not make events happen in fiction but rather that character is created by a plot. That is true. So when we are accustomed to say that a certain attitude or quality identifies and shapes a period (for instance, reason in the Enlightenment, or faith in the Middle Ages), things are backwards. All this suggests is that we have retrospectively carved up human existence in such a way that a plot can be established that requires an age of reason and an age of faith. So Reason and Faith (or the proletariat or Bismarck) become characters who appear to make things happen, but are actually functions of a plot. The whole thing could have been emplotted in so many other ways, and have been dominated by so many different (allegorical) characters. So it helps to ask here: what was this plot good for, and what did it cost in terms of lost possibilities? The economist's notion of "opportunity costs" is very important. What do we have to give up in order to tell a story in a certain way? These are the theoretical and historiographical questions that intrigue me. Your preexisting notion of plot tells you what counts and what doesn't count because the character is a function of plot.

43

What do we have to give up in order to tell a story in a certain way?

In the 1980s we experienced the "narrativist" or "rhetorical turn" in the philosophy of history. I think that the philosophy of history proclaiming this turn points out a very fruitful rhetorically oriented analysis of historical writing. It shows new possibilities of interpretation and restores an artistic dimension to historical writing. On the other hand, however, the result of this fetishization of method is that the philosophy of history overlooks something more important that had happened in historiography itself since the 1970s. It did not allow for the fact that the turn in historiography was made and it made history noble. History started to perform the role of a philosophy of life supporting traditional values. I agree with Franklin Ankersmit's statement in his interview that we should focus on the category of experience. This catches up with historiography and builds a bridge between the theory of history and historical writing.

A change can be observed when one looks into "postmodern" historical writing connected with the anthropology of history. This shift I can describe as a "turn" from macro to micro, from exterior to interior, from history seen as a progressive process to history experienced by man. This transformation is manifested in the microhistories written by Le Roy Ladurie, Ginzburg, and Darnton. Do you also notice this process?

44

There is a movement outward from the nation-state, which once provided a center. (This spatial talk of "centers" is quite imaginary, of course.) The movement is outward at each level to politics, to the social, and then to the personal, everyday life, and then to the human body at the periphery. It is outward movement because each place along the perimeter of this concentric circle is more widely spaced and farther apart from every other thing in that ring. That is to say that the personal is highly fragmented. My personal life is different from your personal life and all of our lives are different. So from that point we are really moving farther and farther apart as the history of personal, everyday life progresses. We see in *The Cheese and the Worms* this fragmentation of experience and in fact experience is highly fragmented. Now you ask about a limit. I speculated not long ago about this notion of limit with regard to Ricoeur's *Time and Narrative*. I noticed a few things there that struck me as odd, primarily in the footnotes where Ricoeur started talking about historians of death—people like Ariès and Vovelle. He speculated that the consciousness of death might be the limit of possible historical representation. I was not certain what he meant. I am still not certain what he meant, although I wrote about what it might have meant, but it was certainly a fascinating example of one major thinker puzzling about limits. I would give a hypothesis about his meaning. In the model we have been talking about—this concentricity of circles getting wider and wider up to the private—one might suggest that death is the most personal, private, and unshared of our experiences. This is a philosophical question of "one's own death." Of course, historians never talk about one's own death: they talk about public ceremonies, the deathbed rituals, wills, etcetera. But I suspect that Ricoeur had something more personal in mind: that the most personal thing and hence the boundary of history in this new movement toward the outside circle that we have been talking about, might be found in the experience of one's own death. Death from the logical point of view appeared to be the edge.

> Ricoeur speculated that the consciousness of death might be the limit of possible historical representation.

> The most personal thing and hence the boundary of history might be found in the experience of one's own death.

Don't you think that if we "touched" such specific and personal topics we should mention categories like the sublime and trauma? Should we get back to psychoanalysis?

> We have never left psychoanalysis.

We have never left psychoanalysis, for better or worse. I have been very much influenced by a certain vision of psychoanalysis. To me

The Interpretation of Dreams, a book I love to teach and love to read, is not about dreams, it is about interpretation. To me this is the great book on hermeneutics. My fascination with Freud is that I see myself there, on every page. I turn the page and I say: "Yes, there I am. What he is describing there proves he knew me." The kind of discourse that Freud produced in *The Interpretation of Dreams* and elsewhere fascinates me because of the way in which he sees the dream as, shall we say, primarily cooked, never raw, not only in its manifest content but in its latent content as well. At all the stages by which he imagines dreams to be produced, we see reconfiguration of senselessness into at least pseudomeaningful forms. Nothing presented to us can be unplotted. The notion that the materials of the dream work are narrativized by something in the unconscious in order to present them to preconsciousness that is present to consciousness in the forms of the dream is a marvelously suggestive way of thinking about what historical thought is. This is why I am interested in Freud's strangely contradictory notion of "secondary revision."

Freud is one of those thinkers that one must not understand through paraphrases or the big statements, complexes and types, and so forth. Yet he is the sort of writer you may go to and just open the books anywhere and look for inspiration. The unconscious is like the "postmodern" or the sublime. It is something that appears in eruptions or disruptions, but once we turn our attention on it, we capture it, write it down, begin to talk about it, we turn it into something very different. This is why we cannot have the notion of the postmodern moment or properly postmodern theory. The present and the moment are tools to make narrative stories, not the materials from which these stories are made.

The notion of conscious-unconscious is just a stage in an ongoing series of repetitions that we have seen in the past two hundred years in Western culture—repetitions of the discourse of the sublime and beautiful. All these unstable dualities concern the thing we cannot grasp in form; again and again new pairs keep coming up. Modern and postmodern fall into that same category. I would like to be very careful to pay respect to the other side, the sublime side, of this paradigm, because once we try to characterize it we have in fact beautified the whole thing, beautified the nightmare, as I would suggest. The moment of present narrativization tends always to close in and swallow up the unstable dualism and turn it into a fully fashioned story or theory, to make the

The present and the moment are tools to make narrative stories, not the materials from which these stories are made.

46 sublime beautiful, to make it coherent, to make it understandable, to make it no longer sublime.

The sublime is unrepresentable by definition, and so in a sense my argument is extraordinarily simple. It is not just literary representation, it is any narrative or logical understanding. In the sublime we are experiencing the present moment as it exists, but it does not exist. We must always beautify it as a way of making sense and creating some kind of ongoing narrative plot.

What is the new purpose for the theory of history?

For me, at least, a new purpose is to explain when, how, and why a reader of history chooses to change the historical text from being a lens to view some aspect of the past into an object itself, with its own structure and historical particularity. This is the crucial question today. If a theoretical consideration of history deals exclusively with the past as the object of historical representation, it will certainly run into all the problems posed by narrativists who cite the ironic splendors and miseries of realism. To claim, on the other hand, that the historical text is merely an aesthetic object or a pure act of will is equally mistaken, and quite arrogant, however defensible it may be. Theory of history today must rest upon the requirement to take both ways of conceiving the historical text into account, even if there are contradictions and uncertainties in doing so. It should recognize a special sort of reader who will toggle back and forth, from naive realism to antifoundational skepticism—from a vision of the past as knowable and comprehensible to a resignation that all we have are figural linguistic accounts. Switching back and forth as we feel the need or desire and as we recognize the importance and truthfulness of our illusory representations—this is interesting.

Switching back and forth as we feel the need or desire and as we recognize the importance and truthfulness of our illusory representations—this is interesting.

Who is the most controversial philosopher of history?

Well, in the United States today, Foucault remains a great force on the generations after him. His work is the basis for current discussions of power, discourse, identity, event—all these things being related to the possibility of historical understanding. Perhaps there is too little controversy about his work. . . . For me, however, right now—Frank Ankersmit. I wish I could read Dutch.

Your book is entitled *Language and Historical Representation: Getting the Story Crooked*. What do you mean by the expression "getting the story crooked"? 47

I appropriated the phrase "to get the story crooked" from a casual comment made by Stephen Bann, whose work I admire very much. It was spoken in Germany across a large conference table in response to a philosopher of history who had just said: "Well, the point after all is to get the story straight." Bann said: "No, the point is to get the story crooked." For me, the statement "getting the story crooked" says two separate things. The first would be: the awareness that stories are made, that they do not come straight either from archives or from experience or from any form of reality and that any self-aware treatment of the artifacts of the past needs some awareness that one's configuration is always going to be crooked in a certain purposeful sort of way. There is in fact no simple straightness to the kind of stories that historians claim to find in the historical past. That is one aspect of it—simply an awareness on historians' part of the configurality of historical work, that you can figure different things in different ways. But the second part, which I consider my own particular point of major interest, comes in the process of reading history. I am very sensitive to the need to read with two different visions: on the one hand reading *through* the text toward some vision, some representation of the past or whatever it is that is being represented there. We can see language then as a kind of telescope that you look through, but a second eye always sees *language as a thing*, as Frank Ankersmit put it. This second eye understands the crookedness of our vision—that language is not a telescope helping us to see straight through to the subject, but rather more a kaleidoscope that breaks up fragments, presents different things to us in different times—a kind of constantly shifting vision that can never be adequately totalized because as you turn a kaleidoscope it is always falling into new situations.

We are concentrating our conversation on theory of history. And as I mentioned, I think that theory of history generally seems to be far removed from historical practice. I would like to ask your opinion of contemporary historiography. What do you think for instance about *mentalité* as representative of a new history?

> Language is not a telescope helping us to see straight through to the subject, but rather more a kaleidoscope that breaks up fragments, presents different things to us in different times—a kind of constantly shifting vision.

Certainly the enthusiasm for the concept of *mentalité* represents a certain moment in the development of a certain new history. I see it, however, as having a negative rather than a positive position. There have been so many "new histories." But the "*mentalité* moment" arose when the third generation of *Annales* historians rebelled against the apparent professional philistinism of their elders, the founders of the movement, with their apparatus of teams, "series," and enumeration. I think the younger ones realized that a "global" history as Braudel and the next generation envisioned it wasn't really very interesting, and became less interesting the more global it became. In a sense, it cost too much to renounce a world of ideas and human expression. So in the face of this boredom, but retaining their anxieties and identifications, they developed the concept of *mentalité* as a sort of reaction-formation, as Freud might say.

The same boredom seems to have driven the second generation to return to narrative, and even anecdote. The boredom seems to have come in stages. First came boredom with the sort of thing one can teach to a student; then, perhaps, appeared *The Return of Martin Guerre*, and finally follows the theoretical justification of how it fits the whole enterprise. Within the horizon of the *Annales* enterprise, I suppose they did the best they could. It is, after all, (or was) a rather procrustean project with many built-in assumptions that could be questioned only at great expense to the whole. It could not, however, answer the question LaCapra posed so well: "Is everyone a *mentalité* case?"

It is perfectly impossible for me to demonstrate with any sort of rational rigor that Dante, or Freud, or whoever you wish, escapes to some extent the limits prescribed by the boundaries and topography of a mental world shared by masses of people. Yet, I believe that Freud is both more than, and other than, the intersection of late-nineteenth-century psychological, social, sexual, Jewish, medical, etcetera discourses. And I believe that no one can demonstrate to me that I am wrong in my belief. Perhaps it is a question here of what kind of world one chooses to be a part of—an ethical question, in other words. So I ask myself, what sort of world are the *mentalité* historians choosing? What future follows from this choice? (Here I am thinking of Immanuel Kant's suggestion in his essay of 1795, "An Old Question Raised Again: Is the Human Race Constantly Progressing") that the future is determined by mental events, essentially decisions about how to

I ask myself, what sort of world are the *mentalité* historians choosing? What future follows from this choice?

conceive the past. Whether Kant was correct or not, it is always worthwhile to ask what version of the future does any vision of the past entail.

Now the one thing I can identify about the history of *mentalité*, as a subset of the *Annales* mission, is that it is a project that can be pursued systematically by many researchers with the hope that their "findings" can be correlated by some future effort into a broader, better proportioned account of how things came to be. In short, some unification of views is at least possible as a goal. Not quite a metanarrative in Lyotard's sense, but some social project. Without that one has studies and monographs, but they cannot be tallied up. Each stands as a separate world of its own. It is the anxiety before such a situation that has led to the elimination of the Dantes and Freuds from the set of topics a proper historian may study. The essence of history as an idiographic *Wissenschaft* was once taken to be its nonrepeatability. This was the neo-Kantian solution—to separate historical from law-producing forms of knowledge. This German solution associated with Rickert and Windelband has fought with the French solution for a century. The struggle defines historiographical modernity.

The history that cannot be tallied up is an aesthetic object. To acknowledge and explore the possibility that this is precisely what histories may well be is surely the essence of the postmodern historical turn. Seen this way, the study of *mentalité* really doesn't differ from the study of individuals or even single texts.

> It is always worthwhile to ask what version of the future any vision of the past entails.

Is there a crisis in historical thought?

Yes, history is in crisis. This is its normal state. Remember, an interest in history is not a natural feeling at all. A culture must have a real and widely shared sense of loss to set up the institutions of research and monumentalization that "history" requires in any form that we would recognize. How large the gap in lived experience must have been for such a bizarre enterprise to have started! So crisis is the start of it all. Without crisis it stagnates. I take this to be the import of Nietzsche's thoughts on history. He wanted to revive the sense of crisis. And Heidegger and his progeny followed him in that aim.

This is, and is not, the crisis to which you are referring. Surely any crisis of history in the 1990s is the crisis of modern historiography, and just as surely that crisis took its form in the crisis of

> History is in crisis. This is its normal state.

> Any crisis of history in the 1990s is the crisis of modern historiography.

The current problems are not the problems of a culture, but of a profession.

historicism a century ago. The current problems, however, are not the problems of a culture (which can do without the work of historians because it is drowning in a trivialized sort of historical environment), but of a profession. What can university historians do to make people care about history in a culture where stories about the past are numberless? What new information, new topics, new media can catch the minds of anyone? What new or old justifications can be offered for preferring such accounts? The dream of a universal history (the Great Story) has rarely been made explicit, but, as I suggested in my comments about *Annales* history, the implicit notion that separate historical accounts can be brought into focus, even in the minimal sense of being multiple perspectives, is crucial to a reasonably healthy historical profession. For a long time it has been clear that professional historians working in a row of offices along a single corridor have little to do with one another, and are doing not only different things but different kinds of things. The mentality/society/economy/nature sequence (or any such system of sublimated materialism) offered a dream of bringing these things into some future coherence, but dreams like this all vanish at dawn. And are dreamed again the next night. The crisis is that we keep inventing these accounts with no convincing justification for doing so. It seems to be instinct. At least, for us. Yet it is absurd to speak of an instinct *for us*, because if it is only our situation, it cannot be instinct.

The really interesting question to ask would be: What does it mean for a culture to be satisfied with an account of the past? Perhaps this was the satisfaction Nietzsche was describing when he mentioned the happiness of cows, who had no historical needs because they didn't know they were going to die? So I suppose that the "crisis rhetoric" that Nietzsche and Heidegger have bequeathed us is accurate enough, if a little overworked. We know we are not cows, and that we shall die. History is in a permanent crisis of normality.

History is in a permanent crisis of normality.

Your professional development is influenced by Hayden White. You were Professor White's student and you have devoted several articles to White's theory. I would like to ask you several questions about Hayden White. We have just celebrated White's sixty-fifth birthday and the twentieth anniversary of the publishing of *Metahistory*. What do

you think about the lasting interest in Hayden White's theory?

I think that *Metahistory* is several books in one. There is first the compact theory, a formalist theory of the historical work described in the first forty-seven pages, and then there are reflections on the course of the philosophy of history from the nineteenth to the beginning of the twentieth century, and then there are the series of specific readings of the historians involved. Your response to *Metahistory* at any given moment will depend on which book you are talking about. As White himself used to point out, *Metahistory* was obsolete at the time it appeared in the 1970s. It appeared in 1973, but I recall that in the later 1970s, and early 1980s, after he would give a lecture he would say (with characteristic exaggeration), "they asked me to come talk about tropology and all these things, and I found the graduate students know more about it than I do." I think that the reason he could say that is that in moving from one rhetorical situation to another, from one game to another game, White brought with him the kind of concerns that came from the first one, the historical game. Students of literature would naturally seem less inhibited than those who had been trained to historian's anxieties.

Let me put it in this way: White published *Metahistory* in 1973 after about ten or fifteen years of being immersed in and frustrated by the level of discourse about historiography. This was mainly in the 1960s, when I was White's student. In his seminars we had read the kind of books that were being written about historical texts, and are still being written in historical terms about historians, and they were primarily political and naive. You would take a historian or a school of historians and you were supposed to ask yourself: what is their political stand toward the French Revolution, toward the working class, revolutionary origins, Napoleon?—that kind of thing. It was difficult to incorporate *Metahistory* within that discourse when it appeared; it was radical, it was a major step forward. It was a major step forward because it brought into historiography certain kinds of allegories from other fields and did it in a very schematic way. The fourfold plots of Northrop Frye, the tropes of Vico, the world hypotheses of Stephen Pepper, and Karl Mannheim's four fundamental ideologies look remarkably simple and even simple-minded when you begin to look at them as a system. But in terms of providing the kind of rhetorical topoi,

52 rhetorical tools that could be applied to the texts of Michelet, Tocqueville, Marx, and Ranke, the system made possible a different look at works that had not been dealt with systematically in other than ideological terms. It provided White with the kind of flexibility that he needed there.

So I think that the first part of *Metahistory* was in fact dead on arrival because it was so clearly patched together for White's own needs and purposes at the moment. Perhaps it was a scaffold to be used and dismantled. Then we move into the readings themselves. White's model and one of his great intellectual debts is to Erich Auerbach and to *Mimesis*. As he taught us back in 1966 and 1967, this notion of taking a passage from a text and unfolding that passage in such a way as to figure forth something much larger was an idea that really intrigued him very much. This is what he tries to do with the readings of *Metahistory*. I think that today we find *Metahistory* (at least I find *Metahistory*) interesting to reread insofar as White has succeeded in bringing his citations to life. What he managed to do was to create an artificial structure that enabled him to handle his historical texts in a new way so that his own originality and insights could come through. Systematically, *Metahistory* has serious difficulties at every point, but rhetorically speaking, in terms of a moment and an audience, a situation and (from White's point of view) a purpose, I think it was and is a tremendous success.

Is *Metahistory* a literary theory of the historical text, or is it a rhetorical intervention into the historiographical debate of the early 1970s for the purpose of changing the habits and ways of thinking of readers of history?

But these are different questions. The question remains: Is *Metahistory* a literary theory of the historical text (that is, is it really a "Poetics of the Nineteenth-Century Historical Imagination"), or is it a rhetorical intervention into the historiographical debate of the early 1970s for the purpose of changing the habits and ways of thinking of readers of history? If we take it in the first sense, *Metahistory* is just as dated as almost every other work that was written twenty years ago. In the sense of rhetorical intervention to change people's ways of reading—not that they follow the exact method of *Metahistory*—in ways that are unimaginable, uncalculable, I think it was a great success.

In your review of *Metahistory* you put White in the circle of "philologist reformers." Could you please tell me, who else can be included in that group?

I was thinking of what I knew about White's intellectual background, the people he studied. His origin is as a medievalist, but then he quickly began to move around (interestingly, within an Italian context—Lorenzo Valla, Vico, Croce). He is another one of these "philologist reformers." Erich Auerbach, for example, is also a philologist-historian. One might even suggest that Foucault partially fits the description. This version of humanism believes that the situation of human beings is determined by literary and linguistic possibilities. The first instance for modern times, in this version at least, comes with Lorenzo Valla and the Renaissance as opposed to the theological or divine authoritativeness of the Middle Ages. The sense there was that we could create the world by creating a true language as opposed to simply copying God's world. This is the kind of thing that White was talking about. And that's what I meant.

This humanist is the person who studies language in such a way as to liberate humanity by pointing out that men indeed are free. White seemed very much influenced by French existentialism and he later confirmed to me that he was at one time passionately interested in Sartre. I made a lot of this hypothesis about his work in that essay, "A Bedrock of Order" (which was a lecture in the first instance at the large conference on *Metahistory* in 1979). For all of this fascination with Foucault, White was in no way part of the death of man, the death of the author, the death of the reader, this sort of postmodern world of subjects as simply colliding functions. He doesn't want to live in that world. And this is why I related him back to Sartre, to existentialism, and above all to the question of choice. The word *choice* comes up in White's work at crucial moments. For example: when he invokes the term *rhetoric* he defines the rhetorical situation as any situation in which choices must be made; the study of how those choices are made and formulated will always be rhetorical. His humanism insists, absurdly in my opinion, but all the better for that, that we are creatures with will, that we make choices, and that these choices are made without any necessarily solid basis in reality, but rather with an armory of cultural conventions that we have been bequeathed and with the mysterious physical personality of an individual.

White says in the introduction to *Tropics of Discourse* that the Kantian faculty of will is an area that has been neglected. I think

> White seemed very much influenced by French existentialism.

> For all of this fascination of Foucault, White was in no way part of the death of man, the death of the author, the death of the reader, this sort of postmodern world of subjects as simply colliding functions. He doesn't want to live in that world.

54   it was already in *Tropics of Discourse*, and he says that he was not
ashamed to call himself Kantian, and not ashamed to emphasize
this notion of will that is precisely the cover for something you
cannot delve beyond. So in an essay called "Hayden White and the
Kantian Discourse," I emphasize will and this sense of choice and
how that leads to rhetoric, the sense of needs of the moment and
situation.

Lionel Gossman is today, like many others, still profoundly
troubled by *Metahistory* and even by the kind of work that he,
Gossman, was himself doing in the 1970s. He has become increasingly insistent, especially in his essay in *Between History and
Literature*, on the importance of the referent and referentiality.
It's a most peculiar situation. He wrote a new essay for his collection of historical essays in which he disavows them! At least this
is how I read it. I read the manuscript of that volume and I was
amazed. I couldn't imagine writing a seventy-nine-page typed
manuscript saying that everything you've been doing in all these
essays you are publishing is, shall we say, not wrong perhaps, but
dangerous. I've never met Gossman but I called him to congrat-
ulate him on the book because I was glad to see it. I admire these
essays and have learned from them. All this discussion is good,
even the worries and concerns that he expresses.

The question of the political and social danger of questioning the referent of history remains a crucial one. In White's work
of the 1980s, particularly in the essays collected in *The Content of
the Form*, he talks about that, and emphasizes that he in no way
belongs to the poststructuralist camp that denies the reality of evidence and historical facts. He seems to pull back from a radical
attack on representation at all levels and to suggest that there is a
kind of special level—emplotment—at which mere documented
happenings gel into the meaning for discourse. It is on this point
that he wants to focus by saying that it is there that the social conventions that determine what kind of plots are available to a culture at a certain time prevail. And it's also in emplotment that he
focuses his notion of tropology. This idea governs the process by
which happenings become documented facts, and evidences are
turned into proper narratives. This applies both across a given
level of discourse in terms of relating parts and wholes and in the
movements between the levels, moving up from what we might

White emphasizes
that he in no way
belongs to the
poststructuralist
camp that denies
the reality of evi-
dence and histori-
cal facts.

call the lexical to the grammatical, to syntactic, to the semantic. Tropes as formalized misunderstandings, one might say, are the models of the processes that govern our understanding. At any given point one has a very large number of possibilities available, and directions to choose from.

Here White is emphasizing his continuing belief in the utility of formal structures and the value of the structuralist project, which pretty much was falling apart in the 1970s under the impact of poststructuralism—Derrida, in whom White has very little practical interest; Foucault, in whom White has had tremendous interest; and Stanley Fish. And that's interesting, because in the United States today Derrida is a limited, passé, concern, but Foucault remains a kind of passionate center for people. White seems to have perceived that early on.

What about Barthes?

White has been concerned with Barthes as long as I have known him. It was simply Barthes's rhetorical originality that was the source of his appeal. White was aware from the beginning that Barthes was always playing with the readers. And in a sense, White is doing the same thing. Each new work of Barthes showed a different writer; from the late 1950s on, from *Mythologies* to the last essay, he was always changing. First you have the modern mythology and all the structuralist business. And then you have *Elements of Semiology*, and you have once again schemes and so forth, but it's different from the former. And then you move on, work by work. And in each work, particularly in *S/Z*, you get this enormous structural framework poised in order to do a quite small job. The reader who was challenged by these texts might think: "I've got to work and work and master the proairetic, the hermeneutic codes, and all of these codes so I can go out and use them." Then Barthes goes on to his next work and says in effect: "Oh, I'm done with all that. I am never going to use that system again." It was the creation of the structure: the theory was just a kind of pretext for the event itself. It was never meant to be part of a big methodology, it was a parody of methodology. Barthes would go on in *A Lover's Discourse* about the way lovers think about their beloved, and then of course he would start reflecting on pictures,

White was aware from the beginning that Barthes was always playing with the readers. And in a sense, White is doing the same thing.

Any theory is suitable for one situation only.

and his mother, and himself. It was the sense of situation, the sense that any theory is suitable for one situation only, which marks the virtuosity of Barthes, that White always has admired. In particular, Barthes's aristocratic casualness about method stands out.

In *Metahistory*, White built a framework that allowed him to go in and be the virtuoso reader he was able to be. His continued work with tropology as a methodology, however, contradicts what I have just said. I find this interesting. After *Metahistory*, for about seven years, White hammered home the idea of tropology as an available master discourse in all those essays that form *Tropics of Discourse* and in a number of other essays that were never collected in a book. He spelled out tropology over and over, extending it, broadening it, adapting it a little bit but keeping it as basically a kind of straightjacket for discourse. And then in the 1980s he basically shelved it. In *The Content of the Form*, his collection of essays from the 1980s, I think "trope" appeared once, casually. Suddenly he turned to something else, and that something else was narrative. He may have sensed that he was putting forth rules for a game that either people were not playing or they weren't playing in the same way he was. He had done what he could. Narrative was where the subject of conversation was, and he is interested in narrative and, in particular, in emplotment. It

Narrative is a code for tropology, or, put another way, tropology is a code for narrativity. At least for Hayden White.

is closely related to tropology. In fact, I suspect that narrative is a code for tropology, or, put another way, tropology is a code for narrativity. At least for Hayden White.

In 1979, when I first wrote on *Metahistory*—my essay "A Bedrock of Order"—my feeling was that for him Northrop Frye's plot structures and the tropes of Vico were virtually interchangeable. Particularly when he came to Irony and Satire—Irony the trope, Satire the plot—it is difficult to tell them apart. He even slips once or twice in *Metahistory* and uses one in a context where the other would be appropriate in terms of the point he is making. I think that White has always thought in terms of Romance as metaphor, metaphor as Romance. Metonymy—well, that's Tragedy, Tragedy—that's Metonymy, and so forth. So the turn to narrative in the 1980s was only a renaming. This "confusion" deepens and humanizes the tropes, which seemed very dehumanized at first. For example, his first readings of Foucault (in "Foucault Decoded") cast Foucault as a tropologist. By the 1980s, Louis O. Mink, Paul Ricoeur, and others had brought about an emphasis on narrative and the notion that humans are basically narrating animals. I think that White believes that.

Could you tell me about Hayden White's attitude toward Ricoeur. White seemed to sympathize with Ricoeur's theory (I am thinking about his essay dealing with *Time and Narrative* in particular). Recently, however, White told me that Ricoeur is passé. What has happened?

Well, I don't think anything happened. I think that White will use Ricoeur as he needs him. I think, for example, that White's essay on Ricoeur in *The Content of the Form* is meant to be what one calls epideictic rhetoric, the rhetoric of praise. It was presented in a context that was celebratory.

I suspect that to some extent White admires Ricoeur as a human being. For White, feelings about people tend to be very important, for all of his ironic facade. I think he feels friendship with people very closely. Nevertheless, he seems to feel a higher responsibility to the future. So in a context here with young people and a debate that has gone beyond Ricoeur, he would say: "Ricoeur is passé, Derrida is passé, Foucault is passé, *Metahistory* is passé, I'm passé." He is saying all these things in order to open up a space in which new things can be said, and in which you and I are free to be critical. In a different context, however, when he is reflecting on a certain kind of meditation about time and about narrative by an individual who is writing not just from the scholarly position but also from a kind of personal and moral position, as Ricoeur—in my opinion—frequently does, White will invoke quite different terms, play different games with different rules, and will channel his discourse into the needs of that moment. That is what I mean when I say that White is a rhetorical personality. It's not that you mustn't take what he says seriously. It's always serious. But you must always look very carefully at the context in which he is saying it.

So, what does the concept passéness mean? Are Shakespeare, or Michelet, or Tocqueville passé? The answer is: yes and no. I think, as White taught us, that the rhetorical responsibility is to create new contexts in which those individuals would not be passé, in which they will be changed in such a way as to serve our purposes in the new context, for the new audience and a new problem.

White would say: 'Ricoeur is passé, Derrida is passé, Foucault is passé, *Metahistory* is passé, I'm passé.' He is saying all these things in order to open up a space in which new things can be said.

White is a rhetorical personality. It's not that you mustn't take what he says seriously. It's always serious. But you must always look very carefully at the context.

What does the concept passéness mean?

58   White does not want to be turned into a monument. He wants always to be part of the action. So he will say in effect: "That part of me is passé. That's gone. I don't remember *Metahistory* because I'm always interested in what's around me right now. So forget everything that happened in the past." In the same sense, Roland Barthes changed with every book. That's my impression of his personality.

What do you consider White to be?

I asked him that once. I asked him what he considered himself and he said: "I am a writer." Just like that. I tried to make sense of that statement a long time ago. It sounded typically flippant and I think at that time he must have had Barthes in mind. I really think there was a period in which he felt that the proper model for the intellectual today was someone like Roland Barthes. Barthes was the first exemplar of a kind of cultural critic, which is another phrase he used for himself in *Tropics of Discourse* where he called himself a cultural critic. He was doing that sort of thing before cultural studies in America became so dreadfully ideological and rigid. He has always maintained an irony and flexibility characteristic of the writer who simply is interested in rhetoric, both as a way of experiencing the world and as a process of production. That's what I would say. White is a writer.

White said: "I am a writer."

Which of these people/theories are related most to White's theory: Ricoeur, Barthes, Foucault, Mink, LaCapra.

The generation born between 1940 and 1947 or '48 produced in America and here in Europe a number of scholars whose work was influenced by Hayden White because these people entered the discourse at just about the moment of *Metahistory*: LaCapra is one of the older ones; Ankersmit certainly; in England, Stephen Bann; in America we have Allan Megill, Philippe Carrard, Linda Orr, Larry Shiner, a few students of White—like me, Sande Cohen, and indeed a number of others.

There are a few individuals closer to White's age, like Lionel Gossman, Bob Berkhofer, and Nancy Struever, who are interested in these sort of things, and all of them show deep concern and distrust and worry about it. There is also a younger generation—

like Ann Rigney at Utrecht—who are doing other things. I see a kind of window: people born between about 1942 and 1948, the real first generation to be influenced more or less directly by White, doing the kind of work that the pattern of *Metahistory* laid out.

The other figures you mention—Barthes and Foucault—were not personally close to White. He knew their work, but I don't think he ever met them. He had a feeling that thinkers are to be known through their work rather than by personal experience. But at a different time and age he might have felt differently about his own contemporaries. I would say that he absorbed their example rather than their lessons. He never wrote much about Barthes, as far as I know. But he spent a good deal of time thinking about and writing about Foucault. Foucault is a very difficult individual to get hold of, but White perceived Foucault's importance very early on and spent time with his books before they were translated. What he tried to do was to turn Foucault into a replica of himself. He doesn't always read individuals that way, but I think that with Foucault, more than anyone else, White was concerned to appropriate this very powerful mind for his own thinking, and indeed to grasp it, in a sense forcing it into the kind of categories that he, White, needed at the time. So Foucault's early work became a sort of lesson in tropology. The later essay on Foucault's rhetoric also shows the kind of things that White was thinking about. He used Foucault as a kind of litmus paper for his own purposes.

You asked about Louis Mink. It's not just that Mink was influenced by White or White was influenced by Mink. I think they developed together as friends. Mink began from a traditional attitude about narrative and what narrative did in history. He thought about it in terms of the Anglo-American philosophical tradition of Gallie and Danto. He began coming up with some very disturbing conclusions. He seemed to say: "You know, I don't know what to make of this, but this is where my thoughts lead." And White grasped those conclusions. I think that his turn toward narrative came from Louis Mink.

> White had a feeling that thinkers are to be known through their work rather than by personal experience.

> I think White's turn toward narrative came from Louis Mink.

Let me come back to Foucault. Foucault is very often considered a precursor of postmodernism. What signs of postmodernism can we find in Foucault's writing and are there

60 **are any similarities between Foucault and White on this subject?**

As far as historians are concerned, Foucault's postmodernism is to be found in his assertion that discourse—the linguistic forms that institutional power takes—lies impenetrably between us and the past. Wherever we look for signs of life, we find encoded and self-referential mountains of texts dictating what counts as life and what doesn't. To my knowledge, Foucault had little interest in the language of discourse—what we would call formal concerns. Perhaps he felt that since the rules of discourse would govern any possible decoding of it from within, so to speak, it was more important to explore the implications of discourse rather than its language. They are quite different.

As a formalist who finds ideological potentials in the forms of narrative, White rarely stresses the discursive wall and its institutions, although he has interesting things to say about historical professionalization as desublimation. But he does seem to grant the cogency of the objection to any sense of an unmediated past or present. In White, as opposed to Foucault, there is more of a Kantian emphasis on the unavailability of things to our experience. His concerns have been with studying how we know. His tropology is his epistemology, and he holds fast to it. In this sense he has little to do with the nomadic thought or the antifoundationalism of the postmoderns, although he is often sympathetic to their speculations. Perhaps his constant encouragement of innovation and experiment in historical representation and the disruptions this inevitably causes derives from his conviction that he possesses a key to the order of texts. It is important to understand that both Foucault and White want order, but also want things that produce disorder.

White's tropology is his epistemology.

Certainly Foucault should be counted as more "postmodern" than White, but doing so must take into account the differing rhetorical situations in which they found themselves. So much of the energy of postmodern theory (back when it had energy) came from its rhetoric of crisis and apocalypse. The French built careers on hyperbole, extreme similes ("like a face drawn in sand"), and a constant vision of the end of one thing or another. Asking for explanations or definitions is bad form in this discourse. White comes from a very conservative rhetorical background as an American medieval historian; every statement he made was challenged and

So much of the energy of postmodern theory (back when it had energy) came from its rhetoric of crisis and apocalypse.

had to be clarified time after time, and not in magazine interviews but rather in university lecture halls in front of an audience of bemused or hostile historians and puzzled graduate students. Both White and Foucault sought a critique of the forms of knowledge—the Kantian project, one might say. The question is what lies on the other side of our world, in the part to which we have no access. Foucault follows Nietzsche in supposing will and power to be flowing "out there," apart from the subjects formed by discourse. White seems more convinced by Schiller's suggestion of a sublime and meaningless chaos of happenings, real happenings, that are given meaning by human narrative (that is, tropological) powers. I think he sees more cogency in the romantics than is common today, although Richard Rorty also appeals to their example.

What is the most important feature of White's theory?

I think it would be the tension between White's attention to the unstable, shifting rhetorical situation and his continuing emphasis on structures and forms that make that moment possible. This tension in White parallels the tension in much American criticism of the last two decades. On the one hand, White is very sensitive to disruptions and free, indeterminate things that occur when you find yourself in a particular situation. This I would call the existential absurdity of moments in time. It's not clear how we got here, you and I, sitting in this room, and it's not clear what we have to do here, or what we are going to do here. There is no script for life. But at the same time we are going to do something here. White wants to make sense of and to appropriate this moment by suggesting that there are social and formal conventions that will guide us in carrying out the work of our worlds, but they pull at these two feelings (the open or existential and the determined or conventional). What I see in White is that tension—you never know which way he is going to go at the moment, whether his emphasis on structures would be leading him in one direction, or whether the sense of openness, the rhetorical options and indeterminacy of a given situation (speaker, will, audience, desire), is going to pull another way. That's why I think it is frustrating to ask for consistency from one situation to another because you don't know in which direction he is going to be moving at any one moment. That tension is the most important, I think.

We can observe White's "development" from *Metahistory* to *The Content of the Form*; that is, from tropics to the narrative itself. However, Hayden White told me that he wanted to extend his theory of tropes.

I try to look for patterns in White and there are many schemes. Even before he knew what the schemes were going to be, he would just go to the blackboards and fill them with charts. These charts didn't mean very much to his seminars. I never figured them out twenty-five years ago; now I know that it's the need to spatialize knowledge that marks a formalist.

He was then trying to deal with a permanent, stable structure that will enable and permit an indefinitely large number of possible situations. In a sense *Metahistory* had the same kind of goal—a generative grammar of historical discourse—that Chomsky was looking for in the 1950s and 1960s in terms of syntactic structures. White still believes in that sort of thing. I'm glad to hear that White is going to extend the theory of tropes, because part of me believes in that project, too. I think it was a very excellent venture. Declaring structuralism and the structuralist project to be dead and over—well, this dismissal is just a moment in time. Structuralism needs to be made relevant again to new needs and new situations. I'm glad to hear that he still wants to do that.

White's theory of tropes is an important part of his philosophy. What is your understanding of tropology?

Tropology is the study of precisely how we are living in error when we use language. When we use words, we are not lying, but we are just in error. We are speaking truth in a form of illusion. Irony is the trope of tropology, but metaphor is the trope of tropes, which is a different thing. Tropology is a self-consciousness about the nature of language use that we might describe as necessary errors. Irony becomes a kind of purely theoretical model and ideal trope of a vision that like all of the others is impossible for us.

Hans Blumenberg has suggested that the human race has survived because of its inability to confront reality directly. We always use substitutions for reality, which he sees as a rhetorical mode of survival. Philosophical anthropology, he suggests, must

Tropology is the study of precisely how we are living in error when we use language. When we use words, we are not lying, but we are just in error.

Hans Blumenberg has suggested that the human race has survived because of its inability to confront reality directly.

be essentially a rhetorical study. I think that tropology, and the sensitivity to the inevitable turning away from reality that it fosters, help with this project. And historical study is clearly a vital form of turning away from reality toward something else that offers us a perspective on reality, which I take to be always present; that is, in the present. This present, however, is impossible to grasp. Historical writing is not only a substitute for the present, but also constitutes one by presenting a version of memory that leads to a version of intention toward the future. The present would seem, then, to exist as the place where a memory and an intention meet. Insofar as past and future, memory and intention, are turns away from the static reality of the present, they are tropes and wishes.

However, memory is a highly suspect form of historical writing, indeed, it is not historical writing at all. It may be historical evidence but it can never serve us as historical writing. And that is because we always experience a present. Ricoeur reminds us that the present is the only thing that exists and that there are three presents: there is the present of the past in memory; the present of the present in experience; the present of the future in anticipation or hope. Even the past is only a mode of a present. This is why I think we find ourselves in the important world of narrative and theory of narrative. What narrative does is to configure a certain form of real or imaginary events in such a way as to produce at the end the sense that we are here in the stable present for a moment. The present is a moment that rules over all past events and dominates their meaning.

What about the problem of historical truth in White's theory?

White has at least two different ways of discussing the question of historical truth, I think. In the first place, in the first section of *Metahistory*, he deals very briefly with the state of the argument up to then in Anglo-American philosophy of history. There were two basic alternative theories: correspondence theory, in which statements correspond to some defineable referents for their reality, one way or another, and coherence theory, in which discourses somehow created their own sense of self-referential coherent truth. Basically, what White did about that is to say: "I'm not going to judge which is right or wrong. I'm not going to play this game." Very frequently in *Metahistory*, White avoids particular kinds of arguments. What about coherence versus correspondence? He simply implies: "I'm not interested at all in that. That language is not relevant to what I'm doing here in a direct way. Read the rest of my work and you can probably figure out where I stand. But if I get caught up in that discourse, playing that game, in that language, first of all I won't be doing the kind of thing that I intend to do; I will be writing different books. Second, I won't be able to move or get very far, because that discourse is already so highly worked out and entangled that almost all the moves in it have already been made by someone." So in a sense the philologist humanist simply sweeps away the old vocabulary: We are not going to take up scholastic argument anymore. But another thing he does in *Metahistory* is to say that already by the eighteenth century, already by Kant, the question of historical truth and historical referentiality have reached the crisis that he describes by running through Kant's three modes of historical thought in his late work of the 1790s.

By the way, another influence on White was a colleague at the University of Rochester named Lewis White Beck—a much older man. Beck was America's leading Kant scholar and was quite interested in Kant's late historical writings, which he edited. Their discussions had an important effect on White's turn in the middle 1960s. Kant described three modes of history: either the human condition is always getting better, or it is always getting worse, or it is what Kant called abderitic (what White called farcical or absurd history), in which case it just gets better, then gets worse, gets better and gets worse, but ultimately moves nowhere. Without directional consistency, it doesn't mean anything. White's point of view on the question of historical truth resembles Kant's solution to that problem, which in my estimation is an existential one. Kant says we have to eliminate the abderitic. God would never create an absurd world. But the difficulty is that we have no basis of evidence for choosing among these three possibilities. How can we know? We can't, Kant concludes. So we have to choose the one that will enable us to move toward the kind of future that we envision as a goal—the utopian vision. Consequently, Kant says, we must choose the future we want, and the kind of history we will imagine will reflect that choice. I think White took these things to heart one hundred percent. That's White's ethical idea. You write the kind of history that enables you to envision the kind of future that you want.

In *Metahistory* White criticizes Burckhardt and Croce severely. In Burckhardt's absurdism it is the idea of nondirectionality that strikes White as being neither right, nor wrong, nor true, nor false, but *wicked*. It is a choice of an absurd world. White seems to believe that one's historical position is a kind of moral choice. At least he asserts this in *Metahistory*. And that moral choice was articulated for him by Kant. He proceeds to say that after the end of the eighteenth-century crisis of historical truth, the tradition builds toward a certain meaning for history. He sees Hegel's philosophy of history as nothing less than an attempt to escape from the historical doubt and insecurity left behind by Kant. He sees that this process repeats itself again in the nineteenth century, leading up to Nietzsche, who is again caught in the situation of historical irony and the desperate need to escape from it. White sees formal reflection on history as proceeding in a series of cycles, leading ultimately toward skepticism, irony, and a new overcoming. A crisis, which was to be gotten beyond. That's the second aspect of the historicizing of the question of historical truth in White. When all is said and done, I feel that White's rhetorical sense of the moment, or *kairos*, is perfectly historical in a traditional sense. So we end back at the question of truth, where we began.

65

You write the kind of history that enables you to envision the kind of future that you want.

We end back at the question of truth, where we began.

Groningen, The Netherlands
26 February 1993

SELECTED WRITINGS

Language and Historical Representation: Getting the Story Crooked. Madison: Univ. of Wisconsin Press, 1989.
A New Philosophy of History, coeditor with Frank Ankersmit. Chicago: Univ. of Chicago Press, 1995.

"A Bedrock of Order: Hayden White's Linguistic Humanism." *History and Theory*, Beiheft 19: Metahistory: Six Critiques (1980): 1–29.

66 "Beautifying the Nightmare: The Aesthetics of Postmodern History." *Strategies: A Journal of Theory, Culture, and Politics* 4/5 (1991): 289–331.

"Hayden White and the Kantian Discourse: Freedom, Narrative, History." In *The Philosophy of Discourse: The Rhetorical Turn in Twentieth-Century Thought*, ed. Chip Sills and George H. Jensen, vol. 1. Portsmouth NH: Boynton/Cook, 1992.

"Naive and Sentimental Realism: From Advent to Event." *Storia della storiografia* 22 (1992): 117–23.

"Afterword: Reading Rhetorical Redescriptions." In *Rethinking the History of Rhetorics*, ed. Takis Poulakos, 241–56. Boulder: Westview, 1993.

"Twenty Years After: A Note on *Metahistories* and Their Horizons." *Storia della storiografia* 24 (1993): 109–17.

"'As Real as It Gets': Ricoeur and Historical Narrativity." In *Meanings in Texts and Actions: Questioning Paul Ricoeur*, ed. David E. Klemm and William Schweiker, 49–66. Charlottesville: Univ. Press of Virginia, 1993.

"After the Fall: October Reflections on the Histories of Rhetoric." In *Writing Histories of Rhetoric*, ed. Victor Vitanza. Carbondale: Southern Illinois Univ. Press, 1994.

"'Never Again' Is Now." *History and Theory* 33, no. 2 (1994): 127–44.

Frank Ankersmit

> *What I am dreaming of*
> *is a historical theory that will*
> *concentrate on the notion of*
> *historical experience.*

Could you please tell me how your interest in historical theory started?

■ When I left secondary school I decided to study physics and mathematics. These were the subjects that I was most interested in and for which I had good marks. You should know, moreover, that I left secondary school in the beginning of the 1960s, so at a time when what we would call a "positivist" mentality was widely shared—also in my family—and that also contributed to my choice for the exact sciences. But after I had studied physics and mathematics with little success for three years, it became clear that I had made a mistake. The conclusion was unavoidable that I did not have the right kind of mind for a subject like that—and history was for me the obvious alternative. It was such an obvious alternative because somewhere in my adolescence I had developed a strong nostalgic yearning for the eighteenth century that was initially inspired by the music of Bach, Mozart, and all the other eighteenth-century composers. As a historian, you sometimes ask yourself in which age you would have liked to live: in my case the question was and is not difficult to answer: the eighteenth century. Indeed, until this very day, I have the vague conviction that the fifty years preceding the French Revolution were the acme of Western civilization. In any case, after my mistake with physics and mathematics and after two years of military ser-

I had developed a strong nostalgic yearning for the eighteenth century that was initially inspired by the music of Bach, Mozart, . . .

I would like to live in the eighteenth century.

68 vice, I decided that I had better turn my hobby into my subject and decided to study history.

But when I started doing history, I was profoundly struck by the immense differences between the study that I had just given up and my new discipline. I really had the feeling of entering an entirely different world, and that is why I have always felt an intuitive resistance against any attempt to dismiss as irrelevant the differences between history and the humanities on the one hand and the sciences on the other. And that is also why I have always had my doubts about attempts made in the 1960s and 1970s to transform history into a (social) science and why I am unable to subscribe to Richard Rorty's opinion that there are no interesting differences between the humanities and the sciences. I should add, though, that to assess Rorty's argument correctly here one should bear in mind that he tends to project the kind of "rationality" we associate with history onto the sciences. To put it succinctly: with Rorty the days of the "unity of science" seem to have returned miraculously, but this time under the aegis of history and the humanities. Now it is history from which the world of science is colonized. However, I believe that in doing this Rorty is the disciple of Kuhn and of this whole post-Kuhnian climate of the historicization of scientific rationality. I am convinced that this historicization of science makes sense only from some metascientific point of view and not from the point of view of the everyday practice of physics, chemistry, or biology. From that point of view, the history of your discipline is largely irrelevant.

> With Rorty the days of the "unity of science" seem to have returned miraculously, but this time under the aegis of history and the humanities.

But to return to your question, what really amazed me when starting to study history was that you could earn a doctoral degree there by merely discussing and expounding the ideas of people like Hobbes, Kant, or Sartre. Having physics in mind, I had always believed that in a doctoral dissertation you would have to discover something new—something that no human being had ever thought of before yourself. And rewriting the texts of the kind of authors I just mentioned—authors, moreover, who one might believe to be intelligent enough to put their ideas on paper in a sufficiently clear and effective way—did not seem to leave any room for those kinds of discoveries. You have this quip of two conservative Prussian generals of the end of the last century discussing science with one another. Then one general asks the other with exasperation: "But what, then, is science in the end?" To which the other general replies: "What one Jew copies from another." Apart, of course, from the anti-Semitism of this little dialogue, this captures how I thought about history when I began to get an idea of what historians ordinarily do.

As you will understand from this, still having the sciences at the back of my mind I was deeply intrigued by a discipline like history and I began to ask myself questions like, what most peculiar kind of discipline is this?, why is it taught at the universities? and why is it intellectually taken seriously at all? Silly and stupid questions, of course, but that is how I became interested in historical theory (where one tries to answer unpractical questions like these) and why I even decided to study philosophy in order to get the right answer to them. I think each historian, in one phase or another of his intellectual career, tends to ask himself this kind of question. But most often they are sensible enough not to let these questions keep them from doing history itself. In my case, these kinds of preliminary questions took on Gargantuan proportions and have prevented me, so to speak, from "growing up" as a historian. I do not mean that as a *Herabsetzung* of historical theory: sometimes you may lose a lot by growing up, but you should recognize things for what they are and not want to make them look nicer than that.

You prefer to use the term theory of history rather than philosophy of history?

I find the word *philosophy*—perhaps unreasonably, for what is in a name?—a rather pretentious term. It always has this resonance of a search for wisdom, which to my intellectual ears still has some association with theology. The word *theory* seems to me relatively free from these connotations. Moreover, *theory* is more accommodating to influences from other disciplines like literary theory, aesthetics, or the history of art and literature—influences that I consider on the whole valuable and even indispensable.

And with regard to avoiding pretensions, there is this definition of philosophy by Locke that says the philosopher should conceive of himself as a kind of underlaborer who has to clear away some of the rubbish lying in the way of knowledge. That is a sensible view of philosophy, I would say. My only qualification would be that the philosopher will never be of any real help in the

70 production of knowledge, not even in Locke's modest way. He rather has to reflect on how traditional philosophical concerns, conceptions, and certainties have to be modified because of the results of scientific research. For example, taking historical writing as a given, the theoretician has to ask himself how historical writing complicates accepted philosophical certainties with regard to the relationship between language and reality. And physics stimulates, as everybody knows, many questions. Hence, philosophy should not be a foundationalist and aprioristic analysis of what goes on in the sciences and the humanities, but aposterioristic and content to ask some general questions only *after* the scientist and the historian have done their job.

Philosophy should not be a foundationalist and aprioristic analysis of what goes on in the sciences and the humanities, but aposterioristic and content to ask some general questions only after the scientist and the historian have done their job.

Who was your main source of inspiration?

When I wrote my book on narrative logic it was Leibniz whom I found most helpful and most inspiring. Narrative logic was, in fact, a logic developed from Leibniz's ontology, and I can still remember my surprise that so many traditional problems of historical theory could be solved in an, at least, not implausible way by having recourse to Leibniz's monadological ontology. Notions like metaphor, point of view in historical writing, and the historian's text and its logical properties, and phenomena like intertextuality and many other things like that, can all be clarified in a coherent and satisfactory way with the help of Leibniz's ontology and his predicate in subject principle. Another interesting aspect of Leibniz is that from his *Monadology* it is possible to derive a metaphysical explanation of both the exact sciences and historical writing. If one wishes to account for the similarities and the differences between history and the sciences, Leibniz's monadology gives you the right background. When elaborating all this, I really had the impression of entering a new and interesting area of theoretical investigation. That is also, more or less, why I am sure that my book on narrative logic is still the best thing I ever wrote.

Colleagues sometimes tell me that in their opinion I have become more radical since the time I wrote that book. But I myself do not think that I have moved much beyond the position defended in that book. One of the pleasant things of the book was that it permitted me to deduce almost mechanically a position on the many topics that are discussed in contemporary historical theory (and elsewhere) from the analysis of narrative language I gave in it. That is also why I never have had the feeling that I have added a lot to that book; what I have written since then is for ninety percent merely a matter of applying the major theses of the book to new problems. It may be, though, that the tonality of my language has become a bit more radical. This has much to do with the fact that I have tended to adopt the rhetoric of deconstructivism and of the relevant French theorists. *Narrative Logic* was a specimen of Anglo-Saxon philosophy of language (as exemplified by Strawson, whom I admired a lot at the time); the things I wrote these last five years sound rather "French," I would suppose. I deliberately opted for this change in tone in the hope of increasing the number of people who might be willing to read my writings. Though the book is sometimes referred to as representative of a certain kind of historical theory, *Narrative Logic* never had the slightest impact even in the small world of historical theorists. Of course, this has much to do with several evident shortcomings of the book itself: I went to the wrong publishing company, the book was poorly produced, written in an awkward and stiff English, and contained a lot of misprints. On top of that I had the misfortune that McCullagh's review of the book in *History and Theory* was the most hostile and most narrow-minded review that was ever published in that journal. The sad irony, by the way, is that I had myself suggested to the editors of *History and Theory* to ask McCullagh to write a review—a perfect example, I'd say, of how one can cut one's own throat. But the worst shortcoming of the book was that I had used the vocabulary and the way of arguing that were customary in Anglo-Saxon philosophy of language to demonstrate "Continental" conclusions. Whereas I had hoped to contribute in this way to bridging the gap between these two philosophical traditions, the result, instead, was that the book fell between two stools: so far as the book was noticed at all, the philosophers of language did not like my conclusions and the Continental structuralists and poststructuralists did not like my way of arguing. So, in fact, the book was dead even before it was born. In any case, what I learned from McCullagh's review was that a meaningful debate with positivistically minded people like him would be impossible. It was not merely a matter of disagreement; rather you could say that all the kind of things that I considered to be the most interesting and challenging problems of how the historian uses narrative language to account for the past were nonproblems for positivists like McCullagh. And that is why I decided I had better try to address those people in the field who speak and write in the language of Foucault, Barthes, and Derrida. The future will show whether I seem to make more sense in that new language than was the case when I spoke the idiom of Anglo-Saxon philosophy of language. I should add, though, that this is no longer of much concern to me, since I am now interested in political rather than historical theory. I have been doing historical theory for some fifteen years now, written five books on the subject, and I think it is only natural then that a certain ennui sets in and that you begin to look for something else.

However, to return to that, one of the predictable results of that change in philosophical style has been that my admiration for Hayden White increased tremendously. It only gradually dawned upon me what a powerful theoretical instrument tropology in fact is. Tropology really is what allows you get hold of a text—as I found out myself when I recently wrote an essay on Tocqueville. In that essay [published in the year following this interview, in *The Tocqueville Review*—ED.] I claim a place for paradox alongside irony. The difference between the two is that irony (like metaphor) is a game with language, with a system of associations etcetera. For example, if you know nothing of Lord Bolingbroke's highly dubious political career, you will not even recognize the irony of Samuel Johnson's statement about Bolingbroke, "that he was a holy man." All this is different with paradox. Think of the paradox of Livius in the beginning of his *Ab urbe condita* when he writes: "Now we come into our period that is unable to suffer both its vices and the remedies for the vices." Associations are only relied upon here in order to unmask them as misleading. Language resists the idea of a nation that wants neither its vices nor the necessary remedies. Yet—and this is crucial—if you look at the Romans of Livius's time (if Livius is correct) this is what actual reality was like. Reality unmasks language in this case; and one might say that paradox is the trope of reality—even more so than the literal statement. As I found out, seeing Tocqueville as

I am now interested in political rather than historical theory.

the theorist of paradox permitted a new analysis of his view of democracy.

You seem to have been very much inspired by Richard Rorty.

You are quite right there. The way I conceive of the task and the aims of philosophy as I described them just now owes a lot to Rorty. It was Rorty who, in my opinion convincingly, showed that philosophers should not look for the foundations of science, of scientific truth, etcetera, but that they should see philosophy rather as a kind of psychoanalysis of science and of our ways of thinking. On the other hand, I regret that Rorty so often tends to make a sudden stop after he has criticized traditional epistemological concerns, without giving philosophers a new bone to chew on. His program is as revolutionary as it is necessary, but it remains mostly destructive and, in the end, one cannot remain satisfied with that.

I must add that I read Rorty's *Philosophy and the Mirror of Nature* at the same time I was concluding the book on what I rather pompously called "narrative logic" and that I mentioned a moment ago. There happen to be some striking similarities between Rorty's attack on epistemology and how I proceeded in that book, and that may help to explain why I was at that time so particularly susceptible to Rorty's ideas—as I still am. I could put it as follows. In *Narrative Logic* I started with the traditional, but now almost universally condemned, distinction between historical research and historical writing. When doing historical research, the historian aims at making true statements about the past; that is, at acquiring the kind of knowledge about the past that can be expressed in singular, constative statements and that can be either true or false. I want to add two comments to that. First, I believe that if one accepts Tarski's variant of the correspondence theory of truth (what is expressed in Tarski's T-sentences), it cannot be doubted that the historian is capable of making true statements about the past. The customary objection that truth is theory-dependent can thus effectively be dealt with, and that is one more reason why I am convinced of the necessity of the distinction between historical research and writing. Second, it may very well be

> Rorty showed that philosophers should not look for the foundations of science, of scientific truth etc., but that they should see philosophy rather as a kind of psychoanalysis of science and of our ways of thinking.

> It may very well be that all true progress in history is progress in historical research.

74

that all true progress in history is progress in historical research. If one compares what we now know of civilizations that have been forgotten for millennia, or of languages that have not been spoken for many centuries, it would be ridiculous to deny that progress is made in the area of historical research. So no one should try to look down on historical research; that really is the cognitive backbone of all history. However, it is not all the historian does. For after having gained this knowledge of the past that can be expressed in terms of true statements—and in the practice of history, as I know from my own experience, this *after* expresses both a temporal and a logical "after"—the historian has to synthesize the results of historical research by proposing a certain view from which we should look at the part of the past in question.

Against this background one can argue that historical research generates the kind of problems that have always been analyzed by epistemologists, whereas historical writing lies somehow outside or beyond epistemology. That was one of the most important theses I defended in *Narrative Logic*. For I tried to show that what I referred to as "narrative substances"—the linguistic entities embodying such synthetic views of the past—do not refer to the past itself, though in the individual statements contained by a narrative such reference to the past is made. So historical writing by its very nature cannot give rise to epistemological questions; of course, I am assuming here a parallelism between epistemology and reference, but since Kripke one often wants the notion of reference to do what epistemology never succeeded in giving to the philosopher, and so this is probably not an unwarranted conflation.

In any case, since I so strongly focused on historical writing and thus bracketed, so to speak, all the epistemological questions (of historical research) that were ordinarily asked by historical theorists, my position happened to be quite similar to Rorty's. Rorty's *Mirror* was therefore a kind of godsend for me. I now was convinced that I was on the right track when cutting through all the epistemological ties between the historian's text and past reality and that historical theorists had always been looking for something that had never existed at all and would never exist. Later on, with the help of the relevant ideas that had been put forward by Gombrich in his well-known essay on the hobbyhorse and by Danto in his magnificent *The Transfiguration of the Commonplace*,

I now was convinced that I was on the right track when cutting through all the epistemological ties between the historian's text and past reality and that historical theorists had always been looking for something that had never existed at all and would never exist.

I still further emphasized the nonreferential character of these narrative substances. I came to see these narrative substances as substitutes or replacements for past reality itself in the way that the work of art according to Gombrich and Danto is a substitute for something in reality. And since substitutes or replacements really take the place of something in reality itself, thus taking on the same ontological status of reality, there was no longer any room for epistemological questions. Epistemological questions now became aesthetic questions. And it is here that I have learned a lot from Nelson Goodman (and from Flint Schier's *Deeper into Pictures*, which proved to be immensely helpful for me in this connection). This is also where I would disagree with Rorty. Following Davidson, Rorty argues that language does not exist and that we should avoid the temptation to reify language. Of course, the substitution view of historical language is completely at odds with this condemnation of the reification of language. But I think that such a reification of historical language is a requirement for recognizing that the historian's work makes any sense in the first place. Let me put it this way: Each discipline requires a specific object of investigation—without such an object of investigation there is nothing one can have knowledge about. But since the language of history on the level of historical writing does not refer to a past reality, historical debate on that level can make sense only if one is prepared to reify the historian's language itself; only then do you have a subject matter. Initially it may seem a peculiarly perverse idea that when discussing the past historians are actually discussing their narrative constructions—their narrative substances I would like to say—but as soon as this reification is interpreted in the way proposed by Gombrich and Danto it surely is no longer a problem. As soon as an aesthetic approach instead of an epistemological approach to the narrative substance is followed, the reification of the historian's language does not turn historical writing into idle self-reflection. This is where aesthetics is superior to epistemology.

This also is where Hayden White comes in. And together with Rorty, White has been my major source of inspiration. The two authors are quite different, no question about that. Rorty always gives you arguments—in spite of his distrust of arguments—and he always gives the impression of knowing exactly what he is doing. White should be read as much between the lines as in what

Since substitutes or replacements really take the place of something in reality itself, thus taking on the same ontological status of reality, there was no longer any room for epistemological questions.

This is where aesthetics is superior to epistemology.

Together with Rorty, White has been my major source of inspiration.

he explicitly says. You must read White again and again. And each time you look at his texts anew, you will discover something in it you had overlooked before, perhaps because you were not yet susceptible to this particular insight. Rorty, on the other hand, puts his cards on the table and the revelation of his books and essays comes as soon as you read them for the first time. But White is more of a genius; Rorty has the transparent clarity of Ingres; White is rather a Turner.

But let me return to what I have learned from White. As you may expect, that has to do mainly with the way he revolutionized historical theory by introducing the linguistic turn here. By doing so, White transformed historical theory from a relatively uninteresting and backward alley in the contemporary intellectual world into a new and challenging area of theoretical reflection. Mainly thanks to him, all the old questions that one had been asking about the relation between the statement and reality could now be asked about the relation between the text and reality. Moreover, by using literary theory to effect the linguistic turn in historical theory, he thus provided the historical theorist at the same time with a sophisticated and well-developed theoretical instrument for dealing with these new and difficult questions. *Metahistory* has been by far the most important event in recent historical theory, and I am sure that without it historical theory would have disappeared from the intellectual scene somewhere in the 1970s or the 1980s and, what is more, nobody would have missed it.

> White revolutionized historical theory by introducing the linguistic turn.

Don't you feel deconstructed by Derrida?

What I found most fruitful in Derrida is how he rehabilitated (mostly in his earlier work) the apparently insignificant detail. He demonstrated that the pivot in an argument, what de Man called the text's "point of undecidability," is often a small and apparently innocuous detail—a detail that in the eyes of the author himself and in those of most of his readers is devoid of any significance and surely not part of the overall essence of an argument or of a text. When I became fascinated some time ago by Ginzburg's *micro-storie* and by the challenge that they embody for traditional historical writing—the kind of historical writing that I had discussed in my book on narrative logic—I found deconstructivism most helpful.

But I must concede that with a few exceptions like *La vérité en peinture* I have lost track of Derrida since *Glas*. I sincerely tried several of his later books but found myself unable to make any sense of them. Since then, his writing has become so hermetic and so user-unfriendly that I lack the courage and the motivation to try to find some useful message in it. His prose has become a kind of private language. Maybe Rorty is right when saying that this is a new and intriguing way of doing philosophy or literary theory — or possibly something entirely new for which we have no name as yet. That may well be. But I must confess that I would like to leave it to the *cognoscenti* to find out about that and to explain then to the vulgar like me what is going on there. I recently read in the *Times Literary Supplement* an amazing story about how Derrida proceeds when writing his books and essays. It appears to be the case that he writes down just about everything that enters his mind when dealing with a certain topic. As a psychoanalyst would say, he entirely relies upon his primary process and he does not allow any interference by some internal, intellectual censor. That explains, I suppose, the breathtaking speed with which his oeuvre expands and the difficulties that it typically presents to the reader of his texts. Of course, in the case of most scholars, such a procedure would lead to disastrous results, and it is only thanks to Derrida's immense erudition, his originality, and his unparalleled capacity for reading texts that he may still claim his prominent place amongst contemporary philosophers. Nevertheless, I would have preferred a Derrida who writes a little less and who is somewhat more inclined to act as a censor of his own writings instead of saddling his readers with that unpleasant task.

> 77

> Derrida's prose has become a kind of private language.

You are interested in narrative. Do you share the opinion that narrative is a cultural phenomenon, as Barthes has taught us—some kind of unification project through which we can look at culture as a whole?

Yes, I believe narrative to be a crucial cultural phenomenon. Think for example of how Auerbach in his *Mimesis*, which I think is one of the most impressive books that have been written in this century, describes how narrative mimesis or the narrative representation of reality permeates the whole history of Western civilization.

There is, however, one feature of narrative that specially interests me. Narrative is an instrument—and a quite effective

> Narrative is an instrument for making sense of the world in which we live.

78   instrument at that—for making sense of the world in which we live. Perhaps nobody was more aware of that than Freud, when he demonstrated that our psychological constitution best expresses itself in how we tell ourselves the story of our life. And your attachment to a certain type of story may even determine whether things that have happened in your past will change you into a neurotic or psychotic personality. Narrative gives you a grasp of reality—though not always one that will guarantee your happiness—it provides you with a certain organization of the many details that are the elements of your life-story.

Perhaps that is what is most essential to narrative and the purpose that it always primarily serves: to get a grip on reality; to effect, so to speak, a certain "domestication" of reality—as White once put it—to change a reality "as such" into a reality that is adapted to our aims and purposes. And from that perspective there is no essential difference from the role of the formula in the sciences, like Newton's "$f = m \cdot a$" (force is mass multiplied by acceleration), which also permits us to organize in a coherent way the kind of natural phenomena mechanics and physics attempt to deal with. What the formula is for the scientist, narrative is for the historian.

What the formula is for the scientist, narrative is for the historian.

This is also where one may begin to have one's doubts about narrative. Telling the past, or even one's own past, is unavoidably a violation of that past in order to effect such a narrative organization of the past—an organization that is not intrinsic to the past itself. As the similarities between narrative and the formula may suggest, this does not at all imply the ineradicable subjectivity of narrative. We even praise the organization of reality by means of the formula of the scientist as an ideal of objectivity—and there is no obvious reason to doubt that matters would be very much different in the case of narrative. The similarities between the formula and narrative suggest that there may very well be such a thing as an "objective violation of reality" by either scientific or narrative language. The opposition between subjective and objective does not run parallel to the opposition between intellectual organization, either by the formula or by narrative, and reality itself. However, as soon as we recognize that narrativization is a "domestication of the past," as White put it in *The Content of the Form*, in which reality has to undergo the violence of narrative language, one becomes interested in the question of the possibility of an awareness of the past that is free from this narrative domestication. And that is why I became so interested in the notion of historical experience and, if I may allow myself the liberty to speak for him, why White in two recent essays drew our attention to the Greek middle voice; that is, the form of the Greek verb that is neither active nor passive. Both in historical experience and in speaking about the past in terms of the middle voice, the "authenticity" of the past is respected. So the really interesting opposition is not the one between subjectivity and objectivity, but the opposition between "authenticity" on the one hand and a reality that has been processed by the linguistic codes of narrative prose on the other.

The really interesting opposition is not the one between subjectivity and objectivity, but the opposition between "authenticity" on the one hand and a reality that has been processed by the linguistic codes of narrative prose on the other.

Don't you think that since the theorists of history have begun to be interested in narrative and have started to look at narrative as a textual whole, historical writing comes much closer to the historian's audience, to his readers, than used to be the case. It is easier—more natural—for people to think about historical reality seen through the prism of stories, since we also know our own lives predominantly in the form of stories. People seem to experience and construct their vision of life not by means of laws and rules but by means of certain kinds of stories (my life was like a drama; mine was like a melodrama, etcetera). And afterwards, people tend to project these experiences on histories.

But do you have the reader of historical narratives in mind?

Yes.

That is a very interesting hypothesis. I have never looked at the matter from that point of view. Most often when narrative is being discussed, the perspective is the relation between the past and its narrative representation. The reader of the historical work is ordinarily left out of consideration, though one exception might be Stanford in his *The Nature of Historical Knowledge*, and, of course, Rüsen with the historiographical matrix that he expounded in his trilogy. Stanford argues that historical narrative is always structured by the requirements of successful communication between the historian and his audience. But when he started actually to elaborate this insight, Stanford quickly returned to more conventional views on narrative. So, on the whole, I would say that there is not yet a pragmatics of historical narrative. And I think therefore that your hypothesis deserves more attention.

A reader is maybe aware that he is reading some kind of story about the past. But this story is no longer a story written by the historian; it has become a reader's story. He puts a new meaning into it, as so often happens in literature. As White told me: After the book has been published the author is no longer the best interpreter of the book. Now it is the turn of reader.

I quite agree with you there. One would fall into the trap of the intentionalist fallacy to say that one ought to concentrate on the intentions of the author of the text. Even if everybody sincerely believed that a certain interpretation of a text gives us the author's intention, you would merely have an interpretation that everybody happens to believe to be the correct one. But by its very nature, this interpretation will always remain just another interpretation—however widely it is believed to be the right one. Like Wittgenstein's wheel in the machine that is moved but does not move anything itself, the notion of the author's intention is useless from an epistemological point of view. The notion does not clarify anything, neither in the theory nor in the practice of interpretation.

But there is another, theoretically perhaps less interesting but nevertheless quite important dimension to the relation between the historian and his audience. I am thinking here of the question of whether the historian should be content to write only for his fellow-historians or whether he should also aim at being read by a large lay public. I think that historians should always realize that just like novelists they also have a cultural responsibility and that therefore their language has to be understandable or readable for a large, interested lay public. This implies that the historian is not so much a discoverer of the past's reality as a kind of mediator (a *hermeneutes*, the Greeks would have said) between the past and the present. You could compare the historian to the guide in a picture gallery who explains a painting to the people looking at the picture. And explaining does not here have the meaning of a penetration into "the reality of the painting," but rather a "giving

The historian is not so much a discoverer of the past's reality as a kind of mediator between the past and the present.

access to the painting." It has to do rather with showing—with making people aware of certain details that they might have overlooked; in short, with what it is like to be a guide. Perhaps you could say that this position of the historian as a mediator also points in the direction of White's middle voice.

But thanks to this "linguistic turn" in philosophy of history, by which historical theory came closer to literary theory than ever since the eighteenth century, history began to be written not only for a scientific elite but in a more popular way for a wider public.

Well, I suppose that you are quite right there. It is true that the linguistic turn in historical theory always went together with the conviction that historical narrative could best be dealt with from the perspective of literary theory, and this certainly suggests a *rapprochement* between historical writing and the novel, which so obviously has no raison d'être outside its readers.

On the other hand, one could have one's doubts about the application of literary theory to historical writing. I am not thinking here of the kind of objection that is customarily made against White that history is a science and not literature. That has always been a most silly objection and is ultimately based on the most naive view of literature; namely, the idea that literature is merely fiction, therefore only gives us lies, and thus could have nothing to do with truth and historical writing. I am rather thinking of two other things. My first point would be that historical theorists often have been too hasty in borrowing from elsewhere; of course, all attempts to transform history into a science, from Buckle to the Cliometricians, are the most obvious examples. But something like that might also be true of a historical theory that makes itself too dependent on literary theory. That is why I have always been a convinced protagonist of historism as it was developed by Ranke and Humboldt; their historism really is the only historical theory that has ever been developed by historians themselves in order to account for historical writing. No borrowing there, and that is why historism has always functioned for me as a kind of "reality principle": you can say all kinds of things about historical writing and you may move in any direction you like, but as soon as you come into outright conflict with historism you may be sure that something must have gone wrong somewhere.

Historism has always functioned for me as a kind of "reality principle."

82   And that is closely connected with a second point I'd like to make. Though I may be confusing levels here, I think one could also use White's notion of the "domestication" of the past for describing the results of seeing history as a science or as a kind of literature. For you could say that in both cases the past is domesticated in the sense that it is forced within the matrix of certain preexisting codes, either scientific or literary. When White uses this notion of the "domestication" of the past in order to criticize such attempts at appropriation, I am strongly reminded of the Foucault of the well-known essay on the genealogical method. Foucault says there that the historian should not aim at explaining the past; that is, he should not try to render the incomprehensible comprehensible, but precisely aim at doing the reverse. The historian should alienate the past from us; he should show that where we think we can recognize ourselves in the past, this ordinarily is a projection and that the past is stranger than we would ever have thought. The historian must show what is strange and alien in precisely those aspects of the past that seem so very familiar and unproblematic to us. That is where Freud's notion of the "uncanny" comes in.

I think literature can often be a good instrument for effecting such an alienation—and I am thinking here specially of the modernist novel. But I am not sure whether literary theory in general is equally helpful in this. The explanation is perhaps that literary theory by its very nature aims at explanation; it wants to clarify what goes on in literature and it is, therefore, intrinsically opposed to alienation as advocated by Foucault. A good example is, of course, the structuralist account of historical writing that White gave in *Metahistory*. The similarities between the Kantian categories of the understanding—the paradigmatic philosophical instruments for the domestication of reality—and White's tropes is too obvious to be ignored. Besides, White himself is quite well aware of these similarities. I believe, therefore, that the Hayden White of *Metahistory* should be seen as subscribing to the Kantian, modernist conception of language and knowledge, and from that point of view I am convinced that most of the criticisms of White that have been made these last two decades are in a quite essential way completely beside the point. The White of *Metahistory* is, in fact, much closer to his scientistic critics than these critics have ever been aware of. The real, interesting opposition is not the opposition between *Metahistory* on the one hand and the adherents of history as a science or the adherents of one form of Collingwoodian hermeneutics or other on the other hand—this is all modernism—but between the modernist approach to historical writing and the later Hayden White who shows us the past under the aegis of the sublime (as in *The Content of the Form*), or who experiments with the notion of the middle voice. I do not doubt for a moment that *Metahistory* has played a decisive role in destroying these more naive forms of modernism—and that is why *Metahistory* is by far the most important book in historical theory since Collingwood's *Idea of History*. But if we look ahead instead of back to the recent past of historical theory, I think more is to be expected from White's conception of the sublime and form, and how he tries to minimize the distance between the past and historical language when proposing to write history in terms of the middle voice. One should notice here above all that White's turn to the sublime and to the middle voice is diametrically opposed to what he argued in *Metahistory*. As his opponents were quick to point out, the tropology of *Metahistory* increased the distance between the historian's language and historical reality. One may think here of White's thesis that one and the same part of the past lends itself to different tropological interpretations. In fact, this is precisely why White became interested in the sublime and in the middle voice. For his critics objected—quite rightly so—that, for example, the Holocaust did not permit of an ironic or satirical interpretation. At least in such cases, the link between the past and the historian's language is not as weak and undetermined as White suggested. And this is what White tried to find a remedy for with the middle voice. He relates the middle voice, as had been proposed by Barthes, to an intransitive form of writing—a kind of writing that does not know the distinction between an "active" author and a "passive" past or a "passive" text that is described or written by the historian. Representing the past in terms of the middle voice is no longer "representing" in the customary sense of the word, but letting the past speak *for itself*. That is the element of reflexivity that is best exemplified by the middle voice. And this is why White's fascination with the middle voice and with the sublime, which has similar effects, points in a quite different direction than *Metahistory*. That does not mean, I hasten to add, that we should now forget about tropology. As

White shows us the past under the aegis of the sublime.

Metahistory is by far the most important book in historical theory since Collingwood's *Idea of History*.

Representing the past in terms of the middle voice is no longer 'representing' in the customary sense of the word, but letting the past speak *for itself*.

White's analysis of the writings of historians and philosophers of history demonstrates, tropology can give us the most surprising insights into the nature of these writings. So I would see the sublime and the middle voice as valuable additions to White's theoretical arsenal, rather than as an abnegation of what he had said in *Metahistory* and in *Tropics of Discourse*. There is room here for a postmodernist eclecticism: sometimes you use this theoretical apparatus, and at other times you use a different one. Your subject matter should determine your theoretical apparatus and you are on the wrong, modernist track when you let your subject matter be determined by your theoretical apparatus.

Your subject matter should determine your theoretical apparatus.

Some intellectual historians, philosophers, and critical theorists believe that history is presently going through a crisis. However, perhaps it would be better not to say that history is in crisis but that it is gradually becoming clear that history as a separate discipline is not adequate to the "postmodern condition" and needs to be united together with all other humanistic domains in one bigger module called "cultural studies."

I think you are right when you say that history is not in a crisis, at least not in the kind of crisis that one had in the 1960s and 1970s and that was occasioned by the joint effort of the *Annales* and the Cliometricians. Though even that "crisis" affected only a small minority of historians. Furthermore, I would also agree with your suggestion that historians might consider a unification of their discipline within one all-embracing, interdisciplinary model. Because of the immense variety of their subject matter, historians ought to have a natural penchant for an interdisciplinary approach. Historians often deal with the history of philosophy, of literature, of art, of economic thought, and so on, and if they want to avoid saying silly things about these topics, they would be well advised to keep in touch with these other disciplines.

But I don't think that historians themselves are particularly eager for the interdisciplinary approach. I think that this has much to do with the aversion historians instinctively have to "theory." This is where history differs from the other disciplines that are taught in the faculty of arts and humanities. All these other disciplines have undergone a process somewhere between the 1960s and now in which these disciplines became thoroughly theoretical. You may think of Chomsky, of structuralism, of deconstructivism, of psycholinguistics, etcetera. History is the only discipline that has successfully resisted all attempts to introduce theory. It is the only discipline that really still is a "craft," rather than a discipline.

The question is, of course, why is this so? Part of the answer lies, I suppose, in the fact that historians cannot be content to write just for their fellow historians. As I said a moment ago, the historian has a cultural responsibility to a large lay public. On the other hand, when selecting their subject matter and when writing their books and articles, historians do not seem to me very much aware of this responsibility. They will even say that too much of it might compromise their independence. So it really must be only part of the answer. And we can be all the more sure that this is an intriguing problem.

> History is the only discipline that has successfully resisted all attempts to introduce theory. It is the only discipline that really still is a "craft," rather than a discipline.

I think that we can observe a strange process here. On the one hand, historical writing tends to move closer to the social sciences, but, on the other, historical theory moves in the opposite direction and toward literary criticism. I am thinking of the popularity of the *Annales* school—of microhistories focusing on small groups and individuals; for instance, the works by Carlo Ginzburg and Emmanuel Le Roy Ladurie. But whereas historians try all the time to escape from literature, usually identified with fiction, theory of history is deeply attracted by literary criticism. I recall the statement by Doctorow who said: "There is no longer any such thing as fiction and non-fiction, there is only narrative."

Well, yes, perhaps. But one should avoid being blinded by theory. Contemporary theorists of history would agree with Doctorow. Nevertheless, the undeniable fact remains that even a child can tell the difference between a contemporary novel and a contemporary book on history—perhaps only Schama's latest book, *Dead Certainties*, might cause some difficulties here. Perhaps one might say that it is a scandal in historical and literary theory that nobody has yet been able to find a theoretical explanation of our faultless capacity to distinguish correctly between the novel and a work of

The absence of fo-
calization is what
distinguishes his-
tory from the
novel.

history. As for me, I have a feeling that the absence of focalization
is what distinguishes history from the novel.

**But maybe this also is a matter of one's aim when writing.
If we are looking for a discipline that can provide us with a
convincing image of the past, both history and literature
can manage to do so, each in a different way, of course, but
both can do it. Let me put it this way: history provides the
facts; theory of history makes us aware that the meaning
of the facts is always a construction by the historian, and
shows how such a construction comes into being in the historian's narrative; but fiction gives us a metaphorical truth
about (historical) reality and also stimulates the illusion
that we can really understand the people who lived in the
past and their world.**

You're obviously right when you say that the distinction between
history and the novel has a lot to do with the intentions and purposes of their respective authors. Nevertheless, I would be much
disappointed if this were indeed all one could justifiably assert
about that distinction. For it would mean that for the distinction
you would have to look behind the text *itself*, whereas the text itself can give us no final clues about that. And, once again, that
seems to be at odds with the facts, since we are so obviously able
to tell the novel apart from the work of history, even if we have
no idea at all about the intentions of their authors. The situation
seems rather to be the reverse: you argue from the nature of the
text to the intentions of the author and not the other way round.
Yet the problem remains that history and the novel can come
quite close to one another and, in the case of the historical novel,
provide us with exactly the same kind of information about the
past. My own view is that you should conceive of history as developing proposals for how to see the past, whereas the novel, in
practice the historical novel, *applies* such proposals to a specific
historical situation. The historical novel is a kind of applied history, and the relation between the historical novel and history is
roughly the same as the relation between the task of the engineer
and the physicist. Taking this view of the relation between history
and the novel would also explain why you never have focalization

in history (as I said a moment ago), while even the weirdest postmodernist novel has focalization. Focalization gives you the "focus" from which historical knowledge is *applied*.

**Could you tell me which contemporary historian is the best
interpreter of the past, in your estimation.**

Well, the twentieth-century history book I admire most is Foucault's *Les mots et les choses*. That is a marvelous book: it has such
originality, so wide a scope, and is so unexpected and so kaleido-
scopic that I could not think of any other book written in this
century that has succeeded in improving on Foucault's tour de
force. Take for instance how Foucault analyzes Velázquez's *Las
Meninas* right at the beginning; that is really stupendous and
breathtaking. And what already becomes clear from this book is
Foucault's unequalled capacity to alienate the past from us, which
is, in my view, the beginning of all wisdom in historical writing
and theory, and though I am sure that Foucault would be ap-
palled by this characterization, I would not hesitate to say that I
admire Foucault most among twentieth-century historians since
he is the best and the most consistent historist of them all.

I admire Foucault
most among
twentieth-century
historians.

**I agree; I also admire Foucault, but he is not an "ordinary"
historian. He can be related to cultural history, like Burckhardt or Huizinga, but what about historians in the more
traditional sense of the word?**

I have a deep respect for John Pocock, whose analysis of political
vocabularies in many ways resembles what Foucault wrote on the
notion of discourse and what Reinhart Koselleck attempts to do
with his *Begriffsgeschichte*. Pocock's *Machiavellian Moment in the
Atlantic Tradition* is a book I admire no less than Foucault's *Les
mots et les choses* because of the archeology of Western political debate that is presented in it. And Koselleck's early *Kritik und Krise*
is a really brilliant book for roughly similar reasons. Furthermore,
I am very much intrigued by Ginzburg's *micro-storie*, though I
cannot say that this would be for me how history ought to be
written in the future. But what is so interesting about Ginzburg's
and about Le Roy Ladurie's *micro-storie* is that they challenge the

notion of a panoramic writing of history that tries to account for as many details of the past as possible in the most effective way. This really is something quite new and unheard of in all the history of historical writing and it requires all the sophistication of deconstructivism to account for what goes on in these *micro-storie*. And since I shall always remain an old-fashioned historist myself, I can add that I greatly admire Meinecke's work—and then I am thinking specially of his *Die Entstehung des Historismus* and his *Die Idee der Staatsräson*. These really are beautiful books, both for the information they give and for the rich and supple German prose in which these books are written.

What do you think about the books by Umberto Eco, like *The Name of the Rose*?

Eco is very good at writing a book that is both pleasant to read and that also gives you a lot of information—in this case about the daily routine of a medieval monastery. Besides, part of the fun of his books is that he leaves you in the dark about his exact intentions. Is the book a parody?—of history, of science, or is he just trying to ridicule one's attempt to place the book in one genre or another?

If I may summarize these remarks, could one say that now perhaps the time has come for the historical theorist to try to write history and that historians should pay more attention to historical theory? I am asking this because you mentioned books that were written by theorists of history as specimens of the best historical writing in this century; for instance, Foucault; but even Le Roy Ladurie or Ginzburg cannot be seen as "ordinary," traditional historians.

No, I don't think that historians
should pay a lot of attention to historical theory.

No, I don't think that historians should pay a lot of attention to historical theory. It would be enough to have some background knowledge of the kind of things that traditionally are discussed by historical theorists. However, it sometimes happens that historical discussions, especially in periods in which the discipline undergoes an important transformation, get a philosophical or theoretical dimension that is not always recognized as such by the

participants. Such discussions may then easily degenerate into a
helpless *dialogue des sourds* as long as that philosophical dimension is not properly identified. Here the immixture of theory in
the practice of history may be welcome.

And what about White's dream expressed in the preface to
Metahistory, **the dream about the reconstitution of history
as a form of intellectual activity which is at once poetic, scientific, and philosophical in its concerns—at it was during
history's golden age in the nineteenth century.**

It certainly is a most attractive prospect and I would applaud an
evolution of history in the direction suggested by White. But,
once again, I would never desire to contribute to such an evolution as a theorist. One should leave history to itself and to its own
devices. My attitude would be somehow similar to Edmund
Burke's position vis-à-vis the French revolutionaries. You should
not construct an ideal state and try to break with the past, Burke
argued, since there is a wisdom and an amount of political experience invested in an existing regime that you can never hope to
surpass by merely abstract, theoretical reasoning. Perhaps I am
more of a revolutionary than Burke in politics, but I am convinced that a fundamentally rational discipline like history is always open to changes that may be necessary under certain circumstances in a way that you do sometimes sadly miss in the
world of politics. So whereas the practice of politics requires the
kind of criticism that is formulated by political theorists, in history Burke's strategy is the best one. Indeed, I am always deeply
impressed by—though it is a rather pathetic word, I nevertheless
use it here—the "beauty" of history as a discipline, by the practical intelligence displayed by historians as a research community,
and by the subtlety with which the discipline has always succeeded
in adapting itself to new requirements and to new challenges. With
some rare exceptions, historical theory should always remain
something ex post facto.

One should leave
history to itself
and to its own de-
vices.

**History is a most accommodating discipline. Hans Kellner
told me that sometimes a certain theory is suitable for one
situation only. So theories seem to have become dispensable**

90 tools that one may change as the situation requires. Could that mean that the current way of doing history and of developing theories of history exemplifies the "postmodern condition"? Do you see yourself as a person who really "experiences" the postmodernism of our time?

I think you gave your question the right formulation. That is to say, I would not say that I am a postmodernist in the sense that you can be a socialist or a vegetarian. For me, postmodernism is not some kind of theory, or theoretical view that you can either adopt or reject; for me it is rather the term we use to characterize the contemporary intellectual climate. Postmodernism is a term much like "the Enlightenment" or "romanticism." And the crucial question to be asked in a time that styles itself as "postmodernist" or "enlightened" is not whether you subscribe to the tenets of postmodernism, the Enlightenment, etcetera, but rather whether you believe such a term—and what it stands for—to be a good characteristic of what goes on in your age. And, as you suggested, that is rather a matter of experience than of rational argument.

Postmodernism is rather a matter of experience than of rational argument.

But then your question itself. Yes, I think that postmodernism gives a better idea of the relevant tendencies in philosophy, the arts, and literature in our time than any alternative. What postmodernism expresses for me is, above all, a recognition that everything nowadays points in the direction of fragmentation, disintegration, and a loss of center. You see this tendency everywhere: in the sphere of international politics, in the impotence of old and firmly established governments to develop institutional models that might react appropriately to a wide array of often contradictory and mutually inconsistent evolutions in contemporary society. Our contemporary world has become a nexus of paradoxes— which undoubtedly is a nightmare for the responsible politician. And all that has its counterpart in historical writing; one need only think of the death of metanarratives as announced by Lyotard, of the interest of contemporary historians in what a previous generation of historians would have condemned as mere insignificant details, of the fact that the traditional confidence in a linear development in Western civilization has had to make room for a conception of the past that resembles rather an incoherent archipelago of self-contained historical or intellectual islands. It is here that recent developments in historical writing—as so often is the case— fairly well reflect developments outside the domain of historical

Our contemporary world has become a nexus of paradoxes.

writing in the proper sense of the term. "Die Philosophie is ihre Zeit in Gedanken erfasst," as wise old Hegel already said, and it is no different with historical writing.

Could you please tell me, what do you predict the future of theory of history to be?

Ah, well, that's the kind of question everybody likes to answer: thinking it over allows you to dream about the future and that always is a pleasant thing to do. But how shall I answer this question? Perhaps the best way of dreaming about the future is to wonder where it might be different from the past and the present. And indeed, there is something that I would like to say from that point of view. No one looking at twentieth-century philosophy of history can fail to be struck by the extent to which it has drawn its inspiration from philosophy of language. One must be honest about one's discipline, and such honesty requires, in the case of historical theory, the recognition that historical theory has most often been little more than a translation to the field of historical theory of developments that had already taken place elsewhere—for example, in the philosophy of science, of literature, in aesthetics, etcetera. As I said a moment ago, historism perhaps is the only exception to that rule. Arguably, historism is the only theoretical *Ansatz* in the history of historical thought that is free from alien elements, elements that do not have their origin in history itself. All the more reason, I would say, to take historism far more seriously than presently is the case. On the other hand, one might object that historism is a spin-off of romanticism. But you could reply that romanticism itself is to a large extent the result of historism and of the new attitude toward the past that was preached by historism.

In any case, most of contemporary historical theory consists of an application to historical theory of insights that have already been developed elsewhere. There is nothing intrinsically wrong with that, I would like to emphasize. On the contrary, if only we recognize how much our understanding of the historical text has been deepened by literary theory, we cannot possibly doubt that a keen awareness of what happens in other fields is indispensable for the historical theorist in all cases. This is how one should assess Hayden White's role in contemporary historical theory—and I think one can safely say that without White's *Metahistory* and

Without White . . . historical theory would have died a premature death. A death, moreover, that would have gone unnoticed in the contemporary intellectual world.

92   the essays and books he wrote after it, historical theory would have died a premature death. A death, moreover, that would have gone unnoticed in the contemporary intellectual world. If historical theory now is a lively and challenging domain of intellectual debate, this is mainly thanks to White and a few other kindred spirits like Lionel Gossman (whose *Between History and Literature* belongs to the best things that have been published in the field since 1945). These most influential theorists—and especially White—have seen to it that historical theory finally and belatedly underwent its "linguistic" (or "literary") "turn" and was thus freed of its intellectual isolation that threatened to reduce it to irrelevance. Thanks to White and Gossman, historical theory ceased to be a kind of intellectual backwater and it became again a challenging intellectual enterprise. We now possess once again, as in the days of Ranke and of Droysen, a historical theory that is *à la hauteur des choses* and that is, in principle, no less sophisticated than other areas of philosophical investigation.

Perhaps this provides one with the best background for dreaming about the future of historical theory. If historical theory nowadays is predominantly an exponent of contemporary philosophy of language and of literature, one might wonder whether historical theory has the potential to inaugurate a new phase in contemporary intellectual debate. That is, one might ask oneself whether the subject matter of historical theory contains something that would allow us, in some way or other, to articulate a new phase in philosophy of language or even to develop a position going beyond the horizon of philosophy of language.

And I think that a positive answer to that question can be given if one focuses on the notion of historical experience. I mean by that the kind of experience of the past itself that has been described by poets and historians like Goethe, Michelet, Herder, Meinecke, Huizinga, or Toynbee and that made such a deep impression on all of them and so much molded their conception of the past. Historical experience is a most paradoxical kind of experience since, on the one hand, only historians with a profound knowledge of the past seem to be susceptible to this kind of experience—it is not something that happens to the *rudis tyro*. In any case, from that point of view one would be inclined to say that historical experience is in harmony with the relevant parameters of philosophy of language, insofar as philosophy of language has always emphasized that intellectual categories (like language, Kant's categories of the pure understanding, linguistic structures, etcetera, and, above all, the knowledge we already possess) determine the content of what we experience. Yet, on the other hand, what becomes clear from the statement of these historians about their historical experience is the complete *authenticity* of the experience; that is, the historian's conviction of having experienced the past as it really has been, "an und für sich," not mediated by existing historical or historiographical knowledge. In historical experience one experiences the radical strangeness of the past; the past is here no construct of the understanding, but a reality that is experienced with the same immediacy and directness as is often ascribed to the sublime. And this is precisely what is so interesting about the notion of historical experience. If philosophers are currently interested in the category of the sublime, this is because in the sublime we experience reality in a way that can never be accounted for within existing conceptions of how language, theory, narrativism, categories of the understanding, or whatever you have, determine our experience of reality and our knowledge of it. That is how Kant himself defined the sublime.

And that is not all there is to it. Galen Strawson recently wrote an essay in the *Times Literary Supplement* in which he said to expect a change in contemporary philosophy from the kind of philosophy of language that philosophers, both Anglo-Saxon and Continental, have been doing since Frege and Nietzsche, to a philosophy of consciousness focusing on how we experience the world and thus become conscious of it. And if one thinks of the number of books that have been written on consciousness in Anglo-Saxon countries these last ten years, this seems a reasonable expectation. Contemporary historical writing would provide historical theorists with an excellent point of departure for developing such a theory of experience superseding philosophy of language. I could best explain this claim by referring to Hugo von Hofmannsthal's essay, "Der Brief des Lord Chandos," dating from 1902. Chandos writes there that he is in a curious mental or intellectual state that prevents him from finding meaning any longer in the kind of abstract and general concepts in terms of which we discern unity and coherence in the world. Everything now disintegrates for him into its fragments and he discovers that he is no longer able to write comprehensive histories like a history of the reign of Henry VIII or of classical mythology. But this

> In historical experience one experiences the radical strangeness of the past; the past is here no construct of the understanding, but a reality that is experienced with the same immediacy and directness as is often ascribed to the sublime.

loss of synthesis is compensated for by a capacity to have an intimate experience of simple and seemingly insignificant things like a jug, a harrow, a neglected dog in the sun, etcetera. Chandos thus discovered the antithetical relationship existing between language and experience. Language always intellectualizes experience and, in this way, reduces it to an uninteresting category—to a mere annex of language and of knowledge. This is why experience has played a subordinate role in the history of philosophy of the last three centuries—even Locke immediately intellectualized experience as soon as he had used the notion for his attack on Cartesianism. To put it differently, one really has to opt either for language or for experience and, if only for that reason, I am convinced that we are entering a new world with this recent interest in experience and consciousness. To be more specific, it is often said that philosophy presently faces a "crisis of representation," and I do think that this notion aptly summarizes a number of problems that contemporary philosophy has got into. Experience, then, may very well prove to be the notion that will enable us to overcome this "crisis of representation."

I am convinced that we are entering a new world with this recent interest in experience and consciousness.

What is interesting, moreover, is that historical writing may help us to show what is at stake in the attempt to move from language to experience. For if one reads Hofmannsthal's "Brief" one cannot fail to be struck by the similarities between Chandos's evolution and developments in contemporary historical writing. In both cases one encounters a process of fragmentation, a paralysis of general and comprehensive concepts, a fascination with the apparently insignificant detail, and, as a result of all this, a rehabilitation of the category of experience—though it must be emphasized that this is a notion of experience that is quite different from the one we have become accustomed to since the days of Bacon, Descartes, or Locke. In short, history might very well prove to be the discipline that best exemplifies what is at stake in this transition from language to experience. So, to return to your question, what I am dreaming of is a historical theory that will concentrate on the notion of historical experience to write a new chapter not only in the book of the history of historical theory, but also in that of the history of philosophy. In this way, Collingwood's well-known statement that it will be the main business of twentieth-century philosophy to account for twentieth-century historical writing might unexpectedly come true.

What I am dreaming of is a historical theory that will concentrate on the notion of historical experience.

You're quite right in suggesting a link with aestheticism. I recently wrote an essay on Richard Rorty. Part of the argument there was that his pragmatist interaction model of language, based on Donald Davidson's work, leaves no room at all for the kind of experience that historical experience is. Perhaps no philosophical system is so utterly hostile to that kind of experience as Rorty's and Davidson's philosophy of language. And if a philosophy so radically excludes a certain philosophical category—like experience, in this case—this begins to intrigue you and you soon find yourself wondering what the explanation for this radical exclusion might be. Perhaps we are all dialecticians (or Foucauldians) in this respect, that we believe that you may have discovered something essential about a philosophical system if you have identified what it so mercilessly and relentlessly excludes. If I am not mistaken, the explanation of Davidson's and Rorty's rejection of the kind of sublime experience that you have in historical experience has a lot to do with their radical critique of all attempts to reify language. But the issue of the relationship between unmediated experience on the one hand and a willingness to reify language on the other is a problem in itself. And I therefore want to restrict myself here to the observation that Rorty's intellectual hero, John Dewey, in his *Art as Experience*, gave an analysis of what it is like to have an aesthetic experience that comes quite close the notion of historical experience as expounded just now. So pragmatism itself, in the person of John Dewey, is capable of creating the "logical space" that is needed for accounting for an unmediated experience of the past.

But when we start to speak about experience, don't we open the door to subjectivism, or even to relativism. Aren't you afraid of that?

First of all, I must say that I have never been able to worry seriously about relativism or subjectivism. As Bernstein, in my view, convincingly demonstrated in his *Beyond Objectivism and Relativism*, relativism is a spin-off of positivism in each of its many variants. So if you have no positivist aspirations, then relativism is a nonproblem for you. But what is more important in this context

If you have no positivist aspirations, then relativism is a nonproblem for you.

96   is the following. If you conceive of historical experience as an unmediated experience of the past, of historical experience as a contiguity between the past and the historian in the same way that
there is a contiguity between our fingers and the vase or shell that
we have in our fingers, then subjectivity and relativism are ruled
out ex hypothesi. Subjectivity and relativism can become a real
problem only after experience has been intellectualized in the
way Western philosophy has learned to do so since Bacon and
Descartes—the contiguity of subject and object prevents this
intellectualization.

**If your view of this shift of interest from language to
experience is correct, does that not mean that the most
important problem in the future will be how we experience
reality instead of how we succeed in representing it?**

You are quite right. And it is true that from the "paradigm" of linguistic theory of history all this talk about experience must seem
hopelessly irrelevant. You might say that what readers of a work
of history expect is a description or representation of the past, and
from that point of view the experience the historian himself has
had of the past is a mere ingredient, a mere occasion for his descriptions and representations. But this, I would say, is begging
the question. I think that of much of contemporary history of
mentalities you could say that it gives you an idea of "what it was
like" to be a country squire in eighteenth-century England, or a
peasant in Montaillou, etcetera, rather than how the relevant history books describe or represent that world. I suppose you could
defend the thesis that much of contemporary historical writing—
as exemplified by history of mentalities—is interested in experience rather than in description and representation.

**When we begin to focus on experience, would that also
amount to a return to existentialism?**

To a certain extent I would agree with you. And it is certainly true
that a lot can be gained from Merleau-Ponty's *Le visible et l'invisible* if one wants to get a grasp of historical experience. However, if I may speak for myself, I have found the Aristotle of
De Anima and *De Sensu* quite helpful. What Aristotle says there

about touch and about the sense of touch being superior to the other senses, I found most illuminating and it has provided me with the "backbone" of my analysis of historical experience.

While we can easily find suitable instruments and theoretical frames for analyzing language, where can we find such tools for studying experience?

In any case, not in language. Here experience precedes language. And it is, in fact, quite strange that we feel so much resistance against the idea of experience preceding language. I quite agree here with Richard Shusterman in his *Pragmatist Aesthetics* that was published last year when he writes that philosophers fail to see this because for us, disembodied talking heads that we are, the only form of experience we recognize as legitimate is linguistic: thinking, talking, writing. But neither we nor the language that admittedly helps shape us could survive without the unarticulated background of prereflective, nonlinguistic experience and understanding. And that is a truth that we all know as a matter of course: first you do the experiencing (for example experiencing the past) and then you write down what you have experienced. Our intuitive resistance against this self-evident truth proves how Kantian we still are, even if we think we have well digested Rorty's attack on Kantian epistemology. And that is true for Rorty himself as well. Think of his discussion in the preface of *Consequences of Pragmatism* with Thomas Nagel on the latter's essay on what it is like to be a bat. Rorty does not like that question and then concludes with the apodictic statement that "language goes all the way down." For analogous reasons, Kant might have said "the categories of the understanding go all the way down." So despite all his antifoundationalism, Rorty ends here by making a deep and respectful bow to Kant—and the same is true for Derrida and the deconstructivists. The greatest anti-Kantians often appear to be the greatest Kantians.

Could one not infer from all this that psychology is the most appropriate discipline to do research into something like historical experience?

Yes, psychology can be quite helpful here. You might think here

Trauma.

of trauma. You have a trauma from something that has happened to you that is so awful, so absolutely terrifying, that you cannot incorporate it in some way into your personality. The trauma represents a part of your past that continues to exist in yourself in a kind of "fossilized" form. This has often happened to the victims of the concentration camps who survived the Holocaust and it is related to the mechanism of "melancholia" that Freud described in his *Trauer und Melancholie*. It may happen that during a psychoanalysis or when the victim of the Holocaust—for example Celan—writes down his memories of the camps in a book or a poem, he reexperiences the terrors of the camps when writing or speaking about them. The fossilized past, that had continued to exist "as such" in his mind, is now reexperienced and to the extent that it is reexperienced it is integrated into his personality. There is also the link here with White's middle voice: for this speaking and writing is an intransitive speaking and writing in which one speaks or writes oneself, so to speak. And since one cannot doubt that one is dealing here with an experience of the past, at least of a fossilized past that has been borne along for several decades, I would not hesitate to claim a close relationship between the middle voice on the one hand and historical experience on the other. Perhaps the middle voice is the best grammatical form and the modernist novel the best textual form for expressing the content of what I call historical experience.

But what about actually experiencing the past? How can we experience the past? Hayden White, for example, argues that we cannot experience the past.

You cannot experience the past if you conceive of the past as a kind of object lying opposite to you in the way you can say that of chairs, tables, etcetera. But the message of Aristotle (and of the middle voice) is that this subject/object model is defective here. As Aristotle demonstrates in his *De Anima*, everything that is of interest about experience has to do with continuity, with a sliding scale between ourselves and the outside world. Positivists think that there is some a priori scheme for demarcating the self from the non-self, schemes that were defined in traditional epistemology; I agree with Aristotle (and with Davidson) that such intuitions as we have about that demarcation are always aposterioristic. And

Could you say where your past ends and where you yourself begin?

could you say where your past ends and where you yourself be-   99
gin? Your relation to your past is like the way Aristotle conceived
of experience as exemplified by the sense of touch.

Anloo, The Netherlands
26 May 1993

SELECTED WRITINGS

Narrative Logic: A Semantic Analysis of the Historian's Language. The
Hague: Nijhoff, 1983.
Knowing and Telling History: The Anglo-Saxon Debate, editor. Middle-
town: Wesleyan Univ. Press, 1986. (*History and Theory*, Beiheft 25.)
History and Tropology: The Rise and Fall of Metaphor. Berkeley: Univ. of
California Press, 1994.
A New Philosophy of History, co-editor with Hans Kellner. London: Reak-
tion Books; and Chicago: Univ. of Chicago Press, 1995.
Aesthetic Politics: Political Philosophy Beyond Fact and Value. Stanford:
Stanford Univ. Press, 1996.

"Historiography and Postmodernism." *History and Theory* 28, no. 2
(1989): 137–53. Discussion: Perez Zagorin, "Historiography and
Postmodernism: Reconsiderations," *History and Theory* 29, no. 3
(1990): 263–74, and Frank Ankersmit, "Reply to Professor Zagorin," 275–96.
"Kantian Narrativism and Beyond." In *The Point of Theory: Practices of
Cultural Analysis*, ed. Mieke Bal and Inge Boer, 155–98. Amsterdam: Amsterdam Univ. Press, 1994.
"The Origins of Postmodernist Historiography." In *Historiography Between Modernism and Postmodernism: Contributions to the Method-
ology of Historical Research*, ed. Jerzy Topolski, 87–119. Amsterdam: Rodopi, 1994.
"Historicism: An Attempt at Synthesis." *History and Theory* 34 (1995):
143–62, 168–74.
"Historism and Postmodernism." In *Postmodernism and Anthropology:
Theory and Practice*, ed. Karin Geuijen, Diederick Raven, and Jan
de Wolf, 21–52. Assen: Van Gorcum, 1995.
"Metaphor and Paradox in Tocqueville's Analysis of Democracy." In *The
Question of Style in Philosophy and the Arts*, ed. Caroline van Eck,
James McAllister, and Renee van de Vall, 141–57. New York: Cam-
bridge Univ. Press, 1995.

Georg Iggers

As historians we should fight against the
instrumentalization of history.

How did you become interested in history?

■ It would be difficult to explain. I have been interested in history
since childhood. Perhaps it had something to do with the turbu-
lent times in which I grew up as a Jewish child in Nazi Germany.
It is also difficult for me to single out any one historian who particularly inspired me. I very early became interested in a broad
spectrum of historical writing from the Old Testament to the
twentieth century. History for me did not consist exclusively of
scholarship but of very diverse forms of historical memory and
historical representation.

History for me did
not consist exclu-
sively of scholar-
ship but of very
diverse forms of
historical memory
and historical rep-
resentation.

Could you please explain your position in contemporary
philosophy of history?

Well, I am not really a philosopher of history. I am primarily interested in historiography. I think my position is probably somewhere between the postmodernist position and a more conservative one.

I am primarily
interested in
historiography.

I take the post-
modernist critique
of historiography
very seriously.

I take the postmodernist critique of historiography very seriously and I realize that there is a problem with every historical text.
I realize that every text has to be understood within a certain historical context. I further realize that no text is totally coherent, that
it contains different contradictory meanings. I also realize that no

author is fully consistent. I think you probably gathered this today from my discussion of Marx, when I pointed out how contradictory Marx's positions were and how these could lead to very
different interpretations, not only because others read him differently but because he is not consistent.

On the other hand, I would go further in insisting on rational
criteria in dealing with a text than either Ankersmit or White
would. I am not convinced that all history can be reduced to pure
metaphor to the extent that Ankersmit is, although I agree that
metaphors play an important role in historical understanding. I
agree with White to a point. White's contribution has been to
show to what extent history as narrative has to be understood as
a literary text. In this sense, White's position is less extreme than
that of Ankersmit.

White in some ways is actually fairly conservative. He deals almost exclusively with the classical historical thinkers, as also does
LaCapra. Like LaCapra, he largely identifies intellectual history
with the classics. One book by White, which I like very much, and
which is now largely forgotten and out of print, is his book *The
Ordeal of Liberal Humanism*. I don't know whether you know it.

Yes. It's from the 1960s?

It's from the '60s. I still use it in my intellectual history courses. I
think it is a very intelligent survey and analysis of modern thought,
but it is also in a sense very traditional insofar as it identifies intellectual history with the great thinkers. The same is true of *Metahistory*, which examines nineteenth-century historical thought in
the works of four master historians, Ranke, Michelet, Burckhardt,
and Tocqueville, and four leading philosophers of history, Hegel,
Marx, Nietzsche, and Croce. I agree with White's emphasis on the
literary character of every historical work. I am somewhat skeptical, however, when you identify it as a purely literary text because
I think it's more.

White distinguishes between history and poetry, or history
and philosophy of history, insofar as he believes that history, in
contrast to poetry and in contrast to fiction, tries to deal with reality. He quite correctly understands that reality is never accessible in this form. What you have are the facts and then the problem is how to get from the facts to the interpretation.

There are approaches to interpretation of which I am very skeptical. One is the classical approach of Droysen, who believes that once you have thoroughly exhausted the sources, the sources themselves will reveal the content. But he really has no method for interpretation and the result is that interpretation then becomes highly ideological. We saw how in the nineteenth century historians went into the archives, applied methods of historical criticism, yet their conclusions were highly partisan. I don't accept Ranke's or Droysen's position that immersion into the sources will lead to an unbiased understanding of the historical past.

On the other hand, I don't fully accept White's approach either. I think White is right in pointing out that every narration involves an ideological component, but the question remains whether all interpretations are equally arbitrary. This is a highly philosophical question and I am not a philosopher. Ankersmit and White hold that, in the final analysis, there is no reality or that reality is, as Kant stated, a "*Ding an sich*" that eludes us.

The fact that an ideological element enters into every historical perception does not exclude the possibility of reconstructing reality the best we can on the basis of the evidence. There is inevitably an element of imagination in the reconstruction of the past, but this element of imagination is not purely arbitrary. Natalie Davis in her introduction to *The Return of Martin Guerre* writes that she had used her imagination in tying together her story, but an imagination that was not arbitrary but was guided by the voices of the past as they spoke through the sources. Thus I think a middle road is possible between Ranke's belief in objectivity and White's relativism.

I think that every reconstruction of the past reflects a different perspective and that there is no final history or final explanation. And yet I think there can be approximations of the past that are not purely arbitrary.

So I would be very critical both of the objectivism of Ranke and the relativism of White. I see certain inconsistencies in White. I am speaking here of *Metahistory*, not of his later work. One inconsistency is contained in his conception of science, which still relatively uncritically reflects an outdated nineteenth-century view. He still makes a sharp distinction between history and science, which is common to nineteenth-century historicist thought; science for him, in contrast to history, is guided by rigorous reason.

I am not a philosopher.

I think a middle road is possible between Ranke's belief in objectivity and White's relativism.

Thus he really is not that far removed from Hempel and Popper. He does not question the possibility of objectivity of science, and in this way is much more conservative than Kuhn, and much more conservative than I am. On the other hand he insists, just like Karl Popper does, that history cannot be a science because it does not conform to what Hempel and Popper call the covering law.

Here again I think I would take a different position. I think, of course, that history is not a science in the sense in which physics is, but physics is not the only model of a science. In this way Hayden White is too deeply committed to the Anglo-American conception of science. There are other conceptions of science in the Continental tradition more open to the study of culture and history. In their sense history can be a science—a science which, to be sure, is more elusive than the classical natural sciences. Here, I think, Hayden White's conception of science is much more conservative than mine and his conception of history is more radical than mine.

> History is not a science in the sense in which physics is, but physics is not the only model of a science.

Metahistory, as White recognizes, is in its highly formalistic approach very much a work that represents structuralist rather than postmodernist thought. I think he is quite right in arguing that historical representation requires narrative. Narrative, as Arthur Danto has pointed out, can be a form of explanation that operates with conceptions of causality. This causality may be psychological. White reduces all narrative to certain tropes and in doing so is somehow fascinated by the number four.

I am not satisfied with his attempt to deal with Ranke, for example, as comedy, or with Marx as irony. Accepting the presence of comic or ironic elements in White's use of the terms, these do not exhaust what Marx or Ranke are doing and it doesn't deal with the question of finding some sort of rational core in their work. I think my position would be one that realizes both the creative aspects and the limitations of reason. I realize the extent to which all historical writing involves ideology, but I think it also involves the attempt to deal honestly with the past. Well, I have not read Ankersmit's book. The only thing I have read was his article on historiography and postmodernism and his exchange with Perez Zagorin and his reply to Perez Zagorin, all in *History and Theory*. I agree with him that there is a metaphorical element that goes into all historical thinking, but I don't think that history is purely metaphor.

White on the one hand rejects the idea of history as a science and on the other hand has a highly scientistic scheme with which he tries to analyze historical discourse.

Here I have the same criticism of Ankersmit that I have of White, except that Ankersmit escapes White's contradiction. White on the one hand rejects the idea of history as a science and on the other hand has a highly scientistic scheme with which he tries to analyze historical discourse.

Do you agree that science can be considered as a science when it does not have its own vocabulary? History always borrows vocabulary from another discipline—sometimes from psychology, sometimes from anthropology, and now it is the time for literature. I mean, history and literature seem to speak the same language.

I think one of the strengths of history has been that it does not have an artificial vocabulary. Of course, there are historians who have tried to introduce artificial terminology into history; psycho-historians have done it, the Marxists have done it, the New Economic History has done it, and Hayden White has done it. But what historians have done for the most part is to use ordinary language.

There is something very arbitrary if you say science has to have a scientific language. I think to some extent in physics or chemistry it is inevitable because you are dealing with abstract concepts. But in history you are dealing less with abstract concepts; you are dealing with a living reality that takes on very different forms.

The professionalization of history did not guarantee a gain in the quality of scientific inquiry. Professionalization involved assuming a certain *habitus*, a way of carrying out scientific research that included routinization, institutionalization, an agreed on way of speaking and writing, etcetera, imitated from the other more established sciences. All these enabled the professional scientist or scholar to speak with an extraordinary air of authority. The use of a specialized language enhanced this authority.

A good deal of sociological language, a good deal of psychological language, etcetera, is basically nonsense.

The so-called social sciences have been worse culprits in this respect than history. I think a good deal of sociological language, a good deal of psychological language, etcetera, is basically nonsense. Some years ago, I read a psychological text that was filled with jargon. I confronted the author. We finally translated it into common language, which only convinced me that virtually every text in the social sciences can be translated into common, ordinary language without losing anything. Economics may prove to be a partial exception.

I think this attempt to introduce a special language is an attempt to imitate the ways of natural scientists. And that involves a contradiction. Hayden White on the one hand definitely insists he is not a natural scientist and that history is not a science. On the other hand, he imitates the language of science. Of course, the question is what do you mean by science? If you mean by science, physics, then what he does is not science because history deals with highly complex human behavior that is guided by value conceptions. But if you try to reconstruct a historical past, if you try to reconstruct the actions and behavior of human beings, I think that you can do that much more honestly without claiming to do science.

The mere fact that history does not use scientific vocabulary does not mean that it cannot deal with the historical past. Ultimately, history has to do with meaning and the interpretation of meaning. But the interpretation of meaning can be an attempt to get back at reality. One thing that in my opinion distinguishes postmodernist historical thinking from modernist historical thinking, as Ankersmit distinguishes the two, is that postmodernism, as represented by Foucault and Derrida, but also by Roland Barthes, raises the possibility that there is no truth at all. All three argue that the author is not a subject with a clearly defined personality who can express clear ideas and has clear intentions. The intentions of the author are contradictory, multifold, and cannot be interpreted. What remains then for them is the text, and the text can be interpreted in many ways. This is not White's position, for whom the text still possesses a given structure that can be analyzed using formalistic criteria, but Derrida's position points in this direction.

This basically means that we can't reconstruct the past. But I think there is a past and the past is very complex, and very ambiguous, and very contradictory. People do act, and although it's difficult to reconstruct what they did and what their intentions were, I think we can take a stab at it.

What I find valuable in the recent critique of traditional historiography, and of concepts of historical cognition, is the recognition of the extent to which ideology plays a role in every historical work, and the extent to which every historical interpretation

If you try to reconstruct a historical past, if you try to reconstruct the actions and behavior of human beings, I think that you can do that much more honestly without claiming to do science.

106 involves manipulation, and reflects power relations. But at the same time, I'm still convinced that there is a past. I recognize the difficulties, the complexities in reconstructing it. I recognize the ideological elements that go into it. I recognize the extent to which knowledge involves power, but I also see the element of objectivity. We can never reconstruct the truth as it was, but we can somehow approximate it.

What is your opinion about applying metaphorical truth? My opinion is connected with the current idea that when we look at a particular sentence, we can think about logical truth, but when we want to interpret narratives as a whole, as White wants to do, we can't apply logical truth. We have to apply metaphorical truth, because it's not complex.

Yes, but the question is whether metaphor is pure fiction, or is an attempt to get hold of reality. I think, it's not just pure fiction; it's an attempt somehow to interpret reality and to find approximate concepts. I see that the borderline between fact and fiction is very elusive. We can have an account that is based very largely on factual materials or the events themselves, individual events that have been established through the critical analysis of sources. And yet when put together as a narrative, they may be highly ideological and may give us a very selective and distorted picture of a society or of a culture. The great novel may often come closer to the reality of a society or a culture than a historical text. I think to some extent the historical text lies somewhere between factuality and fiction. Metaphors, of course, are inescapable in historical narrative, but they may very well be heuristic means for understanding and interpreting a situation.

> The great novel may often come closer to the reality of a society or a culture than a historical text.

> To some extent the historical text lies somewhere between factuality and fiction.

Do you share the belief that we're experiencing a crisis in history?

The question is what do you mean by crisis and what do you mean by history? By history I guess you mean historical thinking, historical writing, historical conception.

Yes.

I don't know, because there is a tremendous interest in history. I am optimistic. What we have seen in the last twenty, thirty years is not a crisis in history but an enrichment of history.

I have just published a little book in German that deals with the relationship of so-called postmodernist historical theory and contemporary historical writing. I think postmodernist theory has raised all sorts of legitimate questions about the ways in which history has been written for the last almost two hundred years.

In social science we have a lot of different orientations, including Marxism, Max Weber, the New Economic History, and a good deal of the *Annales*. I think what they had in common, the *Annales* perhaps not to the same extent, was the belief that there is one history. Since the eighteenth century, we have spoken of history rather than of histories. Of course, the concept of history is very much related to the concept of modernization and the concept of modernization in turn is very much related to the idea of the superiority of Western civilization and the superiority of the modern world. I think this concept of linear progression in history you find even in Max Weber, who was very skeptical about many of the aspects of the modern world but who also thought that there was a process, which he called rationalization, that gave history a direction.

Now this concept of history as a unified process in which the European world is at the center obviously is in a crisis. But this doesn't mean that history is in crisis. I think that in the last twenty-five years there has been an explosion of interest in history. In the early 1970s there was a lot of talk that interest in history was declining, that it was being replaced by the social sciences. If you look at American universities, the number of students studying history on all levels went down from 1970 to 1980 by about fifty percent. It was similar in West Germany. Incidentally, it was not the same in France, where there was tremendous historical interest. Of course, the decline in students studying history had something to do with the fact that there were fewer jobs, but there were also fewer jobs because there was less interest in history. But since the 1980s there has been a new interest in history.

The unrest of the 1960s, reflected in the civil rights movement and in the opposition to the Vietnam War, brought about a reorientation in historical thinking. The interest in national history declined. It didn't disappear, it declined. The same thing occurred

107

What we have seen in the last twenty, thirty years is not a crisis in history but an enrichment of history.

Now this concept of history as a unified process in which the European world is at the center obviously is in a crisis. But this doesn't mean that history is in crisis.

in France. History moved away from the concentration on a center. In France, the *Annales* focused on regional history and historians like Fernand Braudel showed a new interest in global history. His last work, *L'Identité de la France*, a history of France, is interesting, because it's really not a history of the national state, but a history of the many regions and provinces that gave France its character.

What has emerged since the 1960s is a tremendous interest in the history of small groups. In the United States this began with the civil rights movement. The civil rights movement led to an awareness of ethnicity. We had the beginning of black history, and then of the history of other ethnic groups.

One thing that became very important was women's history, and gender history. What we have seen is not so much a crisis of history, but a crisis of traditional views of history. In fact there has been a tremendous increase in historical interest and a concentration on aspects of history that were previously ignored.

> What we have seen is not so much a crisis of history, but a crisis of traditional views of history.

An interesting little book was published about four years ago in German by Lutz Niethammer, and has just been published in English called *Posthistoire: Has History Ended?* It deals with growing beliefs since the nineteenth century that history no longer has meaning or purpose and that therefore we are living in a posthistorical age. It then argues that this is nonsense because the concern with history is very much alive, but it is a different history. We are living in an age that is no longer convinced that history follows a clear course. But why does there have to be one history? Why can't there be many histories? Why can't there be microhistory, the many histories of small groups? Of course, this microhistory takes place in a broader context so that the history of small groups and of the little people is still part of a larger history. To an extent we are beginning to recognize that common men and women have a history, too. I think this is a good development. This interest in the common people, this interest in existential aspects of life, in childhood or death or sexuality, is a good thing in my opinion, but on the other hand, it has too often led to the creation of new historical myths.

> This interest in existential aspects of life is a good thing in my opinion, but on the other hand, it has too often led to the creation of new historical myths.

I find the tremendous explosion of nationalisms since 1989 frightening, also as it has affected historical writing. The revival of historical interest is not a bad thing in itself, but it carries with it the danger that the causes that have led to this interest will create new historical myths in the service of ethnic or other particularistic ends.

But one could say that in theory of history nothing new has appeared since *Metahistory* was published.

I don't think that's true. I should, of course, emphasize that I'm not a philosopher of history. I'm not even a historian in the usual sense. I am interested in historiography, in historiography in the framework of intellectual history. I think that Hayden White is very much aware of things that happened since *Metahistory*. It has been twenty years now since *Metahistory* appeared. The postmodern discussions of the last twenty years have gone a long way beyond *Metahistory*, and in a sense they have deconstructed White. I already pointed out early in this interview how I see White. In many ways White is still quite conservative. He is conservative in his conception of science, and he is also traditional, as is Dominick LaCapra, in his emphasis on the classics. I also think that you cannot deal with the historical imagination in the nineteenth century by concentrating exclusively on a small number of select thinkers, such as Hegel, Burckhardt, and Tocqueville.

Since *Metahistory*, the critique of history, as practiced by Barthes, Lyotard, Foucault, and Derrida, has become more radical. In a recent telephone conversation with me, White disassociated himself from postmodernism and described *Metahistory* as the last gasp of structuralism.

> Since *Metahistory*, the critique of history, as practiced by Barthes, Lyotard, Foucault, and Derrida, has become more radical.

You told me that it is not true that since *Metahistory* appeared nothing new, nothing that could shock historians, has been published. Could you give me some examples of work that has had the same impact as *Metahistory*.

There isn't one single work. As I pointed out, I think there is a large range of historical literature that goes beyond this.

Derrida started writing in the 1960s but he continued writing into the '80s and '90s. Foucault should of course be mentioned here. LaCapra began writing seriously in the late 1970s, as did Ankersmit. Habermas's critique of postmodernism appeared in 1987.

110 And a book that I also find very interesting, although it isn't philosophy of history, is Joan Scott's *Gender and the Politics of History* (1988). So discussion hasn't stopped and I don't think it's going to stop. And of course there are not only these works but there is also a considerable debate that has accompanied these works, as it did Peter Novick's *That Noble Dream*.

Of course some things aren't really philosophy of history but they still have implications for the philosophy of history. I am thinking of Gareth Stedman Jones's book on class and language that came out in the 1980s. I am also thinking of William Sewell's book on language and revolution. I am thinking of Lynn Hunt's work on the French Revolution. These are all things that came out since *Metahistory* in the '80s. They emphasize the role of culture and the role of language.

Do you think that these cultural studies provide the background for a new history?

A lot of history is now being written within the orientation of a new cultural history, but not all of it. Thus political history, too, works much more extensively with symbols, attitudes, and mentalities than it did in the past. But the New Cultural History does not constitute a new paradigm. I don't think there are paradigms in history because there cannot be a consensus regarding methods, much less interpretations, which prevails in the natural sciences. The New Cultural History has a good deal to offer to the history of women, the history of sexuality, the history of leisure time, and so on. But there are also going to be very different types of history and different approaches. There is no crisis in history. There is more multiplicity than ever. What has come to an end is the confidence that history has a clear direction, and this loss of confidence has often been equated with crisis. We have reason to be skeptical of the belief, dominant in the nineteenth century, that history leads to redemption. We've just seen here in Eastern Europe the collapse of a great utopian dream. There was an attempt in 1917 to create a utopia and the utopia turned out to be a horror story, at least a horror story under Stalin and something not very desirable in the post-Stalin period. The twentieth century has been an age in which systematic inhumanity has been driven to unparalleled peaks. On the other hand, I still believe

I don't think there are paradigms in history.

What has come to an end is the confidence that history has a clear direction, and this loss of confidence has often been equated with crisis.

that the Enlightenment tradition, no matter how contradictory, has contributed to a greater sense of human dignity. Horkheimer and Adorno have argued that through its belief in rationality, it actually contributed to new forms of discrimination and inhumanity. But the Enlightenment in fact challenged the legitimacy of age-old forms of domination and inequality as they had been justified in the Judaeo-Christian-Islamic tradition but also in classical philosophy by Plato and Aristotle. The idea that inequality and subordination, including that of women, were parts of the natural or divine order was deeply embedded in the cultures not only of the Western but also of the non-Western world. These assumptions no longer go unquestioned and the great movement for reform and revolution, no matter how tragically their results often differed from their proclaimed aims, have marked the history of the modern world since the American and also the French Revolutions. Particularly in the past several decades, this challenge to old conceptions of legitimate authority has contributed to a historiography that deals with segments of the population and aspects of life that had previously been ignored. A much more pluralistic understanding of the human past has been the result.

You've proved to have a special interest in ideology now. There is some kind of revival of this interest. White told me that his main topic now is to start with the problem of ideological manipulation. Ankersmit told me the same. How can you explain this special interest?

History has been abused and often been used to legitimize power relations. The transformation of history into a scholarly discipline did not change this. The nineteenth-century professional historians used scholarly methods in support of their political and social programs, including their nationalism.

In our day we have seen the use of historical myths for tremendously destructive political purposes, under Nazism, under Fascism, under Communism, but also in the supposedly democratic societies. I don't know Franklin Ankersmit personally. I met him once very briefly at a conference; but I know Professor White and I know that he has very much the same social concerns that I have and that I assume Ankersmit has, too, and that of course makes us very much aware of the ideological misuses of history.

112   Is the main danger of history that it can be used?

As historians we should fight against the instrumentalization of history.

I think as historians we should fight against the instrumentalization of history. But if you're going to fight against the instrumentalization of history, then you also have to have some sort of a concept of what is historical honesty. Here I am a little worried about White's and even more so about Ankersmit's position because I believe the study of the past is very, very complex, but I still think that historical truth can be approximated. Of course, historical studies cannot arrive at definite findings that can be passed on without modification to future generations. To formulate it in very basic terms: if we dismantle the border between fact and fiction, and equate history with fiction, how can we defend ourselves against the assertion that the Holocaust never happened. As a Jew who barely escaped the Holocaust, I'm very much aware of what this means.

Obrzycko, Poland
29 May 1993

SELECTED WRITINGS

The German Conception of History: The National Tradition of Historical Thought from Herder to the Present. Middletown CT: Wesleyan Univ. Press, 1968; rev. ed. 1983.

Leopold von Ranke: The Theory and Practice of History, with Konrad von Moltke. Indianapolis: Bobbs-Merrill, 1973; 2d ed., New York: Irvington Press, 1983.

New Directions in European Historiography. Middletown CT: Wesleyan Univ. Press, 1975.

Aufklärung und Geschichte: Studien zur deutschen Geschichtswissenschaft im 18. Jahrhundert, coeditor, with Hans-Erich Bödeker, Jonathan B. Knudsen, and Peter H. Reill. Göttingen: Vandenhoeck & Ruprecht, 1986.

Leopold von Ranke and the Shaping of the Historical Discipline, coeditor, with James M. Powell. Syracuse: Syracuse Univ. Press, 1990.

Intellektuelle in der Weimarer Republik, coeditor, with Wolfgang Bialas. New York: P. Lang, 1996.

....

Historiography in the Twentieth Century: From Scientific Objectivity to the   **113**
Postmodern Challenge. Hanover NH: Wesleyan Univ. Press, 1997.

"New Directions in Historical Studies in the German Democratic Republic." *History and Theory* 28 (1989): 59–77.

"Rationality and History." In *Developments in Modern Historiography*, ed. Henry Kozicki, 19–39. New York: St. Martin's, 1993.

Comments on Frank R. Ankersmit's paper, "Historicism: An Attempt at Synthesis." *History and Theory* 21 (1995): 162–67.

"Historicism: The History and Meaning of the Term." *Journal of the History of Ideas* 56 (1995): 129–52.

"Zur linguistischen Wende in Geschichtsdenken und -schreibung." *Geschichte und Gesellschaft* 21 (1995): 545–58.

"Historiography and Politics in the Twentieth Century." In *Societies Made Up of History*, ed. Ragnar Björk and Karl Molin, 3–16. Edsbruk, Sweden: Akademitryck AB, 1996.

Jerzy Topolski [signature]

*Postmodernism gives us an opportunity
for changing our mentality.*

How did you first become interested in history?

■ I received my secondary education in Gniezno after the Second
World War. Gniezno had been the first capital of Poland, and hence
it is, as it were, burdened with history. Already, at that time, I was
used to ferreting in the archives of the Gniezno archbishopric,
which had not yet been put in order. Thus the first impulse came
from the place where I lived and studied in secondary school. The
same period witnessed the development of my interest in general
and theoretical social problems. That was why I entered Poznań
University School of Law and Economics. Professor Jan Rutkowski lectured there on economic history. Almost spontaneously I
joined his seminar because I considered him a great authority on
the subject.

The first impulse
came from the
place where I lived
and studied.

**So you turned toward theoretical and methodological
problems very early in your career.**

Yes. Economic history as interpreted by Rutkowski was not de-
scriptive but problem-oriented. In his seminar, empirical discussions always had a broader theoretical setting. Moreover, those
general interests made me interested in sociology. That was why
I started studying that discipline. Among other things I attended
Professor Tadeusz Szczurkiewicz's seminar on Max Weber. Yet
I did not complete my M.A. paper on sociology, even though I

already had a subject matter assigned to me, because by that time I had already received my Ph.D. in economic history.

It was at that time my friendship developed with Andrzej Malewski, who also studied sociology and economics. He was writing his doctoral thesis on explanation. I felt more at home in history and hence I provided him with examples for his analyses. That gave rise to our cooperation. Our discussions came to fruition in the form of the book *Studies in the Methodology of History* (in Polish), which was written after Gomułka's comeback in 1956. At first there were problems with having it published, but finally it appeared in 1960—but without two chapters that contained a critical analysis of historical materialism. They came to be published much later as separate papers contributed to specialist periodicals. *Studies in the Methodology of History* was the first attempt to transfer to Poland the achievements of the analytic philosophy of history. You might remember that the year 1957 witnessed the appearance in the West of *Laws and Explanation in History* by William Dray, and the discussion of Hempel's explanatory model had only just begun. Our *Studies* were received as a revitalizing stream in the muddy waters of Marxist theory mixed with ideology. That gave rise to the idea, advanced above all by Malewski, of our engaging in the so-called empirical methodology of history, which meant the study of the real practices of historians. That was to mark the difference between that methodology and the analytic philosophy of history, which was mainly the work of philosophers who availed themselves of the practices of historians mainly as examples to illustrate their theses. The positivist and analytic base was, of course, common to both approaches. As the first step of our program, we submitted historical materialism to a logically rigorous verification. That was the origin of the then famous paper by Malewski on the empirical sense of historical materialism (in Polish). Reflections on the philosophy and methodology of science aroused more and more interest in Poznań. It is worth mentioning in this context such names as Jerzy Giedymin, Zygmunt Ziembiński, Jerzy Kmita, Krystyna Zamiara, and Leszek Nowak (younger than the rest).

As well as doing my historical research, at that time I began studies in the logical and methodological structure of Marx's *Capital*. I initiated the preparation by the Poznań milieu of *Methodological Assumptions of Marx's "Capital"* (in Polish), written

As well as doing my historical research, at that time I began studies in the logical and methodological structure of Marx's *Capital*.

116 by many contributors. It became the point of departure for later works that critically analyzed Marx's theory. The next step toward a positivist analysis of historical materialism was *Elements of the Marxist Methodology of the Humanities* (in Polish), which had Jerzy Kmita as its editor. Also at that time, Leszek Nowak originated the publication abroad, beyond the reach of Polish censorship, of the methodological periodical *Poznań Studies in the Philosophy of the Sciences and the Humanities*, which exists to this day. Its third issue, edited by me and bearing the title *Historiography between Modernism and Postmodernism*, is to appear soon.

The analytic philosophy of history that was then finding its way to Poland focused its attention mainly on the problem of explanation in history. However, in Poland, it manifested itself in an analysis of the use of the theory of historical materialism in historical research. You were never considered an orthodox Marxist but rather a person who, in a definite political situation, tried to bring out the most fertile directives originating from that theory that could be used in historical research; hence your activistic theory of the process of history, stressing the role and impact of human actions upon that process. How do you now assess such studies? Were they conditioned merely by the political situation?

In post-1945 Poland, interest in Marxism was genuine, but when it comes to historiography it was very superficial.

In post-1945 Poland, interest in Marxism was genuine, but when it comes to historiography it was very superficial. It manifested itself above all by taking up problems inspired by the theory of historical materialism, such as the history of material culture, the history of the masses and of the class struggle, and so on. It was thus merely a certain bias in favor of studying problems important from the point of view of that theory. But a deeper penetration of the Marxist theory, drawing inspiration from it or making it richer, was extremely rare. In that respect it is worth mentioning *Reflections on History* (in Polish) by Witold Kula, which was published in 1958. It was a critique of dogmatic Marxism but at the same time a defense of Marxism as a source of inspiration. Kula opposed vulgar determinism but did not disavow Marxism.

I was also interested in Marx, but I had my own activistic conception of the process of history.

I was also interested in Marx, but I had my own activistic conception of the process of history. It was *not*, I want to emphasize, inspired by Marx's theory. Its core consisted in the distinction between two aspects of the process of history: the motivational (human actions) and the objective (results of those actions). I used this approach in the interpretation of Marx's theory. I still claim that the process of history begins with human actions oriented toward the attainment of certain goals and the satisfaction of certain needs. That is the subjective aspect of the process of history. But these actions also have objective consequences that are not planned by human beings and are not always perceived by them. That process, governed by objective regularities, goes on regardless of human will. And that is the objective aspect of the process of history. Comprehension of history as a whole thus requires an integrated explanation of both of its aspects. In my book *Freedom and Coercion in the Making of History* (in Polish), I tried to present that conception more broadly by referring to examples drawn from history. Of course, I also developed it in my *Theory of Historical Knowledge* (in Polish), which, however, was mainly concerned with the emphasis on theoretical and ideological pluralism that affects the form of historical narratives.

Under the rule of Marxism in the social sciences I tried to "soften" that conception; that is, to make it much less ideological and at the same time more digestible for historians. That was understood in Poland but it was not in other socialist countries. For instance, my *Methodology of History* was translated in the Soviet Union but it was accessible only to a select few. In Bulgaria and Czechoslovakia, translations of my books on the methodology of history were stopped. *Methodology of History* appeared only in Romania, which, as is known, used to stress its independence in foreign policy.

> Under the rule of Marxism in the social sciences I tried to "soften" that conception.

I continue to support my conception of the activistic interpretation of the process of history, and there is no point in substantiating it by references to Marxism. But I still think that Marx was right when he wrote in *The 18th Brumaire of Louis Bonaparte* that human beings make their history themselves but do not make it arbitrarily—not under the circumstances they choose themselves but under the circumstances they received and had transmitted to them. By the way, this is not a new thesis and it is accepted by many. For instance, Johann Gustav Droysen and many others argued similarly. Moreover, I think that one cannot understand the philosophy of science in the nineteenth or the

> One cannot understand the philosophy of science in the nineteenth or the twentieth centuries without reference to Marxism.

118   twentieth centuries without reference to Marxism, because philosophy of science developed either as a critique or as a reference to Marxism. Many ideas originating from Marxism, often not even labeled as such, have been included in the general achievement of the humanities. For instance, students of social history, historians included, will examine the role of the economic factor without bothering about whether it was Marx or someone else who drew attention to its importance. The main lesson here is to avoid dogmatism in explanations.

Self-evidently, writing books at the time when everyone, almost to the very end, was convinced that the system would survive and that there were no prospects of its change (which is to say that changes may take place within that system only), differs radically from writing when one realizes that the system *is* changing. As late as 1986, Czeslaw Miłosz argued that there were no rational grounds to hope that the international system, including Poland's position in it, would change within the foreseeable future. This opinion was also dominant in the West among most renowned researchers and politicians. That was why in the Soviet bloc the dominant attitudes were those of adjustment, which included intrasystemic criticism and "revisionism." That was also the way, I think, in which my work was treated. A researcher could become an apologist of the system, or else recognize the existing state of things as permanent and try to find in it a place for himself that would not be at variance with the values of science, or else, if the situation was mature, actively oppose the system without any certainty whatever that such an action would succeed. Of course, the attitude one adopted was reflected in one's scholarly production. Personally I do not think that I have to disavow anything of what I have written on the methodology and the theory of history. In methodology I was influenced by analytic philosophy, in particular by Popper's hypothetism, and moreover I worked out my activistic conception within the framework of which I tried to interpret historical materialism.

I was influenced by analytic philosophy, in particular by Popper's hypothetism.

We have only recently learned here in Poland about the narrativist turn in the philosophy of history and about Hayden White's *Metahistory*, whereas in the West his theory has been analyzed in detail. Do you think that the intellectuals

in the post-Communist countries are capable of making up
for the lost years when historical and scientific thinking was
dogmatized? I mean, is it possible to change the mentality
of research, the way of thinking that was accustomed to
moving mainly within the scope of the categories of the
theories of historical materialism in the broad sense of
the term?

The post-Communist countries cannot be treated uniformly. In Poland after 1956 Marxism practically ceased to be imposed by the authorities as the only theory in science that deserved support. In that respect we witnessed a return of theoretical and philosophical pluralism. Marxism remained an object of interest for philosophers (which gave rise to its many nonorthodox interpretations in Poland), while historians abandoned its superficial adaptation. The authorities, while discontinuing the imposition of Marxism as the only theoretical and ideological approach in science, continued, and even intensified, the political control of science, and of historiography in particular. The idea was not to diminish Poland's relations with the Soviet Union. Everything that related to Polish-Soviet contacts was subject to strict censorship; hence, so many so-called white spots in historiography concerned with the twentieth century. But that control did not encroach upon the area of the philosophy of history, which could develop. I wrote much about historical narratives in my *Methodology of History* (first published in 1968), pointing in particular to its temporal structure. I was concerned to a still greater degree with historical narratives in my *Theory of Historical Knowledge*. I presented there, among other things, the theses of White's *Metahistory* and pointed to the novel elements in his conception. Many other scholars were watching what was taking place in the philosophy of history throughout the world. The year 1976 witnessed the appearance in Polish of *The Archeology of Knowledge* by Michel Foucault (published as a result of my inspiration and with my introduction). It aroused considerable interest in Poland. Other works by the same author were also published in this country. The positivist way of thinking was still dominant in science and historiography. *Metahistory* was at first coolly received in the West. But it is true that in Poland much is to be done in the sphere of philosophical reflection. The relative retardation of Poland was largely

120 due to a considerable weakening of scholarly contacts between Poland and the West in the 1980s (after the imposition of martial law in Poland). The inflow of many books and periodicals was interrupted just at the time when the narrativist turn you mentioned was taking place. The fact that in Western Europe and in the United States more people are concerned with the methodology of history was conducive to the emergence of separate schools of thought and groups of scholars. Under such conditions there is a stronger polarization of opinions, which is good for a fruitful dialogue. For instance, in Holland on the one hand we have Franklin Ankersmit, who tends to accept postmodernist solutions, but on the other hand Chris Lorenz, who does not disavow realism, and P. H. H. Vries, author of *Vertellers op drift*, who is skeptical about narrativism. In Poland we are now at the stage of transferring new conceptions to this country and of adapting them. In many cases this does not mean implantation on virgin soil but on one that is well-prepared philosophically, with strongly developed phenomenological philosophy, with specialists well trained in logical and philosophical reflection and referring to the renowned traditions of the Polish school. But whether we can keep abreast of the development of the philosophy of history largely depends on the opportunities for training a younger generation of researchers interested in the theory and philosophy of history.

Historians mostly continue to be traditional.

When it comes to the attitudes of historians, they mostly continue to be traditional, which means that they refer to the assumptions that also marked analytic philosophy. The principal ones are the belief that the researcher is independent of the reality he studies; the belief that there is only one truth that reports on the past; the belief that truth can be arrived at by reference to language; and the belief that historical sources are the most reliable road to the past. This domination of the traditional mentality of historians is, of course, not confined to Poland.

What is now taking place in Poland in the milieu of young philosophers, theorists of literature, and art historians might be described as the triumphant entry of postmodernism, which is associated with tolerance, decentralization, abolition of traditional values, undermining of the classical conception of truth, and so forth. Are we prepared for

this dramatic clash of perverse postmodernism with a
traditional society accustomed to traditional values? Is
not the popularity of postmodernist conceptions merely
a superficial reaction to dogmatism and enslavement?

There are in it certainly elements of a sui generis reaction but that applies only to certain milieus in the humanities, and you are right on that point. But historians have so far not been keen on assimilating postmodernism. It is rather passing them by. Even if they become acquainted with works that comply with some requirements of postmodernism, it should be emphasized that these are always numerically dominated by nonpostmodernist literature, by works written in compliance with the traditional canons. They are often merely manifestations of a search for novelties, even if they stimulate thinking. It seems, however, that the scholarly milieus concerned with the humanities (I confine myself here to them only) will apply specific defense mechanisms against the extremes of postmodernism. Historians probably sense that the adoption of the most radical requirements of postmodernism would have to result in the destruction of the kind of historiography that has been dominant for centuries. But it is not my intention to make you think that I underestimate the revitalizing role of the inspirations brought about by postmodernism. I only want to say that in my opinion historians will not accept the end of their writing of history, the elimination from it of the temporal axis, and the obliteration of the boundary between historical and literary narratives.

Could you define in greater detail your attitude toward postmodernism in historiography?

I think that postmodernism is to be treated not as a complete doctrine (which formulation, by the way, postmodernists would not accept), but as a certain trend, or a certain philosophical, artistic, and intellectual continuum, at one end of which one might place the less radical calling into question of modernism (for instance, the postulated change of the subject matter of historical works, doing away with all forms of centrism and Lyotard's meta-narration), and at the other the more radical demands that the category of truth be replaced by that of freedom, or the scattering of senses by their deconstruction (as in the case of Derrida),

122 and the blurring of the boundaries between the various types of intellectual activity (as between historical and literary narratives). According to postmodernists, we should act not so much on the basis of the possibly truest knowledge (in the sense of the classical conception of truth) but on the basis of the practical experience of human communities. This challenge of postmodernism can be interpreted in various ways, more or less radically. For instance, we have the conception of Hilary Putnam, where truth, communities, and social practice function together. However it is, the challenge of postmodernism is a leading challenge, and the world can hardly remain indifferent to it. As I have said, I do not think that historians as a professional community will accept postmodernism in its extreme forms, since that would mean transition from one dogmatism (that of a sole truth) to another dogmatism (that of relativism and a total lack of points of support, be it only historically transient).

I want to make the point that the inspirations originating from postmodernism help us discard certain deeply rooted opinions. It is certainly an intellectual shock, which lets us think many things anew. Many postmodernist ideas will remain as part of the attainment of human thought, but the radical representatives of that trend will probably reach the status of psychohistorians, the status of a sui generis sect whose members are convinced that their teachings are absolutely right. Today, psychohistory, totally pushed to the margin, has almost no support among historians, whereas its representatives still believed not so long ago that they possessed the only good recipe for the interpretation of history. It is, in my opinion, questionable whether radical postmodernists can succeed in eliminating ontology, epistemology (with the legacy of the Age of Reason), and logic from philosophy with its category of truth, set theory, and so on, and in replacing all that by a deconstructing analysis of texts as artefacts that have no authors.

The analytic philosophy of history in its classical form is practically nonexistent. A new philosophy of history is in statu nascendi.

For the time being we can see changes that are extremely interesting and make us rethink many things. So far they have been farther reaching in the philosophy of history than in historiography itself. The analytic philosophy of history in its classical form (imparted to it, among others, by Hempel) is practically nonexistent. A new philosophy of history (narrativist and perhaps postnarrativist as well) is in statu nascendi.

What do you think is most fertile in this new philosophy of history?

As I see the problem, in historical narratives we can single out three principal layers: informative and logical; rhetorical in the persuasive and topical sense; and deep, that is, theoretical and ideological, which controls the formation of the other two layers.

The analytic philosophy of history, which started investigating narratives to some extent only after the appearance of Arthur Danto's fundamental work *Analytical Philosophy of History*, was concerned only with the first of the above layers, which is interested mainly in the schemata of explanation. Since historians did not participate in the work of philosophers of history on the disclosure of the schemata of explanation in historiography (in most cases they were not prepared for the job), that work was dissociated from the historians' practice. That is why it largely consisted in juggling with examples extracted from their respective historical contexts. That meant a one-sided vision, often deformed by a not-too-good knowledge of the practice of historiographers. But those works were not in vain. Nothing has been lost. On the contrary, it is a considerable achievement on which we can build a new philosophy of history.

It would be an exaggeration to examine the historian's work mainly in the perspective of explanation. But it is unquestionable that historians will not renounce explanation; that is, answering the question "why?" The shortcoming of the analytic philosophy of history in the matter of explanation consisted in the belief in the explanatory power of the models discovered in it. In my opinion, an important achievement of the new, narrativist philosophy of history consists in calling into question the cognitive value of those models. For each of them had behind it one and the same myth; namely, the conviction that reality can be described and explained by reference to those models. Hempel stated plainly that we arrive at a complete explanation in history if we succeed in linking the supposed causes with general laws. That method seemed unshakable. But the new philosophy of history made us realize that the search for those factors is a convention, an arbitrary operation. That procedure was marked by an optimism assumed in advance. But in fact in the procedure of explanation there is, by the very nature of things, more rhetoric than in the procedure of

124   describing facts, the latter being in closer contact with its empirical base.

Analytic philosophy gave the impression of greater "scientificity" of explanations. But it must be borne in mind that the search for "factors" that a historian places, for instance, in the nomologico-deductive model is in advance guided by his vision of man and the world and by conventions current in his society, linguistic conventions included. Thus we do not have here any "objective" procedure.

In my opinion the importance of the postmodernist turn with respect to history consists above all in increased skepticism, in calling into question the naive certainty of cognition. That means deconstruction, in a sense.

And what is your attitude toward the problem of truth, which is probably the most thorny issue today?

I wish to emphasize that—contrary, for instance, to the conceptions expounded by Ankersmit in his *Narrative Logic* and by White in his various writings—I think that the concept of truth applies not only to statements about separate historical facts but also to the narrative substance; that is, the historical narrative as a whole. I think so in spite of the fact that to me it seems beyond all doubt that there is no return to the classical conception of truth; that is, to that vision of science that was being constructed for centuries—science that refers to the axis defined by Cartesian rationalism and Humean empiricism. Nor is there a return to the classical analytic philosophy of history. But the restriction of the applicability of the category of truth to single statements combined with its rejection with respect to more comprehensive narrative wholes encounters insurmountable barriers. In historical narratives there are no isolated statements. All of them are interconnected in many ways, and each of them contains more general elements. One may, of course, reflect on the truth of single historical statements. But as soon as they become elements of a narrative, this possibility vanishes. Hence one has either not to apply at all the category of truth to a historical narrative or to conclude that it pertains to such a whole. Of course, in the latter case we have to analyze the extremely intricate problem (not solved to date) of defining the nature of the truth that applies to an entire

> There is no return to the classical conception of truth.
>
> Nor is there a return to the classical analytic philosophy of history.

narrative and not to single statements or their sequences. This means defining the nature of that truth, which might be termed narrational. Such truth would not be the only truth for which one strives when constructing one's narrative and in the light of which one assesses its definite versions. As I see it, that would be a truth with many faces; that is, a pluralistic truth subjected constantly to verification procedures. The arrival at such a truth would be marked by the search for a possibly vast consensus. This is to say that the criterion of the comparison of such truths (functioning as pluralistic ones) would consist in comparisons of the empirical bases of the various narratives and of the effectiveness of their methods. In other words, that narrational truth (whose characteristics we still do not know in any considerable degree) would be both coherential and pragmatic. It would assume rational decisions about it, made by members of given communities. It would also assume a constant exchange of opinions. Even such a truth would not reject being referred to reality, and that reality (or in the case of historians, past reality) could not be treated as something that exists "objectively" with respect to which the historian remains "outside," or as something complete and ready for investigation. It would merely be something that is coconstructed by the historian. Coconstruction does not mean construction. In the former case the empirical base is always present: we are concerned with a game with "reality." In the latter, the formation of suprasentential constructs is not any such name because reality is not present there. Of course, reference is always being made not to reality as such but to our (the historian's) knowledge of it, the knowledge of the sources included.

Reference is always being made not to reality as such but to our knowledge of it.

Thus, even though I am not convinced by the endeavors to restrict the applicability of the criterion of truth to historical narratives, I nevertheless accept as justified the criticism of the new philosophy of history aimed at the classical conception of truth, which is the basic epistemological assumption in the analytic philosophy of history.

Do you think that this "reevaluation" has resulted in a modification of the goals and tasks of the philosophy of history?

I do not think so, although it seems that today, in a period of

126 growing skepticism about our possibilities of understanding the past, combined with a deeper penetration of the process whereby historians study the past and write about it, the tasks are greater, although the goals have remained the same.

The task of the philosophy of history always was (even though that was interpreted in various ways) to make historians realize what they are doing. That is the historian's point of view. For the philosopher of history, the practice of historians and their historical narratives are just an object of study and reflection like any other object.

The task of the philosophy of history always was to make historians realize what they are doing.

But why do you think that the tasks of the philosophy of history are now greater than under the domination of the analytic philosophy of history?

We must, first of all, realize the difference. The basic assumptions that guided the work of the analytically oriented philosophers of history were more or less the same as the assumptions spontaneously accepted by historians. They were based on the conviction that the historian is positioned outside the reality he studies, that there is a single or unique truth pertaining to that reality, and that arrival at the truth is achieved through the intermediary of language, which is a good medium of our understanding. In this way there was no divergence between the philosophy of history and historiography, as far as the basic assumptions were concerned. The philosophy of history reflected the practice of historians as they conceived it themselves (more or less consciously); hence, the classical conception of truth and the mirror theory of language, which guided the work of the analytically oriented philosophers of history, continues to guide the activity of the majority of professional historians. Even though the latter on the whole do not manifest any major interest in general methodological and theoretical reflection, their statements and texts (for instance reviews) show that they are still convinced that they are striving for the truth and for an objective presentation of the past.

Today things are much more complicated. The new philosophy of history has a sui generis mission to carry out with respect to historiography. The point is not merely to draw historians' attention to what they do, but also to restructure their consciousness, which means directing their autoreflection along new paths. That would help historians to look at their own work and its results at a greater distance, to develop an ironic attitude (in the rhetorical sense of the word), to become more open to the truths proclaimed by others, and to make greater efforts toward arriving at scholarly consensuses. This new consciousness should be marked by assent to the circulation of different truths, by the belief that they are equal to one another at their points of departure, and by a lack of an a priori conviction that one is the only person to know the truth.

Further, historians should also discard the belief that sources show us the truth. The more I was engaged in historical research the more I was convinced that that is a myth working to our detriment. That assumption is both utopian and erroneous. But a historian will not himself discard that assumption. It is, therefore, imperative to demonstrate to him that both historical sources and historical narratives are burdened with subjective factors. Metaphorically it might be said that in traditional philosophy the sources are a kind of road that links the historian with the past. But in my opinion there is no such road. There are merely many tortuous paths followed by straying historians. They exchange among themselves contradictory or even intentionally misleading information about where to go, while on the horizon they see only some light blurred by fog.

Thus everything requires incessant criticism. Let me repeat that this new philosophy of history, which still remains nameless (I myself call it neither narrativist nor postmodernist, since it should make different trends merge) and historians as well should discard the classical conception of truth and language. And philosophy ought to concentrate on making historians realize that the assumptions mentioned above are erroneous and that they are not granite-like.

But we can see that the more the theorists try to demonstrate the erroneous character of the assumptions traditionally accepted by historians, such as the classical conception of truth, the more the historians stick to their convictions. There are not many examples of history sensu stricto written in the postmodernist spirit. The few exceptions are the frequently quoted Foucault and representatives of

128 anthropological history: Emmanuel Le Roy Ladurie, Carlo Ginzburg, Natalie Zemon Davis, Simon Schama.

As I have said, the application of the radical postmodernist criteria would practically mean the end of historiography. Just imagine that a historian would like to follow in the footsteps of what Elizabeth Deeds Ermarth wrote in her recent book, *Sequel to History*. That would be a narrative deprived of its chronological axis, philosophical rather than historical, referring more to general problems than to the past and coming close to a postmodernist novel. But that is not what we strive for. Personally I do not assume the necessity of great changes in historiography. Let the historians write as they used to do, but let them also realize what they do and the value of what they write.

Some people treat Foucault as a postmodernist, and in a sense they are right. In any case, he certainly was a forerunner of postmodernism. But we have to consider two trends in his production. One consisted in working out the archaeological method (*Les mots et les choses*) that was later more concentrated on discourse (*L'Archéologie du savoir*). The other consists of works written with strictly historiographical ambitions (for instance, *Histoire de la folie*). The latter are postmodernist insofar as they comply with certain ideas strongly marked in postmodernism, such as the departure from focal topics and the taking up of problems previously treated as marginal; for instance the study of illness, prisoners, and so on. That has, of course, its place in the trend leading to postmodernism. Yet the very method of writing the history of those marginal problems remains traditional. By the way, Foucault wanted to be assigned the status of historian.

> Let the historians write as they used to do, but let them also realize what they do and the value of what they write.

Perhaps that is due to the fact that postmodernism reflects above all a certain intellectual atmosphere; it is a spiritual category that touches upon theoretical and philosophical considerations. But the practice of the historians seems traditional and does not succumb to its influence.

Yes, it is just so. Even Elizabeth Deeds Ermarth wrote her postmodernist work in the traditional language. Take, further, the classical book by Hayden White, his *Metahistory*. I would class it as postmodernist, but in a very broad sense of the term. It is beyond doubt structuralist, too. Its author discloses certain structures of consciousness that, in his opinion, guides the work of historians. They are definite literary models, which suggests that the same historical content may be submitted to conceptualizations of various kinds; that is to say, interpreted as a comedy or a tragedy. Such an approach was undoubtedly novel. It makes one think of Foucault's epistemes, but White went farther as he pointed to the relativism of conceptualization in historiography, which was still absent in Foucault at the time of his writing *Les mots et les choses*.

White's work stimulated further investigations of the mechanisms that explain this and not another construction of narratives by historians. The results are very promising. Let me mention just the very interesting work by Ann Rigney, *The Rhetoric of Historical Representation*, which analyzes the texts of three French historians and their different interpretations of the French Revolution. For instance, while one of them views the revolt in Paris from the perspective of the attacking crowd and shows the heroism of the crowd, the other takes the point of view of those who defended the king and of the royal family, bringing out their sufferings. This shows to the historians that one and the same fact may be interpreted in various ways, and that the truth about it is relative. Hence a certain event may be described, as Rigney does it, by viewing it from various perspectives. One only has to choose the proper rhetoric to convey historical information. In this way, while the fact being described remains, as it were, the same, the way of informing the reader about it varies.

It may be said that the more a given historical narrative is remote from what Lyotard has termed "metanarration," the more it is postmodernist. Thus the works that deconstruct such theoretical concepts as the nation, the state, patriotism, and nationalism are postmodernist. They strive for a scattered description that lacks a central axis. For instance, James C. Scott in his *Weapons of the Weak* tries to reduce the resistance of peasants to individual and local actions whereby he eliminates the concept of collective actions guided by a common ideology. History in such studies (one might also quote similar works concerned with the struggle for independence in Ireland) becomes a collection of separate events governed by their own dynamics. That is, by the way, what a historian should do if he wants to draw a logical conclusion from the conceptions that limit the application of the category of

The more a given historical narrative is remote from what Lyotard has termed "metanarration," the more it is postmodernist.

History in such studies becomes a collection of separate events governed by their own dynamics.

130   truth to statements about separate events; that is, if he wants to
stay on the solid ground of facts and at the same time to discontinue the creation of a fictional—in the light of those conceptions—superstructure over them.

But then do you think that the works of Le Roy Ladurie and Ginzburg may be linked to postmodernism?

It is not essential whether they can be so linked. But it is beyond doubt that the microhistories by Le Roy Ladurie and Ginzburg (life in Montaillou and the story of the miller Menocchio) allow us to understand the past better, and that most probably explains their popularity with the public. For if a historian writes a synthetic work, then he uses historical data at a more general level and thus loses contact with individual people. If, however, he descends to a lower level, microlevel, one might say, then the reader more strongly senses history through the intermediary of his text. The historian then finds it easier to identify himself with people who lived at the time he describes. History in this way reaches the reader more directly, without the various ideological interventions of the historian. In such a case the reader's freedom is greater.

But to revert to your question, *Montaillou* and *The Cheese and the Worms* were not intended as postmodernist books, even though they express certain new trends in the humanities. They are sui generis harbingers of new approaches. That is why, even though they are written in the postmodernist spirit, they do not discard metanarration, for which postmodernists criticized them. Le Roy Ladurie and Ginzburg brought human individuals closer to us. Because of them we see those people in their direct actions and with their everyday worries. In this way those people are very close to us.

Undoubtedly postmodernism must be credited with a certain return to existentialism, which restores the ideas of sensing history, of identifying oneself with people who lived in the past, and emotional bonds between the historian and the persons he writes about. Does this mean a return to Diltheyan understanding?

To some extent it does, but the problem is more complex. Positivism, by putting history on an equal footing with the natural sciences, dehumanized it. But structuralism did the same. Foucault expelled the author. Derrida did more or less the same. This reveals two trends in postmodernism—one of them linked with this dehumanization and the other turning toward the individual. In positivism, there are regularities, there are processes, there is history written with a capital *H*, and human beings exist only as its element. It is the same in structuralism. But it seems that historians, if they succumb to the influence of the intellectual atmosphere of postmodernism, would rather follow that existential trend.

What do you think about the marriage of history and literature? Many researchers would like to remove the barrier separating these disciplines from each other. Although the difference between them seems self-evident, it is difficult to find clear-cut opinions on what that difference really is.

I think that there is one essential difference between historical and literary narratives, and also several differences that are relative in character. Contemporary reflections on the philosophy of history and postmodernism make us realize that the boundaries between these two types of narrations become blurred at many points. The essential difference between historical and literary narratives is that the historian cannot invent individual facts. He cannot deliberately include in his narrative fiction pertaining to what originates from the empirical base. A man of letters, on the contrary, may include the description of such facts in his text. Historical and literary narratives are similar when it comes to their interpretation and the suprafactographic level. There is no qualitative difference there. On the other hand, if we are referring to the category of truth, in a historical narrative the empirical base should be "true," and in the case of a literary narrative the author may only aspire to truth that might be termed typological (pertaining to types of situations, events, human beings). That is not linked to the requirement of factographical truth. This boundary, while it may seem clearly marked, in practice is not. Hence, that which is above the empirical base is constructed by the historian in a manner that resembles what a man of letters does.

The essential difference between historical and literary narratives is that the historian cannot invent individual facts.

132   There are also differences of degree between historical narratives and belles lettres. I shall mention the two most important
ones. One of them pertains to the very conception of narratives,
and the other to their temporal content. The "becoming" of history is shown to a much greater degree in literary narratives. It
shows the mechanisms of decision-making by human beings, it
includes dialogues and penetrates human consciousness. A historian has no such opportunities, especially because of the lack of
appropriate sources. Droysen complained about that by emphasizing the fact that a historian can never penetrate the human psyche in the way Shakespeare did. This is not something imma-
nently linked with the historical narrative, but is a result of the
nature of the empirical base of historical research. The historian
would probably be willing to enliven his narrative, for instance,
with dialogues, but he is not allowed to do so because he is not
allowed to invent things. Dialogues may be found in historical
narratives if the sources make that possible. Le Roy Ladurie
quotes many of them in *Montaillou* because he found them in the
documents of the Inquisition. Perhaps *Montaillou* has become a
best-seller exactly because it comes closer to literature.

The second difference pertains to the way of handling time.
In a postmodernist novel the author does not bother about the
chronological axis. He freely travels through time. On the contrary, the historian always, even in the case of a synchronic narrative, must refer to dated time. He is bound by it, although he may
refer to it in a manner different from the chronicler and the an-
nalist because he views the facts he studies in a temporal perspective. Arthur Danto saw in this the main characteristic that singles
out historical narratives. That is really the case, but an author of
historical novels can also view in retrospection the times he describes. That is why the basic difference between historical narratives and literary narratives, and at the same time the main characteristic of the former, consists, in my opinion, not in that they are
written in a temporal perspective, but in that their factographical
base is not fictional.

**Do you not think that the obliteration of the boundaries
between belles lettres and historiography is due to the**

shifting of the center of gravity from the method whereby 133
reality is cognized to the goal of cognition? Should we conclude that the goal consists in the acquisition of the knowledge of reality, its sensing—then both historiography and
belles lettres (fiction, poetry) can attain the goal?

Agreed, but that is a quite different problem as it pertains to the
cognitive values of the various ways in which we conceive reality.
I find it self-evident that, for instance, Balzac's novels may give
their readers a more tangible knowledge of the epoch than dry
historical works do. I do not see in that the difference in the cognitive value of belles lettres and historiography. In my opinion it
is historical novels that are the most dangerous. The authors of
such novels cannot distance themselves from their knowledge of
what occurred later than the time in which the novel is set. That
is why they ascribe to the characters in their novels the consciousness that they themselves have. The historian, of course,
also knows the consequences of the facts he describes because a
historical narrative is always written in a certain temporal perspective. But he is not allowed to ascribe such consciousness to
historical persons. As I have said, the historian reports on history,
while the man of letters shows the becoming of history. Therefore, the strong point of a historical narrative (its author's knowledge of what occurred later) is the weak point of a literary narrative that describes the past.

> I do not see in
> that the difference
> in the cognitive
> value of belles
> lettres and
> historiography.

**Would you tell me which of the books that you have read
recently have intrigued you most?**

My job requires that I should become acquainted with many
books of various kinds. The majority, or even the overwhelming
majority, of them I assimilate professionally, but I enjoy only few
of them. I am now reading *Foucault's Pendulum* by Umberto
Eco, but I find it less attractive than *The Name of the Rose* by the
same author. I would give pride of place to Le Roy Ladurie's
Montaillou. I have found it really astonishing. The book by Ann
Rigney, *The Rhetoric of Historical Representation*, and that by
Marcello Flores, *L'Immagine dell'USSR*, where he describes the
attitude of Western intellectuals to Lenin's and Stalin's Russia, are

134   interesting, too. I am also reading an excellent book by Elzbieta Kowecka, *The Court of the Most Frugal Magnate in Poland*, about the Polish magnate Jan Klemens Branicki, who lived in the eighteenth century.

And what is your opinion of the work of American historians?

American historiography is very diversified. Good modernist historiography, precise and quantitative, continues to be successful. For instance, a couple of days ago, I received from Robert W. Fogel an excellent work originating from the methods of cliometrics, which also makes historical sense. Its title is *New Sources and New Techniques for the Study of Secular Trends in Nutritional Status, Health, Mortality, and the Process of Aging*.

In my opinion *The Embarrassment of Riches* by Schama is an example of postmodernist historiography. The evocation of certain images and the use of art I find very interesting and inspiring. I have been similarly attracted by *The Return of Martin Guerre* by Natalie Zeimon Davis. Such books enable us to grasp the past emotionally.

Recently it often happens that authors whom we associate with postmodernism avail themselves of art, especially painting, in their research. Do you notice a specific transition from modernist verbalism to postmodernist visualism? Perhaps in the future, instead of comparing our life to a novel we shall speak about it as a film. I mean the characteristic mixing of times, the sensual conception of truth, and the specific, frame-like treatment of reality.

I think that the future may be just such. In my methodology of history, on which I am now working, I emphasize very strongly the fact that we must also take into account the visual layer of narratives. The historian not only writes his narratives but also evokes images. Moreover, one might also evoke audial and even olfactory impressions.

And yet, in spite of the fact that so many interesting things are now observable in the philosophy of history, and in

historiography itself, some people claim that there is a crisis in history.

I do not think that history is in a state of crisis. I do not even think that traditional historiography is in a crisis. It is merely that the contemporary philosophy of history makes us realize that there is a contradiction between the fundamental assumptions of historiography and those of the new philosophy of history. Whether that hiatus means a crisis is a question of how we define crisis. I think that we shall witness the coexistence of the various ways of writing history, postmodernist included. That would be very good.

I do not think that history is in a state of crisis.

The title of your essay, "A Non-Postmodernist Analysis of Historical Narratives," in _Historiography between Modernism and Postmodernism_, suggests that you continue to focus your attention on the writing of history. But do you not think that recently we see a lesser interest in language, discourse, and narration?

Agreed. But my point is not to arrive at some one-sidedly narrativist methodology, but one that would also avail itself of the achievements of the analytic philosophy of history. I have termed my analysis of narratives nonpostmodernist to emphasize that I do not discard the category of truth (even though it is not the classical conception in its naive version), and that I do not discard the author and ontology, either. I see that historical and literary narratives are also close to one another, from the rhetorical point of view. In this way I place myself among the contemporary theorists of historiography somewhere near the left pole, which is the less radical one.

But in the sphere of postmodernist conceptions?

I do not think so. My conception is not postmodernist although it accepts much of the postmodernist striving for the abolition of dominant ideas and for the freedom of choice. But I do not discard epistemology and truth.

My conception is not postmodernist.

You show an interest in the theory of Hilary Putnam.

Yes. I think that although his conception of truth has no place in

Putnam's conception has a remarkable future in the philosophy of history.

postmodernism, which after all is obvious, it is something that marks the new intellectual atmosphere of our times. In my opinion that conception has a remarkable future in the philosophy of history.

I wish to emphasize that I consider the postmodernist shock very invigorating. But too far-reaching relativizations that originate from postmodernism deprive one of points of support, for which one is always looking. Absolute freedom does not mean freedom.

Well, postmodernism is after all a situation born of crisis. Nietzsche, to whom postmodernists so willingly refer, stressed that it was necessary to make something new emerge from nihilism.

Perhaps it is just for that reason that everything has been called into question. For the time being we see chaos, from which a new quality will emerge.

Postmodernism gives us an opportunity for changing our mentality.

We should arrive at some synthesis in the philosophy of history. Postmodernism gives us an opportunity for changing our mentality. For instance, it suggests that a narrative should be interpreted as some form of practical wisdom, its own conception of the past, which the historian submits for discussion.

Can postmodernism become a new philosophy of existence?

Postmodernism, at least for some time, may become a way of approaching the problems of human existence. Personally, I also like pluralism and tolerance. But I fear that postmodernism may suffer the fate of a sect closed to critical arguments. There have been such things in history.

But it seems that there is a still greater danger: postmodernism is a good substratum for relativism, not in epistemology alone but in the sphere of morality as well.

The category of truth is also a moral one.

That is exactly why I firmly oppose discarding the conception of truth. To me the category of truth is also a moral one. It means, for the historian, the exhortation to be honest and to serve human beings, who cannot rest satisfied with lies or substitutes for

truth. I treat the category of truth as one of the points of support
that human beings need in life.

137

Poznań, Poland
23 October 1993

Translated by Olgierd Wojtasiewicz

SELECTED WRITINGS

Methodology of History, trans. Olgierd Wojtasiewicz. Warszawa: PWN,
1976.
Teoria wiedzy historycznej [Theory of historical knowledge]. Poznań:
Wydawnictwo Poznańskie, 1983.
*Historiography between Modernism and Postmodernism: Contributions to
the Methodology of Historical Research*, editor. Amsterdam: Rodopi,
1994.
The Manorial Economy in Early-Modern East-Central Europe. Aldershot,
UK: Variorum, 1994.

"Historical Narrative: Towards a Coherent Structure." *History and The-
ory*, Beiheft 26: The Representation of Historical Events, 1987:
75–86.
"The Concept of Theory in Historical Research." *Storia della Storio-
grafia* 1 (1988): 67–79.
"Was ist historische Methode." In *Historische Methode*, ed. Christian
Meier and Jörn Rüsen, 100–113. München: Deutschen Taschen-
bach Verlag, 1988.
"Polish Historians and Marxism after World War II." *Studies in Soviet
Thought* 43 (1992): 168–83.
"Types of Historical Narratives from the Point of View of Their Tempo-
ral Content." In *A Special Brew . . . Essays in Honour of Kristof Gla-
man*, ed. Thomas Riis, 73–89. Odense: Odense Univ. Press, 1993.
"Historians Look at Historical Truth." In *Epistemology and History*, ed.
Anna Zeidler-Janiszewska, 405–17. Amsterdam: Rodopi, 1996.
"The Commonwealth of Scholars and New Conceptions of Truth." In
The Idea of the University, ed. Jerzy Brzezinski and Leszek Nowak,
83–103. Amsterdam: Rodopi, 1997.

*There is a lot of open future
in the past.*

Could you tell me how your interest in history began?

■ It began by reading historical novels in high school and not by historical instruction in the classroom. On the level of academic development my original interest was not history but philosophy. I wrote my Ph.D. in philosophy. My subject was Johann Gustav Droysen. He is a historian, but he wrote one of the most important texts on the theory of history, his *Historik*. My thesis lies across the border of both disciplines, philosophy and history. My main interest was in philosophy, but during my student years and while starting to teach at the university I felt a little bit uncomfortable in philosophy. It was often too far away from the so-called real problems of life, so that I thought that doing philosophy alone was not sufficient. For me history was a place where reality could be brought close to philosophy. My philosophical interest was deeply influenced by the kind of philosophy taught in the late 1950s and early 1960s in Cologne. Philosophy was presented mainly in the form of history of philosophy. So there has always been a historical impact in my academic interest.

My main interest
was in philosophy.

What/who was/is your source of inspiration?

For me one of the main sources of questions has been religion. Normally religion is a place to get answers. For me, religion is

For me one of the
main sources of
questions has been
religion.

a place to ask questions. Maybe this is the reason I think that the only way of treating history correctly is doing it in a philosophical way, because then it is always related to fundamental issues of meaning and significance. The place of significance and of meaning traditionally is religion. But in modern societies religion has a very ambiguous role. So it may even bring about more questions than give answers.

Another source of inspiration for me has been the German philosophical tradition: philosophers like Kant, Schiller, Hegel, Fichte, and modern philosophers like Heidegger and Husserl. My main inspiration comes from German idealism, from Jürgen Habermas and Max Weber.

My main inspiration comes from German idealism and Max Weber.

Do you not think that the ideas presented by the philosophers mentioned here (I am thinking first of all of German idealism) are perfectly suited to the "postmodern condition"?

In some respects they are. Schiller's famous inaugural lecture as professor of history, "Was heisst und zu welchem Ende studiert man Universalgeschichte," e.g., includes elements of an argumentation we may call postmodern. It contains his insight that history is something constructed by the human mind and not simply by the reality of the past. The same is true of Kant's short text on universal history, "Idee zu einer allgemeinen Geschichte in weltbürgerlicher Absicht." This text inspires me much more than the postmodernist concept of history or of "posthistoire."

But the game of using philosophers for our own purposes in a postmodern context has its limits. The tradition I am speaking of is a tradition of philosophically explicating reason as the highest gift of mankind in dealing with history. Opposite to this, postmodernity is characterized by a radical criticism of reason. This criticism is important because we know that reason has played an ambiguous role in modern history. In the name of reason, millions of people were killed. But on the other hand we should not forget that in the name of antireason, of irrationalism—Nazi ideology is its most significant example—even more people were killed. Going back to the tradition of the philosophy of reason, mainly to Kant, may bring about an awareness of how to conceptualize reason, with its criteria of truth, in the theory of history of today. In order to avoid disastrous ideological consequences in the frame-

Reason has played an ambiguous role in modern history.

140 work of the cultural orientation of practical life, we need a specific kind of reason.

You present a skeptical attitude toward narrativist philosophy of history and to postmodernism. You are not a postmodernist. You are also not involved in the analytical tradition of the theory of history. So, what is your position in contemporary theory of history?

I wouldn't say that I am skeptical of narrativism. In the German context of historical studies and metahistory I have always argued in favor of narrativism, because I am deeply convinced that historical knowledge has a narrative structure and that this narrative structure epistemologically defines its distinctive nature as a specific field of human culture. The logic of narration is a basic factor of historical consciousness even on the prelinguistic or metalinguistic level of visual perception.

Narrativism is a very important advance in the theory of history. It has brought new insight into the distinctive nature of the historical disciplines in the humanities. Historical consciousness conceptualizes reality by the mental procedure of narration. But at the same time I try to continue the tradition of methodology and theory of history that is concerned with rationality and reason in dealing with the past and with historical experience. I criticize narrativism when it neglects methodical rationality and criteria of truth, and I criticize the scientific approach to history when it neglects narration as a fundamental procedure of historical consciousness.

I would characterize my position as an attempt to synthesize two approaches in theory and methodology of history that are opposed to each other in the present-day discussions of historians and philosophers. I try to bridge the dichotomy between narrativism on the one hand and scientific rationality on the other.

In my recent work I have been trying to develop an entire concept of "historical culture" in order to bring about a more complex reflection on historical consciousness, historical thinking, and the role history plays in human life. In this attempt to conceptualize historical culture I have tried to go beyond the limits of the academic discourse on historiography and historical thinking. I have been looking for the practical function of histori-

Historical knowledge has a narrative structure.

I try to bridge the dichotomy between narrativism on the one hand and scientific rationality on the other.

cal memory in human life as well. From this point of departure, metahistory brings about a new awareness of the noncognitive dimensions and operations of historical consciousness, mainly in respect to politics and aesthetics.

Which philosopher is closest to your own ideas?

In respect to the tradition of metahistory, the German historian Johann Gustav Droysen is closest to my thinking. In a way I understand myself as his student. I wouldn't say that I am epigonic in repeating his way of inquiring into the fundamentals of historical studies and in arguing in favor of their distinctive nature as an academic discipline in the context of the humanities. It is my attempt to bring the specific historical experience of the twentieth century into the argumentation scheme of Droysen's *Historik*. When confronting experience, mainly that of the Holocaust, in the reconstruction of the discourse of historical studies, the issue of the "rupture of civilization," as Dan Diner has interpreted the Holocaust, arises. The question is how to perceive the senselessness of the Holocaust in the mental procedure of making sense of history.

> Droysen is closest to my thinking.

Metahistory has to keep asking the question: what makes sense in history? Arguing in favor of reason and rationality in historical studies leads to a lack of meaning in respect to the negative historical experiences of our century. Confronting the negativity of historical experience in the twentieth century makes it necessary to reorganize our idea of historical thinking vis-à-vis the experience of the lack of meaning in history. That might be a typical German attitude. You know that many German intellectuals are obsessed by the Holocaust.

I do not think that it is typically German. The Holocaust is maybe one of the most evident examples under discussion. We have to revive a philosophical anthropology and look for a "new philosophy of history" that can help people find the meaning of their existence.

You are right. When Max Weber formulated his famous thesis on the universal process of rationalization, he spoke of "disenchantment," thus pointing at a growing sense of senselessness. The sources of significance are drying up, as Jürgen Habermas

142

described it recently (*Austrocknen der Ressource Sinn*). Historians cannot create values. They are no prophets, as Max Weber said, and he is absolutely right. It is nonsense to say that history has the task of creating meaning. It can't create, it only can translate meaning. What we can do is commemorate past in sources of meaning. In the mirror of the past we can see what sources of meaning and significance we have. We have to preserve the products of past sense-making as a help for people in present-day life. This is one reason I think history of religion is enormously important. There is a deficit in the so-called "new cultural history": We need more information about the religious life of people. We need more knowledge about the practical dimension of religious significance in human life.

Generally, we should pay more attention to the symbolic forms of the everyday life of people in the past. There are many books dealing with it. I think French scholars dominate in this field. So, I would say, back—for instance— to Eliade.

Quoting Eliade today is very important, because we can use his works in order to make clear what is necessary. Eliade, and others like Rudolf Otto, portrayed the premodern world as a source of significance and meaning and contrasted it with the meaningless world of modern societies. The underlying antagonism between a meaningful premodern world with religion and a meaningless modern world without religion is not very convincing to me. Revocation of a lost world full of cultural treasures is a typical modernist attitude of the intellectuals of the 1920s, with a very problematic, antimodern impact. Eliade recollected religion as a source for meaning and this is necessary today just as it was necessary in the '20s. But he did it in an ahistorical and one-sided way; ahistorical since he composed the premodern world into one picture with no internal temporal dynamics; one-sided since he presupposed a fundamental lack of religious creativity in modern societies and completely overlooked its specific sources of meaning and significance. Eliade de-historized religion and in this respect we should not follow him, although it is still very fascinating to recollect the spiritual forces of religion in premodern and even more in archaic societies. We have to historize religion and present it in a temporal movement, with its internal temporal dynamics. Only in such a perspective does it really have something to say beyond a simple compensatory role. Compensating for lack of meaning by means of historical memory is not very meaningful. In order to speak about religion, we must have a temporal interrelationship between past and present. In his sociology of religion, Max Weber has presented us with a more convincing paradigm for treating religion historically.

> Compensating for lack of meaning by means of historical memory is not very meaningful.

In your new book, *Studies in Metahistory*, you write about the role history plays in human culture. Do you think that the classic task of history as *magistra vitae* is changing now?

I would say: yes and no. No, because we know that the slogan *historia vitae magistra* reflects a specific kind of historical thinking that is characterized by the words of the English politician and historian Lord Bolingbroke: "History is philosophy teaching by examples." History has a very specific role in this kind of thought. It presents single cases of what happened at a specific place and at a specific time, and these cases demonstrate ("teach") general rules of human life and conduct. So knowing history means being competent in handling the rules of practical life; namely of politics, but of morality as well. History teaches these rules and at the same time it teaches an ability to apply the rules to concrete cases and to generate general rules out of single cases.

> "History is philosophy teaching by examples."

This is a very specific mode of historical thinking. I believe that it came into being together with the cultural achievements of advanced civilizations. Some first elements can already be observed in Babylonia. Then it became the dominant cultural form of historical thinking and historical memory in all advanced civilizations till the development of modern societies with modern historical thinking. In my theory of four fundamental types of making sense of history by narration, *historia vitae magistra* stands for the exemplary type. In modern societies another type of historical thinking prevails, so *historia vitae magistra* is no longer a slogan characterizing historical thinking today. The main reason we can't follow this slogan is that history doesn't teach us rules with supratemporal validity to be studied and tested in the wide field of the experience of the past in order to be applied to present-day situations; on the contrary: it teaches us that the rules themselves change in the course of time.

> History teaches us that the rules themselves change in the course of time.

"Yes" means, in respect to your question, that history never-theless plays a necessary role in the cultural orientation of practical life. Without history, people are unable to organize their lives in the light of temporal change and development.

These are theoretical considerations. Do you think that professional historians are aware of these matters?

Professionalization in historical thinking has brought about a gap between the work of specialists and the role historical memory plays in cultural life. But on a very fundamental level, even professional historians follow the guidelines of orientation needed in practical life. Where do the really inspiring questions for historical studies come from? What initiates new, fascinating, and interesting questions? They come from the life context of historians. For instance: today we suffer from the unintended consequences of modernization, of so-called progress. Progress has been more and more put into fundamental, critical doubt. Therefore, historical studies have started to ask new questions; for example, the question of the cultural and social costs of modernization, the question of how people culturally come to terms with the constraints on their lives. Questions like these have led to what is called now "new cultural history," to microhistory, to history of everyday life. This new kind of questioning has generated a completely new idea of the historical meaning of the past. The new meaning of history (beyond progress) is an answer to the challenge of a new experience of time in present-day life. New concepts of historical interpretation are not simply the result of questions raised by experts in an academic field. When we look into the history of historiography we can see that every substantial change in historical thinking went along with a change in the present-day life of historians.

The new meaning of history (beyond progress) is an answer to the challenge of a new experience of time in present-day life.

Is this why you are especially interested in historical culture at present?

Historical culture means the role historical memory plays in our lives in general. It covers the whole field of social life: life of the people, of groups and societies, even of whole cultures. Historical culture is human life insofar as it is influenced and determined by the memory of the past. Everybody needs some memory in order to get an orientation in his or her practical life, an orientation vis-à-vis temporal change.

Without a relationship to the past we cannot develop any future perspective in our practical life. So, in fact, history is a necessary element of real life. Without history, without historical memory, people cannot live. History furnishes people with an idea of temporal change in human affairs. In line with this idea they can organize their practical lives as well as themselves in respect to their identity. This cultural function of history—orienting practical life and manifesting identity—is essential; it is a basis, a root (and a legitimation) for what professional historians do.

Without historical memory, people cannot live.

When historians speak about their discipline, about methodological and theoretical problems, they often overlook or even forget the roots of their work in practical life. They forget that in practical life memory has an essential role to play in orienting people's lives vis-à-vis the experiences of temporal change and development.

I would like to ask you about microhistorians. Emmanuel Le Roy Ladurie, Carlo Ginzburg, and the others, represent a very specific and, I think, the most attractive way of writing about history in the present day. When we read such stories, we can identify ourselves with people living in the past. We can almost "touch" the past. Is this a sign of the return of ideas popular in nineteenth-century philosophy, presented by Dilthey, among others?

In fact, history today presents a different kind of past. It gives us more intimate ideas of the lives of ordinary people in the past. What makes it so fascinating? I think the fascination of these presentations, Le Roy Ladurie's *Montaillou* or Ginzburg's *The Cheese and the Worms*, lies in the fact that they present counterimages to our present-day life experience. *Montaillou*, as well as the world of the miller Menocchio, are counterimages for a modernized society. *Montaillou* presents a Rousseauist time of human life (close to "nature" in the sense that it is far removed from modernity). This historiography is full of projections and it has a very specific cultural function. It furnishes people who are frustrated by the "progress" of the modern world with a compensation. It com-

History today presents a different kind of past.

146   pensates for our experience of social life by the image of a completely different, premodern lifestyle with the eternity-like quality of the *longue durée*. It may even help people to bear their experience of modernized life forms, knowing of an alternative existing in early modern history.

The same is true of Carlo Ginzburg's miller Menocchio. If you look at this sympathetic miller's qualities, you may find that he accumulates many qualities that the intellectuals of '68 wanted to become cultural values in their society by revolution. For me this is, at least, one of the reasons for the success of this book. It presents a historical image, the realization of the ideals of the '68 generation. They have lost their future in the past. This is compensation: loading the past with disappointed hopes for the future.

The characters in microhistorians' books are very close to us. We notice that they felt in the same way we do; they were not so different from us.

That may be the way many people read and understand *Montaillou*. But I am not so sure whether Le Roy Ladurie would say that this is a message of his book, because we have learned from the French *Annales* school that even feelings have structurally changed.

Le Roy Ladurie gives us a description of a structure of social life. I am not so sure that we can find out very much about the feelings of these people. We find forms of life, forms of communication that come close to subjectivity: subjectivity is a category of this presentation. It increases our awareness of the subjective factor in the process of history. This is one of the advantages of the so-called "new cultural history," in the second generation of the *Annales* school.

Moreover, these books are very nice to read. They are almost like novels.

Well, historiography has always been a kind of literature. What has changed is our awareness of this dimension of historians' activities. For more than one and a half centuries historical studies claimed to be a scientific discipline and there is something true in this. There has been a process of scientification in the development of historical studies from the end of the eighteenth century onward. In the course of this process, the rhetoric and literary structure of historiography became more and more overlooked and even suppressed. This is changing now. We should not forget, however, that in 1902 Theodor Mommsen got a Nobel Prize for literature for his *Roman History*. That historiography is literature is not new. What is new is our awareness of the literary quality of history writing.

We think that books, like those we are speaking about, are remarkable because most of the academic production of texts is so bad, in respect to its literary character (I don't exclude the texts of metahistory, of course), that we are enthusiastic if we find a book that fulfills some standards of literary quality.

But I see more problems than advantages in this respect. Speaking about the literary form of historiography, we have to compare historiography with what we call "real literature." Doing so, we can see that historians still use forms of narration that are very traditional. We know that the narrative structure of the novel has changed completely. I think one of the most prominent examples of a substantially modern form of narrative is Franz Kafka's novels. Can you imagine a piece of historiography that represents this kind of modernity?

This brings me to one of the key issues in theory of history, as far as I understand this reflection about what historians do: What is the reason Kafka writes in this very specific way? Because he tries to meet a certain fundamental experience of modern life—the experience of a growing senselessness in human affairs, in human communication. One may say that Kafka represents senselessness in a very meaningful and elaborated way. Why don't historians use the same strategy in writing history? (Or do they have a better feeling for sense and meaning than poets? I don't think so.)

Living in the twentieth century, we know what senselessness means. We have the essentially negative experiences of the history of the twentieth century before our eyes. The core of these experiences is the Holocaust: is Auschwitz. How do we deal with this experience? How can we still keep up traditional forms of a mean-

> That historiography is literature is not new. What is new is our awareness of the literary quality of history writing.

> Do historians have a better feeling for sense and meaning than poets? I don't think so.

148 ingful narration vis-à-vis this historical experience? This is a critical question I have to ask myself.

In my attempts to develop a systematic theory of historical studies I was very deeply engaged in explicating the cognitive mechanism that brings about reason in respect to our relation to the past. And I am still engaged in this issue of reason. But my problem is: how to bring the negative experience of the Holocaust into this concept of reason?

We have come to this question when looking at the literary structure of historiography, and, I think, we have to ask about the possibilities of historiography that can be compared with the substantially modern forms of narration as we find them represented by Kafka. We don't have many examples of presenting history in a form that is similar to this modern form of narration in literature. But there are some. For instance, in Germany we have a very interesting book, which confronts us with quite an unusual form of presenting history, significantly not written by a historian but by a team of a sociologist and a filmmaker. I am thinking of the book by Oskar Negt and Alexander Kluge, *Geschichte und Eigensinn*, where the authors try to present history in a completely different way from what has been done by historians. It has been a great success on the book market and it was completely neglected by historians.

It is interesting that the most fascinating historical books are mostly written not by historians — or, better, not by traditional historians. When I asked people interested in history and theory of history about their favorite historical book, they spoke first of all about Foucault, Le Roy Ladurie, and Ginzburg. But that is not "pure history," that is a mixture of history, philosophy, art, psychology, and sociology.

Indeed these presentations lie across the limits of disciplines. Who is Foucault? Is he a philosopher? He developed a specific concept of history in which modernization is presented in a completely different way from what we are used to, and this is fascinating. It is a counterconcept to the traditional idea of modernization. But this kind of fascinating historiography, written across the limits of pregiven genres, is not so new. Think of Voltaire.

He was one of the most prominent historians of the eighteenth
century. He was a poet and a philosopher. Looking at these examples we may ask where the best chances for innovation in historical thinking are. I would not say within the realm of historical studies.

If you want to develop novelties in a discipline, you run the risk
of becoming an outsider. For me, this is the one of the reasons
for the fact that you cannot find many prominent German writers presenting new and fascinating historiography and concepts
of history. In my country the pressure of adjustment in historical
studies is very high and new challenges and new ideas very often
come from other fields like philosophy, sociology, or even literature, from a mixture of different disciplines. But who gets a chance
to cross the borders of disciplines? The chance for a career lies
within these borders, not beyond them. I am not so sure if a scholar
like Hayden White would have got a history professorship in Germany. Even today, many German historians think that he is anything but a historian. Why did Anton Kaes, a prominent historical
expert in the new medium of film, go to the United States? It is
an important and open question how historical studies should
treat its limits as an academic discipline, in order to bring about
novelties, new and challenging concepts and visions of history.

> If you want to
> develop novelties
> in a discipline,
> you run the risk
> of becoming an
> outsider.

**Do you not think that when historical studies bring about
some new concepts of history, as we observe some at present, it is very difficult for professional historians to follow
these novelties, to put these ideas into practice, if we assume that they want to do so?**

Your question brings me to my special business: theory and methodology of history. I think that reflecting on what one is doing
should belong to the normal practice of historians. Then the professionals might get some knowledge about the rules, perspectives, concepts, and strategies of interpretation. This is the main
task of theory and methodology of history: to bring about a better self-awareness on the part of historians. Within the framework
of such a self-understanding theory of history, an insight into the
relation between the experience of present-day life and our relation to the past may come about. The professionals should have

> The main task
> of theory and
> methodology of
> history: to bring
> about a better self-
> awareness on the
> part of historians.

150 open eyes for what is going on in present-day life in order to get a relevant insight into history. They must become aware of the main problems of present-day life in order to bring about a commemoration of the past that is really relevant for the cultural life of today. All the great historians had this sensibility. Look at Burckhardt. He critically observed the process of modernization in his time and this enabled him to get a very deep insight into European culture and politics.

There is a structural relationship between the awareness of present-day life, on the one hand, and the capacity for historical insight, on the other. This is trivial, but in historical studies historians should develop an attitude that cultivates this relationship. This can only be done academically, and for this purpose, I think, theory of history, or metahistory, may be necessary and useful.

But we can observe an evident inconsistency between the point of view on history and historiography that is being presented by philosophers or theorists of history and that presented by historians themselves. Why is this the case?

Historians tell stories. This is what all historians do.

Very often people who are able to do something, who are experts in what they do, do not really know what they do. In fact, historians tell stories. This is what all historians do. They produce stories of different kinds, of course. And now the theorists come and tell them something about narrative structure. Many historians then say: "No! This is not what we are doing, because we know what a narration is: it is different from what we do. Narration is telling a story as Ranke and the historians of the nineteenth century did. We do historiography in a different way. We do it with quantification, with statistics, with structural analysis, and with a lot of other methods that lead far away from simply telling stories." Metahistory tries to convince them that "narration" means something different, something more general and fundamental: a logical structure in historical studies, which comprises the post-Rankean attitudes in historical studies. Historical thinking in general is deeply structured by the form of narrative.

Now you may ask: What is the use of such a metahistorical knowledge of the narrative structure of historical studies? What may be the result of an insight into one's own practical work in history? In respect to narrative structure, it may at least bring about a wider awareness of the importance of the linguistic form of historical thinking. Historians become more aware that the whole process of bringing about historical knowledge is shaped by specific language-operations, giving knowledge of the past a narrative form.

Normally we teach students that they have to extract information from the source material, and after this they have to make a good interpretation of the information, and after having done this they can simply write down what they have found. Thus they get the feeling that writing down is not very relevant; that it is just an execution of what they have already compiled in their minds. They think they can just put down on the paper what is in their minds. This is a normal attitude. What we don't teach the students and what they don't learn and don't get into their professional self-understanding is the fact that knowledge itself gets its form *as* knowledge through a specific linguistic forming and writing.

This is, of course, a truism for metahistory. For the practice of history it is still something to be recognized, however. So metahistorical knowledge must have consequences for the teaching of history to students. We have to teach them much more about writing or the rhetoric of historiography.

When traditional historians hear the word "rhetoric" they become upset. Why? Because they think rhetoric is the contrary of academic rationality; accepting rhetoric means the contrary of being a good scholar. A good scholar means: to follow methodical rules of research, to go to the archives, and to make a good, empirically based interpretation of what happened in the past. Rhetoric is something completely different. It is against reason, it is against rationality; it is just playing around with words. This common opinion of professional historians is completely wrong. There is a specific rhetoric of reason and we have to teach the students this rhetorical structure of their own practice. Thus they may get a competence in dealing with linguistic problems in presenting the past to an audience today in different forms like texts, lectures, or even videos, and so forth.

> Accepting rhetoric means the contrary of being a good scholar.

> There is a specific rhetoric of reason.

From this perspective, how do you find White's *Metahistory* as a milestone in the theory of history?

152   *Metahistory* is a book that emphasizes exactly this point—that history is a linguistic procedure. In this respect it is a great book. Unfortunately, the way Hayden White tried to explicate the specific linguistic regularities that guide historiography as a linguistic procedure is misleading, because the concept of tropes does not explicate the distinctive nature of historiography. It does not clarify what is specifically historical in dealing with the past. Hayden White teaches us to see the literary and linguistic form of historiography. This is important and necessary. But pointing to metaphor, metonymy, synecdoche, and irony as basic principles for giving meaning to facts by bringing them into a narrative order doesn't elucidate the specifically historical quality of this order. Historiography has the tropes in common with other narrative literature that is not at all historical. This is my point. We need a better insight into the specificity, let's say the "historicity," of historiography.

I for one tried to develop an alternative by working out a general typology distinguishing four different kinds of making sense in history. It is very close to Hayden White in respect to his emphasizing fundamental and constitutive criteria or strategies of bringing significance and meaning into knowledge of what happened in the past.

What can you say about the problem of truth in the case of White's theory?

I agree that one has to look at the totality of a text, at the entire story in the context of other stories, but speaking about truth, in respect to Hayden White, is a problem. I am not so sure whether he is very sympathetic to the criteria of truth. In a discussion with me he said it would be better to speak of morals or politics instead of truth. This is one of the reasons why the professional historians still are doubtful about his *Metahistory*. I share this doubt because I think that, as long as historical studies are done as an academic discipline, we have to speak about truth and we have to reflect and strengthen the cognitive strategies that stand for objectivity and truth. This issue is different from linguistics or rhetoric, but following Hayden White we keep it out of mind. We forget the procedures in historical thinking that have been developed in the process of the so-called scientification of historical studies.

As long as historical studies are done as an academic discipline, we have to speak about truth.

You will not find any enlightening remark on historical method
in Hayden White's thinking about historical studies.

In metahistorical discourse we can observe a very interesting
shift of important issues. In the process of scientification historians forgot the linguistic and rhetorical strategies of historiography and replaced them by an awareness of the very skilled procedures of research methods. Method as a strategy of research
replaced rhetoric. Today, it is just the contrary. We have a growing awareness of rhetorical and linguistic strategies and a shrink-
ing awareness of rationality, of method, and of the cognitive procedures that stand for truth and objectivity.

**A consequence of the narrativist philosophy of history
could be the theses that, first, there is no reality worth analyzing outside of interpretation; second, historiography is
a "play" between such interpretations; third, we can speak
only about the truth of interpretations being rhetorical or
metaphorical in nature; fourth, the truth of interpretation
lies in its persuasive power.**

You are right. History, historiography, historical memory is a play
around different texts, but these texts always deal with experience.
Does it make sense to speak about experience in respect to history? An experience is traditionally an instance of truth. Something is true when it is based on experience.

An experience is
traditionally an in-
stance of truth.

**But experience is always a subjective category of an individ-
ually perceived world.**

You go to an archive and you look for a death rate or a birthrate
of a society in the past. And then you find information.

**But "naked" numbers, pure statistics, do not say anything.
You—as a historian—have to provide this material with
meanings and you can do it only by interpretation.**

This is true, but nevertheless, sometimes, the sources tell you
something that you did not expect, something that is against your
concept of meaning. You are right, the sources don't tell you the

154

significance and meaning of the information they present to you. But on the other hand, you cannot make the meaning and the significance just "out of your stomach." There is a very complex relationship between the information in the source material and the procedures of interpretation that bring about meaning. There is even more "objectivity" in meaning and significance than the usual argumentation about subjectivity is aware of. Looking at historical interpretation, we often can find something already pregiven in meaning and significance in the interpreted past. Droysen has called this pregivenness of meaning in the source material "tradition" and distinguished it from the pure "relict" character of sources. The point in historical interpretation is that we can't completely reduce tradition to relict. Meaning is already embodied in social reality and this is the case with the witnesses of past social reality as well. We can't completely or sufficiently create historical meaning just by ourselves, without going back to experience. Meaning and significance in respect to the past are already embodied in our social reality.

There is a very interesting question about what reality really is in respect to the work of historians. Most of the so-called postmodern theorists have a very crude, positivistic epistemology. In this epistemology a fact is defined by the cognitive strategies of the natural sciences where facts as such have no quality of meaning. In history it is different. Is meaning and significance factual or is it fiction? Using a crude positivistic epistemology, the answer is clear: since facts are meaningless by definition, meaning is fiction. This hidden epistemology in metahistory must be criticized. It does not make sense to use the categories "fact" and "fiction" because meaning and significance lie beyond the presupposed difference between them; they lie across this dichotomy. When we define fact in a very crude and narrow way, as it has been done traditionally in the philosophy of science, then all the relevant elements in historical thinking are fictional. "Fictional" normally means beyond, far away from experience, but this is not the case in historiography. Historiography is based on experience, otherwise historians would never go into archives—

Most of the so-called postmodern theorists have a very crude, positivistic epistemology.

It does not make sense to use the categories "fact" and "fiction."

Historiography is based on experience.

Looking at its appearance in our lives and, of course, through the source material.

You are right, we cannot go beyond a subjective perspective into a completely "objective" reality. We can't go through subjectivity into the real, objective essence of the past just by taking into account that the source materials are always presented in a subjective perspective and by methodically taking away the subjective perspectivism. But, nevertheless, we have the strategies of source-criticism that enable us to get reliable and valid information about what happened in the past at a specific place, at a specific time. We can answer the questions, what? where? when? why? and so on. This is very often overlooked in the current debate about theory of history. Unfortunately, the methodology of historical studies, on the other hand, very often overlooks what is emphasized in the other kind of reflection on historical studies; namely, the constitutive role of human subjectivity, of values in historical interpretation.

We have a schizophrenia in the theory of history of today. We have a sharp awareness of and reflection on the linguistic, rhetorical, narrative procedures bringing history very close to literature. We also still have, but not so much emphasized on the level of theory, a recognition of the technique of historical research, of quantification, statistics, of a lot of auxiliaries helping historians to get valid information out of the source material. There is no convincing relationship between the two sides; it is like schizophrenia, it is not at all mediated.

For me, metahistory has to meet a double challenge. On the one hand, when we do methodology of research, we have only a very narrow concept of what produces the reason and truth of history. We reduce methodology to a technology, omitting fundamental questions of significance and understanding. On the other hand, when we reflect on the linguistic procedures of historical narration that bring about meaning and significance, we overlook the prospects for reason, objectivity, and truth in the narrative procedures of bringing about historical knowledge and historiography. I think we have to look much more for a synthesis of these two perspectives rather than continuing the already established antagonism between them.

The state of contemporary theory of history, characterized by you as "schizophrenia," is in fact a fault of the narrativist

We have a schizophrenia in the theory of history of today.

156   philosophy of history. Do you think that this very modern
and currently fashionable narrativist approach is dangerous
for the discipline of history?

For me the greatest danger of narrativist history is the possibility
of losing our knowledge of the classical role historical studies as
an academic discipline can play in cultural, mainly in political, life.
This role has been called "critique." Through its possibilities of
checking images of the past, of testing concepts that were used to
interpret the given situation through historical memory, historical
studies are an instance of control, of critical reflection. Presenting
its cultural strategies only in such a way that you get the impression—"Well, it's only literature; it's a way of making sense through
literary and rhetorical strategies"—makes us overlook the critical
potential historical studies have developed through its scientification. We can simply say that some images of the past are not true,
simply not true (for example, the legend of the stab in the back
after Germany's defeat in the First World War).

**Perhaps we are afraid of it prematurely. There is a narra-
tivist (postmodernist) philosophy of history, but does a
postmodernist historiography exist?**

What does postmodernism mean in historical studies? Postmodernism is a very ambiguous concept. By postmodernism you can
understand a very radical position that is characterized by a substantial lack of methodical rationality and by an arbitrary relationship to the past. From this point of view, historiography is just literature and nothing else. It must be a fine text (with aesthetic
qualities) and then it is OK. Yet it should at least fulfill some functions of entertainment. Since there is no such thing as truth and
plausibility, it is completely open to what people (or critics) want
to know about the past. Apply this concept to the Holocaust and
the questions of the so-called revisionists, and you see its limits.
There is something like evidence, information, experience, and
there is no doubt that it happened.

But there is a much better sense of postmodernism in historical studies. Postmodernism may mean a fruitful and convincing
criticism of traditional "modern" concepts of historical thinking.
For instance, the concept that there is something like "the" history as one unit of temporal changes and developments. Or that

there are methodical capacities of the human mind that enable us to control the development of the human world in the future by finding out its laws in the past. Both concepts are very close to ideology. They must be criticized because something like "the" history is nothing other than one single history that has been generalized into history as a whole. And all attempts to govern history have caused disastrous developments—the contrary of the intended ones.

There is another important criticism of postmodernism. It is related to the specific concept of methodical rationality, claiming that through method one can get an insight into the essence of history (Ranke's famous words—"wie es eigentlich gewesen"). Postmodernism in this respect means fundamental perspectiveness. So postmodernism means that there is no such thing as the one, single, entire history; there is not only just true and valid insight into what really happened. This criticism has opened up the prospect of multiperspectivity. It has brought more discursive elements into the whole business of the historians. It has made historical studies more dynamic. In this respect, postmodernism is an advantage for historical studies. It has brought about new categorical conceptualizations in respect to historical experience.

Postmodernism has made historical studies more dynamic.

To give an example: Walter Benjamin is very famous and popular in the field of literary criticism. Historians do not very much use his ideas about history in the discourse about historical studies. (In Germany you can find only one fascinating book that tries to introduce Benjamin's theory of history into the history and theory of historical studies.) But Benjamin presents some arguments about historical thinking that are worth debating intensively among historians. For example, his idea of a "historical moment" beyond any genetic relationship between past and present that cracks open the category of development that sees history as a closed chain of time, combining past, present, and future. In such an argumentation I see a chance for a categorical improvement in historical thinking. Another example—I would not say for postmodernism, but for a conceptualization of history that goes beyond the traditional, modern concept of history for which the category of progress, of development, is very typical—another example may be the time concept of *kairos*. I would very much like to introduce this idea of a condensed time into the theory of history as a very important and useful category of historical significance, in respect to the specific temporal structure of the real-

Benjamin presents some arguments about historical thinking that are worth debating intensively among historians.

158 ity of human life. With the category of *kairos* we may conceptualize important themes in history. For instance, in the history of human and civil rights we may use the category of *kairos* for the late eighteenth century, the time of the first declarations of human and civil rights as essential elements of constitutions. We may also use the concept of *kairos* in a negative sense in respect to experiences like the Holocaust. These categories of "the historical moment" or of *kairos* may bring about new perspectives, new insights into the temporal structure of history.

Looking at the "development" of theory of history (and not only theory of history) I have an impression that it is based on the permanent rethinking and reinterpretating of certain categories and ideas. For instance, Fredric Jameson's famous formula "To think everything through once again in terms of linguistics" signaled the linguistic turn. Recently Frank Ankersmit suggested that we should change the subject and attend to the category of experience. Maybe the time comes for "rethinking everything once again in terms of experience"? Maybe it can provide a deeper insight into reality?

Experience is not a very good category for historical thinking because it lacks specific temporality.

There is no language without experience. Experience is not a very good category for historical thinking because it lacks the specific temporality that is a necessary condition for historical thinking. We must enlarge the perspectives of our questions. Enlarge language with time. Enlarge language and time with experience. In this combination we should discuss the question, What is a historical experience?

What is it in your opinion?

I cannot give you a very short and clear answer. I can give you an example of new questions we have to debate, to discuss in the field of theory of history. It is a very simple question: Can we see history? Is history something to be realized in the dimension of aesthetics?

Can we see history?

This question brings me back to the issue of historical culture. I think that, at least in modern societies, historical culture has three dimensions: a cognitive one, a political one, and an aesthetic one. Theory of history has mainly dealt with the cognitive dimension. In the last ten or twenty years it went beyond the cognitive dimension and came close to the aesthetic one by speaking of language, poetics, and rhetoric. But aesthetics is more than only language. It includes elements of prelinguistic experience and communication, something like visual and sensual perception. We don't know what is possible in this realm of visual perception in respect to history. We have to start basic research into the aesthetics of historical consciousness, mainly into the visual perception of history. If we see, for example, a historical painting, do we really see history, or do we impose the historical significance of what we see from outside the visual perception? I think there is something that we can call a specifically historical perception. It is something very elementary for the eyes and I think we can at least identify essential elements of historical perception. A necessary, but not sufficient, condition for a historical perception is a visual awareness of a qualitative difference of times. A simple example: Walking along a street, you look at the houses and sometimes you get a visual experience of different times. You can see one house belongs to a different time than the next house. Very early, children must have the perception that their time is different from the time of their parents and that the time of their parents is different from that of their grandparents. This is a very essential experience. For me such an experience of time difference is a necessary condition for a historical experience on the level of aesthetics. It seems to be a universal phenomenon that people think the older something is, the more remarkable it is. When you can see something is old, it gets a specific quality, even for the eyes.

This is essential for what I call an aesthetic experience of history, but we do not know very much about it. The reason for this lack of knowledge is that the most elaborated disciplines in respect to aesthetics, mainly art history, are not so much interested in history. Of course, they do a good deal of historical research. Art history puts works of art into historical contexts by iconographic investigation. But at the moment the interpretation comes to the genuine aesthetic quality of a painting or of another piece of art, that which makes it a great work of art, history is a matter only of external conditions—not an element in the essence of the artistic quality.

We do not know very much about an aesthetic experience of history.

160   At the level of aesthetic values, the interpretation is limited to a synchronic relationship between the viewer and the work. Time and history have vanished into genuine aesthetic experience and communication. This is a completely different relationship from a historical one. At the level where the quality of the work of art, its essence, is dealt with, we should ask for history in a new and fundamental way. This may bring about an enormous achievement in historical culture.

Recently, for many researchers, a work of art (a painting, in particular) is a point of departure for their considerations. Have you noticed that visualization plays a more important role in scientific reflection now? We are all the time in the world of symbolic forms of expression, but there is a shift: art instead of language, painting instead of words. Should we start to look at history from the point of view of aesthetics?

Asking for the aesthetic dimension of historical culture may lead into an aestheticization of history.

Asking for the aesthetic dimension of historical culture may lead into an aestheticization of history. Such an aestheticization is not so new in history. We can study the problem of aestheticising history, for example, by interpreting the works of Jacob Burckhardt. Looking at the tradition of aestheticizing history we may identify a fundamental problem: since the three dimensions of historical culture, which are cognition, politics, and aesthetics, are necessarily interrelated with each other, aestheticizing has consequences for the political and the cognitive dimensions. There is a tendency to deal with the aesthetic dimension of historical culture at the cost of the two other dimensions. It may lead to a depoliticized and irrationalized version of history, with disastrous consequences for practical life, which gets its orientation from it. The same is true of emphasizing the cognitive or the political dimension at the cost of the other ones. A cognitive strategy in historical culture, which instrumentalizes the other, leads to dogmatism. Emphasizing the political dimension of historical culture may bring about a tendency to instrumentalize the cognitive and aesthetic elements of historical study for political purposes and thus enforce a blind will to power in historical memory.

    The growing importance of aesthetics in history may have similar consequences with respect to the relationship to the two other dimensions. We should study instances of aestheticization that can teach us what this means: that aestheticization may lead to a depoliticization and irrationalization of historical studies. Depoliticization is very dangerous for politics, because we need a specific kind of historical orientation in order to make a reasonable politics. Depoliticizing history throws it out of the political field, where history plays an enormous role in legitimizing and criticizing political domination. History is an important factor in the legitimacy of political rule and domination. Depoliticized, it leaves the field of legitimacy open for ahistorical or even antihistorical principles and argumentations. It deprives legitimacy of the test of historical experience. To give an example: the film of Hans-Jürgen Syberberg on Hitler presents a highly aestheticized version of the historical experience of the Nazi time, and in doing so it completely depoliticizes this experience and enforces an essentially irrationalistic attitude toward it. Saul Friedlander has indicated the problems of such an attitude by showing how close it comes to some elements of Nazi ideology.

This is not an argument against the new issue of the aesthetic dimension of historical culture. I for one have started some work in this field, and it leads me a little bit away from the cognitive dimension of historical studies, where I have worked for a long time to develop a theory of historical studies as a factor of rationality in historical culture. I do not follow the fashion of disguising rationality and reason. On the contrary, I am looking for elements of reason on the level of the aesthetic perception of history.

The classic philosophy of art—for example, Kant's *Critique of Judgment* and Schiller's *Letters on the Aesthetic Education of Humankind*, not to speak of Hegel's *Lectures on Aesthetics*—has already taught us that aesthetics is close to reason, that it is a necessary condition for reason in the field of the cultural orientation of practical life.

Just another remark on reason in the noncognitive field of historical culture. I would say that history can play the role of reason in politics through its function of legitimation. Legitimation in modern society has to do with reason, because legitimacy in modern society is related to the cognitive element of a free and discursive consent of citizens to political rule and domination. Traditionally, this element is formulated as a basic principle of a constitution. This brings us to the history of human and civil

Aestheticization may lead to a depoliticization and irrationalization of historical studies.

I am looking for elements of reason on the level of the aesthetic perception of history.

162   rights. Human and civil rights were introduced into this field of legitimizing political domination as an element of reason. In a way you can say that the system of human rights is an equivalent in the field of jurisprudence and constitutional law to the categorical imperative. What has this to do with history? As long as we look only at the fundamental rights of our constitutions as being fixed and settled systems of rules we have the problem of how to deal with the experience of temporal change in the social and political structure of our life. Additionally we have the problem of how to meet the challenge of cultural diversity vis-à-vis the universal validity of human rights. Historicization in our intellectual dealings with them may help us to solve these problems. This may teach us that history can bring an element of reason into politics.

Reason means, of course, to limit political power, to domesticate it. Frank Ankersmit is working in this field of political theory. It would be a very interesting debate with him whether and how he combines the political, aesthetic, and cognitive elements of historical thinking, mainly in respect to the role history plays in political legitimacy. But do we know very much about the role history really plays in politics? I note that there are only two books in Germany where we have results from research on the use of historical arguments in politics. One is a dissertation by a student of mine. She investigated debates in the parliament of the German Federal Republic from the 1950s to the 1980s and inquired about the historical argumentation that politicians used in these debates—how they used history. This has given us some knowledge of what the politicians really do with history—what function history really plays in politics. We must know this when we discuss the orientation function of history in practical life. Knowing it, we may meet it as a challenge for our business on the cognitive level, in the cognitive dimension. In fact, whatever we do, we are a part of politics in historical culture. There is a very famous example of the role history can play in public opinion—the so-called German historians' debate. Studying this debate you can see that the participants are not aware of confusing the political and the cognitive dimension of historical culture in respect to the interpretation of the Nazi time in Germany. One of the chief participants, Jürgen Habermas, mainly argued politically. His opponents argued at a cognitive, scientific level. In some way they

could not really communicate. The debate was a fascinating example of noncommunication based upon the fact that the participants spoke in different dimensions of historical studies. They were
not able to bridge the gap argumentatively between politics and
cognition in historical culture.

**Does that mean that this problem—the noncoherency be-
tween a cognitive and a political dimension of historical
studies—will be at the center of interest in theory of history in the future?**

I would say that for me theory of history has to bring about more
insight into the complex relationship between the three dimen-
sions of historical culture I have mentioned, and doing so we have   We have to rethink
to rethink a very old question: What makes sense in history? Sense,   a very old ques-
significance, and meaning exist in the relationship among the   tion: What makes
three dimensions. Neither aesthetics, nor politics, nor cognition   sense in history?
alone makes sense in history, only a synthesis of all three do so.
But what and where are the synthesizing principles? This is a
completely open question. Answering it may be the future of the
theory of history. Trying to answer it will bring us close to the old
questions of philosophy of history.

**Almost all the time we have been speaking about the past
and the present, about the relationship between the past and
the present, but what about the future?**

Historians deal with the past because people need a future perspective in their lives. We never deal with the past for its own sake.
It is my deep conviction that history is fundamentally relevant for
the future. We look into the mirror of the past in order to get perspectives on the future.

Today our historical relationship to the future is mainly   Today our histori-
shaped in the form of a critique of future perspectives. We are de-   cal relationship to
constructing deeply rooted time concepts in which the future has   the future is
the image of being already prestructured by the past. The idea   mainly shaped in
that the future is a part of temporal development that starts from   the form of a cri-
the past, goes through our time, and then goes into the future   tique of future
unbroken has had an enormous cultural power. It is the typical   perspectives.

time concept of modern societies. It is related to the idea of "the" history, which combines past, present, and future into one entire development. We are deconstructing it. We are breaking it into pieces.

But only criticizing pregiven future perspectives in the way we deal with the past is not sufficient. What will happen when criticized future concepts have lost their cultural power? What I do not see in influential works of historiography is an element of the future already incorporated into the past. The past is mainly presented in a counterimage as something different, into which we may project our hopes and expectations, thus towing them away from the future of our own world. This past engulfs the future and does not release it into a perspective to be filled by activity. The future remains open. But there are always elements of the future in the past that are still to be realized. I think there is a lot of open future in the past that is worth disclosing.

There is a lot of open future in the past.

Bochum, Germany
11 November 1993

SELECTED WRITINGS

Grundzüge einer Historik. 3 vols. Göttingen: Vandenhoeck & Ruprecht, 1983, 1986, 1989.

Zeit und Sinn. Strategien historischen Denkens. Frankfurt a.M.: Fischer, 1990.

Geschichte des Historismus: Eine Einführung, with Friedrich Jaeger. München: Beck, 1992.

Konfigurationen des Historismus. Studien zur deutschen Wissenschaftskultur. Frankfurt a.M.: Sohrkamp, 1993.

Studies in Metahistory. Edited and introduced by Pieter Duvenage. Pretoria: Human Sciences Research Council, 1993.

Historische Orientierung. Über die Arbeit des Geschichtsbewußtseins, sich in der Zeit zurechtzufinden. Köln: Böhlau, 1994.

Historismus in den Kulturwissenschaften. Geschichtskonzepte, historische Einschätzungen, Grundlagenprobleme, co-editor with Otto Gerhard Oexle. (Beiträge zur Geschichtskultur, vol. 12). Köln: Böhlau, 1996.

"Theory of History in Historical Lectures: The German Tradition of   **165**
Historik 1750–1900." *History and Theory* 23 (1984): 331–56.
"Jacob Burckhardt: Political Standpoint and Historical Insight on the
Border of Postmodernism." *History and Theory* 24 (1985): 235–46.
"The Didactics of History in West Germany: Towards a New Self-
Awareness of Historical Studies." *History and Theory* 26 (1987):
275–86.
"Historical Narration: Foundation, Types, Reason." *History and Theory*,
Beiheft 26: The Representation of Historical Events, 1987, 87–97.
"Historical Enlightenment in the Light of Postmodernism: History in
the Age of the 'New Unintelligibility.'" *History and Memory* 1, no. 1
(1989): 109–31.
"Rhetoric and Aesthetics of History: Leopold von Ranke." *History and
Theory* 29 (1990): 190–204.
"Auschwitz: How to Perceive the Meaning of the Meaningless—A Re-
mark on the Issue of Preserving the Remnants." In *Kulturwissen-
schaftliches Institut: Jahrbuch 1994*, 180–85.
"Trauer als historische Kategorie. Überlegungen zur Erinnerung an den
Holocaust in der Geschichtskultur der Gegenwart, demnächst."
In *Erlebnis, Gedächtnis, Sinn: Authentische und konstruierte Erin-
nerung*, ed. Hanno Loewy. Frankfurt: Campus, 1996.

*Aesthetics is inseparable
from science.*

Could you tell me how your interest in the theory of history began? Who was your source of inspiration?

■ I attended Wayne University—now called Wayne State University—in Detroit, Michigan. I was a veteran of World War II and so was one of hundreds of returning veterans who, older and more serious students than universities had perhaps ever seen in such numbers, created a wonderful intellectual atmosphere. I studied art, for my ambition at the time was to become an artist, but I had strong intellectual interests as well and took courses that particularly interested me. My interest in history was inspired by a powerful and visionary teacher, William Bossenbrook, whose courses in medieval history and in the Renaissance were tremendously exciting. Bossenbrook read very widely in philosophy and brought his reading to bear on the subject at hand. The immediate postwar years brought existentialism to America and I found that philosophy very compelling, especially in the way Bossenbrook used it to illuminate the past. His classes are impossible to describe, but one felt that nothing was irrelevant and that he saw everything somehow connected with everything else. He had an assistant named Milton Covensky, who read even more than Bossenbrook. I remember going to Bossenbrook's office and hearing the two of them trying to mention a book the other had not read. It was very intoxicating. In my book on history, I acknowledged Bossenbrook, saying in effect that inspired by his example I would have

I studied art, for my ambition at the time was to become an artist.

been a historian, save for the discovery that he was unique. Other history courses were altogether dull by comparison. Unfortunately, so were the philosophy classes at Wayne: there was a terrible professor named Trapp, who insisted that one could take advanced courses only if one first took his introductory course in philosophy, which I refused to do: one did not go through four years of war to tolerate that kind of petty authority. So art was a good subject to major in, all the more so in that there was a gifted historian, Ernst Scheyer, who opened vistas for me, and in fact became a friend. I could never have gotten close to Bossenbrook: he was really like some sort of shaman.

Anyway, I did a great deal of reading in the philosophy of history: Spengler especially interested me, and so did Toynbee. Toynbee was indirectly important because I read the reviews as they appeared of the one-volume abridgment of his *Study of History*, which were very negative. I learned what criticism was from that: the defects in Toynbee never would have occurred to me and I realized what reading seriously amounted to. I read Collingwood, and got something of Marx and Hegel from Sidney Hook's writings. Hook impressed me greatly for the clarity of his style and what at the time struck me as the power of his mind. I later saw through that kind of argumentation, but at that stage I was quite dazzled. I hoped to study with Hook at New York University after graduation, but since I had no philosophy as an undergraduate, they refused to admit me. But Columbia was then as now interested in students who knew something outside philosophy, and so I went there. It was at Columbia that I worked with Ernest Nagel, and his course in the philosophy of the social sciences gave me structures to work with in thinking about history.

Do you think that some experiences from your life influenced your interest in the philosophy of history and of art?

Oh, very definitely. Going into the Stable Gallery and seeing all those boxes by Warhol was a real revelation and my philosophy of art was a response to that. Another example came from my experience as an artist. The artist Mark Rothko said about abstract expressionism that it would last a thousand years. It lasted about twenty years instead and was replaced by something so radically different that those whose philosophy of art was formed in the

Seeing all those boxes by Warhol was a real revelation and my philosophy of art was a response to that.

years of abstract expressionism could barely make the transition. I wrote about that because I lived through it: it made me sensitive to deep historical changes. Those again are in the objective order of things.

I think one difference between Nelson Goodman and me, on the one side, and most philosophers of art, on the other, is that we made philosophy out of our own lives. Nelson after all was an art dealer, and the question of forgeries was a natural problem for him. You cannot just make philosophy from the philosophy other philosophers have made. In truth, everything that has happened to me has found its way into a piece of writing: my work really is a running intellectual autobiography, though of course it doesn't especially read that way.

Everything that has happened to me has found its way into a piece of writing.

How did it happen that you turned your interest from the theory of history to the philosophy and history of art?

Well, I did have the ambition to be an artist, and I pursued this ambition for some considerable time through graduate school and beyond. In fact I was making and exhibiting art well into the 1960s, when I stopped. I stopped in part because the art world changed, but mainly because I found myself so interested in writing philosophy that I did not want to do anything else. But my practical knowledge as an artist led to my doing the philosophy of art: I was asked, because of that knowledge, to present a paper on aesthetics to the American Philosophical Association in 1964. Paul Ziff was supposed to have done this, but found he could not, and they turned to me. That paper was called "The Artworld," and it became rather a famous paper, since the institutional theory of art took its rise from my text. I knew then that I would someday write a book on the philosophy of art and I believed it would be part of a large system of analytical philosophy. I published a book in epistemology in 1968 and in 1973 a book on the philosophy of action, which was again a subject I more or less invented, granting that the rudiments of my ideas were suggested by some arguments of Wittgenstein and by Elizabeth Anscombe. An analytical philosophy of art was to be next, and I wrote my book sometime in the late 1970s. But I no longer thought of it as an "analytical philosophy of art." I called the book *The Transfiguration of the Commonplace*, and I was very lucky with it, for it took its place alongside Goodman's *Languages of Art* as the founding text for a renaissance in the subject. It is on the ontology of art, prompted by the work of Andy Warhol, and tried to work out some answers to the question of why his *Brillo Box* is a work of art though it looks so much like Brillo boxes, which are not works of art at all. The question of history became acute at that point; namely, why were artworks of this sort possible in 1964 but not at an earlier time? And this leads me to the problem with White: I think there were really objective possibilities in the art world, and some account has to be given why this is so. In any case, that is the issue that at the moment occupies me most.

How do you consider yourself? Are you a philosopher of history, philosopher of art, critic?

I don't believe philosophers should specialize, because the answer to a problem in one field may be more apparent in an adjacent field. Then there are all the analogies you lose out on. I try to keep the whole of philosophy somehow in mind all the time. But I also don't believe philosophers should only know philosophy. My philosophical writing on art is interesting to nonphilosophers because of the density of its examples. And that led to my becoming an art critic. I don't necessarily think of the critical pieces I publish in the *Nation* as applied philosophy, but often they are philosophical analyses worked out for concrete instances of art. I suppose I like to be known as an analytical philosopher, mainly because there is a commitment to logical analysis and clarity of exposition. I don't of course subscribe to the antimetaphysical or antisystematic programs of earlier analytical philosophy.

I like to be known as an analytical philosopher.

Where do you place yourself in contemporary philosophy (philosophy of history)?

I have a philosophical system, but not a philosophy. In this I am as usual the opposite of Rorty, who disbelieves in system but has a philosophy. Dick and I are good friends, but we disagree about everything. He is very much like Foucault in wanting to discredit whatever impedes human growth, but he does not have Foucault's burden of dangerous drives. His life is quite a normal one, and he is a most congenial man with a great deal of curiosity and

I have a philosophical system, but not a philosophy.

170 hope. I think he thinks anyone can be anything. I am very much more pessimistic. He thinks everyone should be like The Artist, but he does not know what artists really are like. I am postmodernist enough to believe that no one should be defined by structures imposed upon him or her through gender or race or whatever; no one should be excluded from anything by virtue of those kinds of factors. But that does not mean that there are not internal limits. Not everyone really can be an artist in any sense worth thinking about. Or a philosopher. There really are gifts and limits; it is not all the work of society. My antecedents were Jewish, and Jews had a hard time overcoming external barriers until recently. My cousin was unable to become a philosopher for those reasons (he went on to became a famous psychiatrist). Still, the absence of external limits leaves intact the fact that some people are more gifted than others. I think Rorty feels that human beings are as plastic in this sense as Foucault thought the world is.

I think my philosophy of history was pretty original, as was my work on action, and on the philosophy of art. And my books on Nietzsche, Sartre, and the Orient are still read. I have gone after whatever interested me, or whatever I thought I could say something about, which makes me in no way representative of a philosophical school. Rorty thinks of me as a Cartesian philosopher, and it is true that Descartes taught me a way of thinking that on the whole is basically correct, though it would be crazy to say my work brings his thought forward. I have learned from everyone—Hegel, Hume, Kant, Quine, Frege, Russell, Nietzsche.

The only label I am comfortable with is "analytical philosophy." The only label I am comfortable with is "analytical philosophy." But that, as I say, is a commitment to clarity and logic, nothing more. I give myself all sorts of privileges as a writer. In fact what I really want to be known as is a writer, who writes mainly philosophy and art criticism. I am very much a professional philosopher, but I want to write in such a way that everyone can read and enjoy my things. Sometimes, as a kind of joke, I tell people I am a "man of letters." I have no gift for narrative, but I would want my books at their best to have the structure of novels.

I really want to be known as a writer.

I would want my books at their best to have the structure of novels.

What is your favorite book?

I don't have a favorite book. There are books through which I think things—Descartes's *Meditations* is a case in point, or the

Bhagavad Gita. Sometimes I wish I could see the world the way it is seen in the *Tao Te Ching*, but I find I cannot always see the world that way. I suppose I love [Proust's] *A la recherche du temps perdu* and E. M. Forster's *Passage to India* and Henry James's *The Golden Bowl*. For a book really to be a favorite, it would have to be about life as I live it. No philosophical book I know of is like that. I admire Wittgenstein's writing, but not his thought. I love Jane Austen's novels, especially *Persuasion*, and maybe George Eliot's *Middlemarch*. There—that's quite a list.

> For a book really to be a favorite, it would have to be about life as I live it. No philosophical book I know of is like that.

What is your opinion about postmodernism? Can we connect this "phenomenon" with a crisis of human values? Postmodernism calls for the rethinking of everything once again in different terms—in terms of linguistics or maybe in terms of experience. Should we really rethink everything through once again?

I think the best way into postmodernism is through the recognition that modernism was after all a style, mainly of art and architecture, possibly of poetry and music, which lasted about eighty years, but which became pronounced with the fauves and cubists, then the futurists and constructivists and suprematists, then art deco, minimalism and hard-edge abstraction. I put the surrealists and the abstract expressionists on a tangential line. Mainly, modernist art is marked by clarity of form, appreciation of machinery, pure hue. Leger is a sort of paradigm modernist. I think modernist attitudes penetrated life: cities, for example, should be rational and clear, like the buildings that form them, and of course it affected the way machines were designed, households were thought of, and the way people dressed. Coco Chanel gives the modernist look in garments: women wearing them look like soft machines. It also implied a sort of mechanized politics, a sense that we might relate to society the way parts of a machine relate to the whole, as in early Russian modernism. Fascism and totalitarianism, I am afraid, are modernist political forms. They finally seek to fit human beings into structures, and cherish uniformity—hence cherish the uniform, as in Maoist China. I would suppose that modernist philosophy would be logical constructivism, with Carnap's *Logische Aufbau* as its prime exemplar. In general, modernism was revisionist, rational, and in a certain wide sense of the term, aesthetic.

> Modernism was revisionist, rational, and aesthetic.

172   Postmodernist philosophy was by definition antiformalist, with Wittgenstein and Austin spokesmen for the thesis that ordinary language is alright as it is and does not need to be reconstructed. Pop art advanced the same thesis—that the ordinary objects of ordinary life were as meaningful as objects get. And I think politically that when people stopped thinking of themselves as having a place—woman's place, "knowing your place" if you are of the lower classes, "not getting out of line" if you were a student, not trying to "pass" if you were a black or a Jew—the attractiveness of the totalitarian state began to crumble. I think the vanishing of "place" and the celebration of the ordinary finally brought about the collapse of Communism. So postmodernism is at the very least a world of placelessness, and, because the higher ideals as specified by the state belonged to modernism, postmodernism enjoined a pattern of life that can easily be read as a sort of selfishness, which became institutionalized in Reaganism, and a pattern of art that is a sort of deep pluralism. It involves the erasure or the blurring of boundaries—between the genders only to begin with. I think one sees it in eating today: all the cuisines get mixed up. Then there is a lot of cross-dressing. Then there is the discouragement of *machismo*, the effort to get men to acknowledge their feminine side, and women to acknowledge their masculine side. And art becomes completely boundaryless: something can be painting, sculpture, performance, all at once.

Of course this may be felt as a crisis of values. Everyone either grew up a modernist, or had parents who were modernists. So what one learned from that is not of much use in a postmodern world. But I think it a marvelous time to be alive. Of course, it has its drawbacks. I think the erasure of the boundaries of warfare, for example, are showing up in Bosnia, which is a war against civilians.

As far as your suggestion that postmodernism means we have to think everything through in terms of "linguistics," I am uncertain. There is to be sure the idea of a "text" that has become so central in Continental philosophy. And we are enjoined to think of society and ourselves as texts, and hence our relationships to one another insofar as part of the same society as largely textual. I feel that this makes us understand ourselves as parts of a larger structure once more—just as Frege said that a word has meaning only in the *Zusammenhang* of a sentence, so we have meaning

Postmodernism enjoined a pattern of life that can easily be read as a sort of selfishness, which became institutionalized in Reaganism, and a pattern of art that is a sort of deep pluralism. It involves the erasure or the blurring of boundaries.

only in the *Zusammenhang* of larger texts; viz, families, societies, institutions, and the like. Well, that may be true. But it reintroduces the concept of place all over again. It sounds like a kind of organic modernism. But how deep and totalistic the idea of text is is a problem for philosophers to think through.

How deep and totalistic the idea of text is is a problem for philosophers to think through.

Maybe we cannot think about postmodernism in a logical way. I mean in terms of scientific logic. I can say that postmodernism expresses, rather than says. The obsession with language and discourse—as Frank Ankersmit told me—is passé and we should change the subject. Thus maybe there is a time for studying experiences. Can we say that postmodernism is existential? It wants to communicate but not only in a verbal way (which is of course limited). Maybe that is the reason many theorists are interested in visual art (in painting for instance). And now there is a space for the philosophy of art. Do you think that your ideas could be adapted to the philosophy of history?

Do you not think that we jump over from a modernist verbalism—by means of narration—to a postmodernist visualism? Maybe in the future instead of comparing our life to a novel, we will compare it to a movie. So we have a picture instead of a verbal story?

This seems to be less a question about postmodernism than a postmodernist question—all sorts of things jammed together, a sort of multimedia question. And I am not sure I know how to answer postmodern questions.

Ankersmit is probably right in saying that a certain mode of philosophical analysis is passé, what Rorty in his early anthology called the linguistic turn, where the thought was that by what Quine called "semantic ascent" the questions become more tractable. Nobody much thinks that way. Nor does anybody think that in describing "what we say when . . ." (as the Oxford School recommended) we have said all there is to say in philosophy. Those were interesting and valuable efforts, still worth knowing how to do, but they are not universally interesting and valuable. So linguistic philosophy, which a decade or so ago was considered the heart of philosophy, is now, if not marginal, certainly of limited worth.

Linguistic philosophy, which a decade or so ago was considered the heart of philosophy, is now, if not marginal, certainly of limited worth.

174

I tentatively agree with you about experience. Tom Nagel's important paper—or at least important title—"What's It Like to Be a Bat?" brings out that there is something it is like to be which is very difficult to put into words. And these days people say such things as "You wouldn't understand: it's a black thing." Or women may say that there is something it's like to be a woman—a mode of experience that can only be lived by someone who in fact is a woman. Since feminism is archetypically postmodern, I suppose you could say that postmodernism "starts to be more and more existential." To be sure, this need not be altogether personal: blacks would presumably understand "black things"; women share whatever it is to be a woman, and so, perhaps, don't have to explain things to one another (and maybe can't explain them to anyone not a woman.) Still, bringing this to consciousness is a start in getting others to respect and acknowledge it, and that can be all to the good. A man who learns that there is something that it's like to be a woman might learn to be considerate of just those feelings—or at least appreciates that he has to take them into account if he is going to have a harmonious relationship. And that certainly makes for greater happiness for as long as it continues to be true that there is something that it's like to be, etcetera. And then I suppose there is such a thing as what it's like to be me.

Feminism is archetypically postmodern.

I perhaps would go along with Ramsey in saying: if you can't say it, you can't whistle it either—but I think discourse probably has to be supplemented with something else in order to communicate. Perhaps that is where your thought about the visual as against the verbal comes in. But I am not sure that you have to go all the way to the visual arts, though a lot of feminist artists today certainly make the effort to show how it feels to be a woman. And I guess they think men can understand this art. (A lot of it, on the other hand, is pretty awful.)

I find your assumption that narrative is to modern as visual art is to postmodern doubtful; you have to remember that "modern" was a style of art, and that modernism is probably best exemplified in modern art. That art was paradigmatically geometrical, and glorified formal values. "Narrative" was strictly as forbidden as "literary," or "decorative." Postmodern art allows itself narrative when it wishes, and is almost systematically opposed to formalist aesthetics.

So far as adapting my philosophy of art to a philosophy of history is concerned, I have in a way already done that in talking as I have about the "end of art," meaning the end of a certain narrative that ends in the moment of transfiguration, when art passes, just as Hegel anticipated it would, into philosophy. I feel that narrative was internal to the historical unfolding of art, which is a main reason why I have become a narrative realist, and stand against writers like White and Carrier, who still think of narrative as just a way of organizing things. My thought was that narratively driven art has come to its end, leaving us in the posthistorical phase others in fact speak of as postmodernism. My real belief is that ours is an era of deep pluralism—and that postmodernist art, narrowly so-called, internalizes this pluralism into itself, producing disjunctive works, photographic, painterly, sculptural, and so on, all at once.

I have become a narrative realist.

Do you feel seduced by a postmodernist way of thinking? Do you consider yourself a postmodernist?

I am uncertain that there is a postmodernist way of thinking at all, to tell you the truth. In rejecting modernism, which really was a style, one may in fact regress to something premodern. The style of postmodernism is not to have a coherent style. An artist like Gerhardt Richter is an exemplary postmodernist artist—realist, abstractionist, etcetera, etcetera. I don't think you can have something like that in history-writing, but you could have it in life: as in Marx's vision of being a hunter in the morning etcetera, where one is not one with any particular practice, but turns from one practice to the another, as the mood takes one.

As a philosopher I am more modernist than not. I still find the general idea of constructivism rather compelling, which means that one builds structures up out of elementary units. I developed a theory of action with a concept of basic actions—actions that have no further actions as components of themselves—and a parallel theory of knowledge. That means one has to identify the structures through which basic actions get transformed into higher order actions, and similarly with cognitions. In history, the notion of narrative sentences implies a concept of what one might call basic events. As a philosopher, that is the way I think about things, and I am convinced that it reflects a very basic structure of thought. But I am in a qualified way postmodernist in my refusal to specialize: you can (and should) be an epistemologist in the morning, an aesthetician in the afternoon, an action-theorist

176
I have never been
seduced by what
people identify as
postmodernist
philosophical
styles.

in the early evening. And I am a deep believer in pluralism in art. I have never been seduced by what people identify as postmodernist philosophical styles, for example, writing as Derrida practices it. Or Lyotard. Nor do I suppose anyone trained in analytical philosophy capable of being seduced that way. As you can see, my character is not consistent, being modernist here, postmodernist there. I suppose that makes me in fact a postmodernist by definition.

What was your opinion of White's *Metahistory* when it appeared? At that time you presented a different point of view about how history should be explained and understood. Did you think that this book put theory of history on a new track—I mean that it started the "narrativist turn" in the theory of history?

It is something of a curiosity that White and I went to the same school, and indeed were both of us disciples of Bossenbrook. White in fact published a *Festschrift*, to which I contributed. We did not really know one another in Detroit, however, and he was really a historian. I imagine that it was because he was Bossenbrook's student that he was liberated from the conventional way of historical thinking, as was I: that was truly the way that teacher inspired us.

White's inspiration came from rhetoric, mine, you might say, from logic. Because of Nagel, who was the best thinker at Columbia, I got immersed in the philosophy of science, and in fact I published an anthology with Sidney Morgenbesser in the philosophy of science that is still in use here and there. Of course, the master thinker for us was Carl G. Hempel, and in particular the latter's famous paper "The Function of General Laws in History." I thought and I continue to regard this a correct way of thinking about historical explanation, and in my own book, I tried to show that there was a deep equivalence between the Hempelian model of explanation and a narrative model of explanation. The point was that narrative is not a deep alternative to scientific explanation, but rather that narratives and scientific explanations are constructed on the same logical principles. There may be a difference pragmatically, because of the epistemologies of time-indexed information. Narratives really do refer to the position in time of the narrator in regard to the events narrated, and this makes some immense pragmatic difference. The central thought in the *Analytical Philosophy of History* was that of "narrative sentences," defined as about at least two time-separated events, in which the earlier is described with reference to the later, because of which the description cannot be known and perhaps cannot be understood by someone contemporary only with the first event. "The Thirty Years War began in 1618" refers to the end of the Thirty Years War, and nobody in 1618 could have known the war would last thirty years. Nobody perhaps knew it was even going to be a war.

I found White's account ingenious rather than compelling. I thought it interesting that there should be those four rhetorical tropes, but I wondered why four, and why those four. White's views got to be philosophically important because he inferred from the fact that there is no objective reason for choosing one trope over another that how we organize the past is wholly up to us, and from that the inference was drawn that there is no objective way the past is ordered. Narratives are just ways among other ways. I think there really are objective organizations of events in history, that there are realities to which narratives correspond. So in a way the difference between us is a distant relative of the realism/antirealism controversy in the philosophy of science. Of course, that is a very hard issue to resolve—but I cannot imagine that the existence of alternative tropes contributes to the resolution at all. I feel that there are gaps between White's systematic tropology and antirealism.

> I think there really are objective organizations of events in history, that there are realities to which narratives correspond.

Hayden White started the process that I would like to call the "aestheticization of history." Return to cultural history in its nineteenth-century form seems to be the object of a dream: for enthusiasts of the new cultural history, Huizinga and Burckhardt are exemplars and objects of study. The old debate about the status of history and the relationship between history and literature has been revived. I think maybe your proposition of replacement: aesthesis and cognition, instead of art and science (proposed in your article "A Future for Aesthetics"), can help to solve this problem. Both historical and literary narration similarly touch the essence of reality. Fiction seems to be a metaphor for life.

178   In that article I sought to unhook aesthetics from art and establish the way in which it really belongs to cognition and in particular to scientific cognition. I tried, if you recall, to emphasize the way in which scientific illustrations not only show us how things look but how we feel about them. My examples were the engravings from the *Micrographia* of insects. The old microscopists may not have realized how deeply their perceptions were tinctured by an aesthetic, but it is perfectly visible now, just as the aesthetics of present-day science may come to be visible to a later generation. Nothing can be more connected with normal aesthetics than narratives, with the suspense, resolution, fulfillment, and catharsis inherent in the medium, whether fictional or factual. We want to see the thing unfold even if we already know that. Children love to hear the same story, again and again. Stories cast spells, capture and hold the imagination, and they reinforce the feeling that the world is ordered and intelligible at once. Psychologically—aesthetically—there is probably no great difference between history and myth: the myth almost always explains something we were curious about, or should have been: how the kangaroo got its pouch, how the rabbit lost its voice. The mythteller always concludes this way: "And so we see how . . ." The *so* is *thus* and the *thus* is the particle of logical demonstration. *How did we get this way?* is a request for a story, a myth in less advanced cultures, a history in our own. But my general point is that once we see that aesthetics is really inseparable from science, we will see that the old notions of a "scientific history" that is purged of aesthetic considerations was a history purged of human interest. My argument, remember, in *Analytical Philosophy of History* was that the whole structure of explanation was co-implicated with interest in the so-called explanandum. Erase interest and you erase structure.

Aesthetics is
inseparable from
science.

Can we say that now we are not exactly interested in the interpretation of the past but rather we try to present how people in the past experienced their "reality" or—maybe—in this way, how we experience our "reality"?

The relationship between what was happening and how people experienced what was happening is extremely complex. I am not in the least certain that the past reality consisted entirely in people's interpretation of their present. The stock market crash of 1929

was undoubtedly caused by many individuals all at once losing
confidence in the market, and acting in a panicky way. But when
the market crashed it really crashed, and many people were ruined,
and many businesses were bankrupt. It is true that a business or
an investment is in some measure a matter of perception—but
the effects were real. The "sexual revolution" of the 1970s was in
large measure due to the way the Pill turned out to be an effective contraceptive, liberating women—and men—from the burden of parenthood. The response to this was a license to experiment sexually, and it dissolved a great many myths about women
and their differences in this respect from men. But there was still a
fair amount of chemistry involved, as there is physiology involved
with AIDS. Right now it is snowing in New York. This will affect
greatly how people live their day and night.

How do you rate the value of metaphor in the representa-
tion of reality?

I have written twice on metaphor. The main account is in *The
Transfiguration of the Commonplace*. Metaphor is of course a rhetorical trope, and rhetoric has the function of moving the minds
of one's readers. It is an open question whether we can altogether
avoid rhetoric in describing things—or in showing them, since
you think there might be a contrast. The important logical feature of metaphors is that they refer to an object and to a mode of
representation, virtually flattening the object into a representation of itself. Since reality becomes part of representation in such
cases, it is hard to separate representation from reality, and hence   With metaphor, it
hard to separate rhetoric from reality: the way we see things be-   is hard to separate
comes part of what we see. That leads easily to a "there is noth-   representation
ing hors du texte" sort of theory. In fact everything is hors du   from reality, and
texte, but human reality is reality woven into a text-like fabric.   hence hard to separate rhetoric from
reality.

Do you think that it is possible to avoid speaking about the
world in terms of the subject-object?

The thought sometimes expressed that Continental philosophy has "overcome" the subject-object dichotomy is simply reck-
less philosophizing. It is true that there are certain descriptions
of things that involve interpretation, and, on certain views of

180   interpretation, the "object" cannot be abstracted from these descriptions, nor from the meanings assigned it under interpretation. To say that the object could not exist without the subject's
interpretations is, however, merely false. The gaps of Cartesian
philosophy are always there.

**Which theorist of history presents a point of view that
can be compared with yours? Which historian presents the
best way of studying history? Which one do you personally
like best?**

I am really a loner, I'm afraid, though in general I admire the way
Hegel thought. I think Vasari a tremendous historian, with a deep
sense of objective narrative. Among contemporaries, I think a
great deal of Simon Schama. I think I would read anything he
wrote. Fred Beiser is a great historian of philosophy, because he
deals with the little guys. I cannot think off-hand of a feminist historian I particularly admire, but feminism puts history in a fresh
light.

**Are you going to write something about the theory of his-
tory or does only the philosophy of art attract you?**

"Only" the philosophy of art? Seriously, I have two projects. I am
supposed to give a series of lectures in 1995 at our National Gallery in Washington. They are obliged to be on the visual arts, but
I intend that they shall be on the history of the visual arts, philosophically considered. After that—if there is an after that—I have
a cherished project on the philosophy of mind. I have published
very little on that, but have some novel things to say. My most
important essay is in a somewhat obscure volume edited by Ralph
Cohen on the future of criticism. It is called "Beautiful Science
and the Future of Criticism." I don't think I have heard from a
single philosopher about that piece, but occasionally people in literature have been taken with it.

**Do you personally feel the change in principles? Intellectu-
als seem to be in the worst position in such situations. I
think a dangerous symptom is that we often tend to move**

from epistemological relativism (which in fact is needed for
our thinking) to moral relativism. Postmodernism is the
epoch of "deviants." Full of paradoxes and ambiguities,
postmodernism, connected with instability and relativism is
like a paradise for "heretics." Hayden White was considered
a "deviant" in the 1970s, Derrida in the '80s. Foucault very
often is given as the best example of a new "model" of an
historian. But he is a typical "heretic." Certainly he is not
a traditional historian. He is like a sensitive artist, who by
exploring past reality tries to touch the truth about the
world.

I have a difficult time with the concept of epistemological relativism. Given the standard analysis of knowledge as justified true belief, then of course knowledge will be relative because belief is so heavily indexed for time, place, information, and so much else. There are beliefs you cannot have at a certain time—nobody could have had a belief about DNA in the eleventh century. It is difficult for us today to believe the world will come to an end in 1000 A.D., since it didn't. But then truth isn't relative that way, and belief isn't knowledge unless true. What holds for epistemic beliefs holds of course for moral beliefs—but there is no moral knowledge because there are no moral truths. That does not make for moral relativism, of course, since consensus is as wide as it is. Take the case of human rights: rights are *declared*. The declaration of human rights in the United Nation structure is *universal*. It defines what a dignified human life is. An intellectual who cannot keep epistemology and moral theory in their proper spheres does not deserve to be called an intellectual. An intellectual so-called who says it is alright, if you are a Serbian, to rape Muslim women—alright for them if not alright for us—is about as muddled as it is possible to get.

> There is no moral knowledge because there are no moral truths.

Your description of postmodernism sounds very much like a description of mannerism ("full of paradoxes"). I don't see it as a paradise for deviants: there is no heresy without orthodoxy, no apostasy without dogma, but neither orthodoxy nor dogma are postmodern possibilities at all.

> There is no heresy without orthodoxy, no apostasy without dogma.

I think you dramatize things in calling Hayden a "deviant," or Derrida for that matter. Both of them are highly regarded members of the academic community. Both of them raise important

182 questions—or re-raise questions the Sophists raised—in original and interesting ways. But Derrida prepared students for the *agrégation* in the Ecole Normale. You cannot get more orthodox than that. He is a walking anthology of French academic values. I have little to add regarding Foucault. I'll go along with considering him a new kind of historian. But there is a difference between originality and deviancy. And Foucault did after all hold a chair in the Collège de France: what he achieved was not perceived as discontinuous with historical practice. I think one has to put him alongside Braudel: Braudel stressed continuities under seeming change, Foucault stressed discontinuities under seeming continuity. Together they put in question certain older ideas of historical periods, or, if you like, of historical events. What was striking about Foucault was the degree to which he thought it possible to demonstrate the politics of cognition, which meant, to him, that intellectual critique was equivalent to political subversion. That made him cynical about truth-claims in general, even in his own case. And that in turn committed him to a critique of truth rather like Nietzsche's. He paid little attention to what life would be like if he were to succeed, or perhaps it did not greatly matter whether or not he succeeded: it was enough to call everything into question and then to live as though one were free of it. I find it therefore very doubtful that he was interested in truth. He was interested in freedom, and felt it his task to destroy the very ideas of truth in order to lead the life he thought destroying truth made possible. He was interested in the sense of truth in which a man finds out the truth of himself under an ordeal. There is a combination of Faust and Nietzsche in his personality: Nietzsche in the sense that truth was dead; Faust in the sense that he sought to live out his terrifying fantasies. Foucault is one of the scariest human beings I know, and one of the most dangerous.

Foucault is one of the scariest human beings I know, and one of the most dangerous.

Do you share the opinion that presently we are experiencing a crisis of history? For example, Gertrude Himmelfarb in her book *The New History and the Old* insists that the crisis "is so deep that it may signal the end of Western civilization." Maybe history as a separate discipline is passé?

There is a difference between a crisis and the end of a certain epoch. A crisis is really a critical moment, where it is unclear whether or not something can continue: an ill person lives or dies when the crisis occurs; a war is won or lost; a business fails or recovers. But when an epoch begins another one has ended. You have to make your mind up which it is. I argued that modernism was an epoch, and that it ended. So postmodernism was not a crisis for modernism. There are no crises for the dead. So it is not a symptom of a crisis either. Nor is it a symptom of the new epoch—it is the new epoch. Nothing is a symptom unless something is a disease, and I am very cautious in projecting medical metaphors onto social conditions. I think postmodernism is an attitude for very sophisticated persons who are very comfortable crossing and erasing boundaries. It is also an era composed of questions to which everyone knows none of the old answers will do. Not a bad time to be alive for the adventurous in spirit.

I don't quite see the inference from a crisis in history to history as a discipline becoming passé, not unless the crisis in history just is the threat of history as a (separate discipline) becoming passé? The only thing that might connect the two points might be the emergence of theories like White's, Rorty's, and Foucault's that discount the very concept of truth. History as a discipline becomes threatened if there is no truth to tell—but then so is every discipline threatened. There just get to be stories we tell one another, but unless we also feel those stories to be true, the propensity to listen to them withers, and history withers with it. Is that the issue? Is that the crisis? (I did not read Himmelfarb's book.) Now and again someone comes along and says something like the Holocaust never happened. That is not a threat to history as a discipline because, for the most part, such persons first of all put forward a No-Holocaust theory as the historical truth, and then get involved in issues of evidence. Such fanatics would not be in the least grateful to Rorty, who tells them they can tell the stories they like, or to White who hands them a license to emplot. But I am reluctant to consider White, Rorty, and Foucault as putting an end to Western civilization! With variations in detail, their positions can be found in the ancient world and so just are part of "Western Civilization." There are of course a lot of theories like those that insist on the death of the author, or that "there is nothing outside the text," which must seem threatening. But these really are philosophical positions that seem at a certain moment terrifically exciting. They are part of the fabric of civilized discourse, not an

Postmodernism was not a crisis for modernism. There are no crises for the dead. So it is not a symptom of a crisis either. Nor is it a symptom of the new epoch—it is the new epoch.

184

Contemporary
philosophy feels a
lot like fourteenth-
century philoso-
phy: scholastic,
hairsplitting, arid,
and of no conse-
quence for anyone
outside the game.

How to keep in-
tellectual work go-
ing on when there
is not that much
more to find out.

end to it. No: I don't feel a crisis there. What would please me would be if philosophers, who are equipped to deal with these kinds of issues, were to get involved with them rather than the rather tired agendas of professional philosophy. In truth, contemporary philosophy feels a lot like fourteenth-century philosophy: scholastic, hairsplitting, arid, and of no consequence for anyone outside the game.

The domination of discussion by these theories, on the other hand, really does reflect some very puzzling and difficult questions about what should be read and how it should be read and why it should be read. And that in the end is to be an issue of the point and nature of higher education. No one today can doubt that there is some sort of crisis in higher education, if by that we mean a loss of direction or at least a loss of certainty. Raising the issue of truth really means raising the issue of education in the most radical possible way. But someone is going to have to find an answer to the question of why truth—Truth capital T—should have become the target on which so many lines of subversion converged. It is like cutting away the ultimate justification for inquiry.

Here might be one way of looking at it. The year 1992 marked the five hundredth anniversary of the birth of Piero della Francesca. There were a lot of books published to mark the occasion, most of which agreed on the bare facts. It is hardly likely that there could be a fact known to one specialist unknown to the others. But there was all that pressure to publish books. This put immense pressure on coming up with different interpretations. And Nietzsche's dictum "There are no facts, only interpretations" all at once licenses interpretations of every sort. And writers like White, Rorty, and Foucault seem like an answer to a prayer; namely, how to keep intellectual work going on when there is not that much more to find out. Then there get to be feminist interpretations, gay interpretations, all kinds of readings. This is not a crisis but the response to a crisis; namely, coming up against the limits. It is a way of learning to live within those limits. Derrida's philosophy promises the possibility of infinite interpretations. Small wonder he is so popular! It is as though he issued working papers for the entire academic profession. I could see how what you call "history as a separate discipline" could look passé. The number of new facts relative to the number of possible interpretations is infinitesimal. "Truth is dead" is a dramatic way of describing this.

The fascinating question for the philosophy of history—for the theory of history, if there were such a thing—is what must the objective structure of present history be like in order that an explanation like this should be possible?

What do you think about microstories? Le Roy Ladurie's *Montaillou* and Ginzburg's *The Cheese and the Worms* were best-sellers. How do you explain the great success of these books?

I have no particular views on microhistory, but tend to think that it is because it reads like a kind of journalism, and takes us into the minds of actual people, that we so enjoy it. And the surprising truth is that they are altogether people like ourselves, with some few beliefs that happen not to be ours, but still not so different that we have much difficulty in understanding their behavior. And it is, moreover, of the greatest value to see what it was like to be living through certain events—what the Great Depression was like in terms of the people who had to come to terms with unemployment and not knowing when or how it was all going to end. Thomas Nagel sloganized the concept of consciousness by saying that to be conscious is for there to be something it is like to be whatever one is—his example was a bat. To be historically conscious is for there to be something it is like to live through certain events. These events otherwise tend to become abstractions. "What was it like . . . ?" is a very poignant and fascinating question. Philosophically it is interesting that, whatever it was like, ordinary men and women lived through the event, and however different their lives were, they remain close enough to us that there is no problem in understanding their feelings, their responses, and their conduct.

What do you predict the future of the philosophy of history will be?

Well, the subject so far has been pretty marginal, mainly because philosophers tend to think in universal and hence nontemporal terms. I think my own work brought into the discussion the idea of seeing events "under a description," which I first found in Anscombe. And this made its way into action theory, especially in the

186

A certain kind of
materialism will
have to give way.

History as a mode
of being.

work of Davidson. What now has to be done is to recognize that descriptions themselves are historically indexed, making it clear finally that we are through and through historical beings. This connects with the point that beliefs are historically indexed: there are beliefs than cannot have been held at certain times. And once that is seen, a certain kind of materialism will have to give way; namely, a materialism that thinks of us merely as a material system whose laws are the same in all times. The laws change as our historical position changes, and the more that is appreciated, the more attractive the philosophy of history as a subject will become. It will become attractive because it will be perceived as central to what has always preoccupied philosophers. Of course, it will not have a lot to do with history-writing. It will rather have to do with history as a mode of being.

The questions were sent to Arthur C. Danto by Ewa Domańska on 29 October 1993. He composed his answers 26 and 28 November in Brookhoven Hamlet, New York.

SELECTED WRITINGS

Nietzsche as Philosopher. New York: Macmillan, 1965.

Analytical Philosophy of History. Cambridge: Cambridge Univ. Press, 1965. Rev. ed., *Narration and Knowledge* (including the integral text of *Analytical Philosophy of History*). New York: Columbia Univ. Press, 1985.

Analytical Philosophy of Knowledge. London: Cambridge Univ. Press, 1968.

Analytical Philosophy of Action. Cambridge: Cambridge Univ. Press, 1973.

Jean-Paul Sartre. New York: Viking Press, 1975.

The Transfiguration of the Commonplace: A Philosophy of Art. Cambridge: Harvard Univ. Press, 1981.

The Philosophical Disenfranchisement of Art. New York: Columbia Univ. Press, 1986.

Encounters and Reflections: Art in the Historical Present. New York: Farrar, Straus & Giroux, 1990.

Beyond the Brillo Box: The Visual Arts in Post-Historical Perspective. New   **187**
York: Farrar, Straus & Giroux, 1992.

"The Decline and Fall of the Analytical Philosophy of History." In *A
New Philosophy of History*, ed. Frank Ankersmit and Hans Kellner,
70–85. Chicago: Univ. of Chicago Press, 1995.

Lionel Gossman

*The goal is not knowledge
but the good life,
not theory but practice.*

**Let me start our "conversation" with a few questions:
What was the subject of your study? Who was your source
of inspiration? Can you mention some philosophers, literary critics, or writers who influenced your way of thinking?**

■ I studied French and German language and literature. I thought
I would like history and took a course in European history in my
freshman year at the University of Glasgow, but I did not like it
at all. It seemed void of any philosophical self-consciousness. I
couldn't figure out what those who studied this material were really interested in. The focus of the course was diplomatic history.
I wasn't ready for it. At the time, I wanted to find "meaning" in
history (I was barely eighteen, we had just emerged from a war
that had always been presented in "meaningful" terms, rather than
as a simple power struggle, and we wanted to build a new world).
Now, I have taken my distance from history conceived of in those
philosophical terms, but I remember what a thirst for sense—and
for social justice—I had as a young man and I try to have understanding for those, especially the young, who still feel those things
intensely. Recently, I met Norman O. Brown. I don't know if that
name will mean anything to you. He is the author of *Life Against
Death* and *Love's Body*, two books that everybody read in the
1960s, along with Marcuse. They remain very lively works, though
I doubt that they now have many readers. They elaborate a strange
mixture of Freud, Marx, and a kind of Dionysiac Christianity: ex-
hilarating and emancipating; intoxicating, perhaps. Norman O.
Brown retains, at eighty, a kind of boyish enthusiasm for specula-

At the time,
I wanted to
find "meaning"
in history.

tion, for philosophical solutions, for the adventures of the mind. He asked me whether I wasn't looking for a vast synthesis that would accommodate everything, and volunteered that he had always sought such a synthesis and was still seeking. I replied that I had at one time, but that now I found it was more important for me to learn to live with contradictions, or at least with incompatibilities, those of my own personality and psyche as well as those that concern philosophical positions. I often have to acknowledge the validity of incompatible positions. Hume's skepticism and pragmatism and Hegel's or Marx's pursuit of a total systematic theory; the existentialist (potentially elitist and undemocratic) emphasis on *Bildung* and the positivist (potentially reductive, alienating, and bureaucratic) emphasis on *Wissenschaft*. I don't find that there is a choice to be made between these and other similar pairs. You have to move back and forth from the one to the other, correcting the one with the other. Hence *Between History and Literature*. Hence maybe my current work on nineteenth-century Basel, which I see as a culture that acknowledged the claims of both pragmatism and principle, the present and the past, humanism and technology.

To return to my education. I studied French and German language and literature, then, not history. But my approach to literary study was much informed by history. I fell under the spell of Lukács, whom I discovered by accident in the library of the German department at Glasgow. (How he got there is a mystery, since the German department, with the exception of one scholar, was extremely conservative.) I never really read Marx, except for the very easy texts and some of the correspondence. My "Marxism" was entirely Lukácsian—that is to say, penetrated with German idealism. To this day, the German tradition both attracts me powerfully and repels me. For a time, around 1953–54, I was keenly interested in Raymond Williams as a kind of homebred social and cultural critic, but he never had the impact on me that Lukács had. I am no longer a Lukácsian, but I still have a lot of sympathy for his concerns, and I will always be grateful to him for having aroused me from my undogmatic slumbers. What was it that appealed to me? The intense longing for community, wholeness, totality. Something I now see as basically religious. Real Marxism is more hard-nosed, and in that sense a useful corrective to the potential for *Schwärmerei* in Lukács (this despite his excellent dialectical

I replied that it was more important for me to learn to live with contradictions.

I studied French and German language and literature.

190   skills). Lukács provided a fairly well articulated framework for my interest in culture, not as something given, but as something problematical, something always rooted in a historical condition, usually of exploitation and injustice, and inevitably, to some degree, complicitous with that condition, even when particular works are directly or (more frequently) indirectly critical of it. I later came to use the rootedness of history in literary and linguistic practices in order to undermine the complacent claim to scientific objectivity of history, while at the same time using history to undermine the notion that culture is pure and disinterested. My intention has never been to present history simply as disguised fiction or to present culture as simply disguised power and interest. Such extreme reductionism stems, I suspect, from a disappointed desire for purity. My intention is only to enhance awareness of our imperfection in order to make people more self-conscious and also more modest and realistic about what can be achieved.

My intention is only to enhance awareness of our imperfection.

There is no truth or value that allows us to dispense with the opinion and judgment of others. In the end, my appeal is for recognition of the role of intersubjectivity in all cultural production.

My appeal is for recognition of the role of intersubjectivity in all cultural production.

I have strayed far from your initial questions. Let me just add to the list of formative influences, besides Lukács and—to a far lesser extent—Raymond Williams, Sartre, who forced me to confront (but did not help me to resolve) a conflict between Marxism and existentialism, both of which spoke powerfully to me; René Girard, who was my colleague at Johns Hopkins in the late 1950s and 1960s; certain essays of Roman Jakobson and Albert Lord's *The Singer of Tales*; Lotman's *Introduction to Structural Poetics*; Ingarden's phenomenological studies of theater and cinema; a fabulous work with the unpromising title of *Der Übergang vom feudalen zum bürgerlichen Weltbild* by Franz Borkenau, a member of the Frankfurt School; Lucien Goldmann's study of Pascal, *Le Dieu caché*; the work on the rhetoric of argumentation by Chaim Perelman; and Stephen Toulmin's books on reasoning. (A motley collection!) I am sure I have absorbed, as my whole generation has, something of the work of Jacques Derrida, whom I knew well when he was a regular visitor to Hopkins, but in the end I think the Lukácsian strain, corrected by formalism, has been the main one, and it goes back to the preoccupations of German classicism and neohumanism. The impact on me of a selection of

letters between Goethe and Schiller on questions of epic and
dramatic, etc. as well as of Schiller's *Letters on the Aesthetic Education of Mankind*, all of which I read as an undergraduate, was
enormous and has been enduring. I still go back to that stuff, and
I recognize it and respond to it in the work of some very recent
critics—for instance, a young Italian scholar in comparative literature at Columbia by the name of Franco Moretti, for whom I
have the highest regard.

I have gone on for too long and have strayed unpardonably
from your questions. Probably in a few minutes, I will remember
some important influence that I have suppressed. But that is the
way it goes. We never know as much as we would like to know
about anything, including—maybe especially—ourselves.

How do you see yourself? Are you a historian (intellectual historian), philosopher, critic (literary critic)?

I see myself first and foremost as a teacher. I spend most of my
time working with students, undergraduate and graduate, and—
more recently—contributing to the running of my university. I
enjoy writing a lot, and I see that part of my activity as another way
of participating in the general work of human culture. I care a lot
about the way I write, about using language well. Though I can't
aspire to real literary distinction, I think that maintaining a generally decent standard of language usage, a kind of high-quality
language craft, so to speak, is important. That aim corresponds to
an ideal of culture that we have inherited from the classical period
and the Enlightenment and to which, on the whole, I remain at-
tached, as I've explained in the preface to *Between History and
Literature* and in the short autobiographical essay I contributed
to a recent collective work (*Building a Profession: Autobiographical Perspectives on the Beginnings of Comparative Literature in the
United States*) that I edited with my friend Mihai Spariosu.

I'm not particularly concerned with defining myself professionally—or in terms of a discipline. My job, in the first instance,
is to contribute to the *Bildung* of Princeton students. I do that
by studying with them texts that our culture has generally considered to be enriching and formative. Not all such texts. Chiefly
texts in the field in which I am supposed to have specialized—

I see myself first
and foremost as a
teacher.

namely, French literature. I am permitted to interpret that broadly rather than narrowly, so that I get to teach historical and political writings, travel works, etc., as well as novels, poems, and plays, and I am also permitted to select for study works that are not well known but that I believe to be capable of enriching, challenging, and forming their readers. I look at texts from a variety of points of view—formal, historical, philosophical, political, ideological. My ultimate goal is not explanation or analysis—it is not knowledge. Analysis and interpretation are for me only means by which readers, with all their contemporary concerns and questions and with their particular individual talents, can be helped to enter into dialogue (often critical dialogue, or even debate) with texts. Through such dialogues, I believe, we form and reform our own ideas and values. I see my scholarly writing, such as it is, as part of a similar enterprise, only on a broader scale. So, in the end, I should probably call myself a teacher, a philologist, possibly a cultural historian or critic, certainly not a philosopher, and probably not a historian.

> My ultimate goal is not explanation or analysis—it is not knowledge.

How do you find your position in the present debate on philosophy of history and historical writing?

I've tried to sketch out a position in the essay entitled "Toward a Rational Historiography" in *Between History and Literature*. I don't want to take up your time by going over it again. The gamut of historical writing extends from large synthetic works, which probably express or at least imply a view of the world and a set of values, to detailed investigations that seem so technical that some scholars consider them "historical erudition" rather than "historical writing." Essentially, my position is that this is a continuum: "historical erudition" is not completely free of value judgments or independent of worldviews, and "historical writing"—if the word "historical" is to signify more than that the writer constructs a "story" out of nuggets of "fact" (or what passes for such)—is more than the expression of values and a worldview, but is subject to criticism in terms of plausibility, evidence, argument, and so on. It's conceivable that a work that was found to be deeply flawed in terms of plausibility, evidence, and argument could continue to be effective as the representation of a worldview, but would we still consider it to be history, except in a formally generic

sense? And would the standing of the world view presented in the **193**
work remain unaffected by flaws in the historical argument?

You mentioned formalism as one of your sources of inspiration. In the United States at present we see a special interest in Russian formalism and also in Bakhtin. Could you please tell me the reason for this situation, in your opinion? Which formalist's ideas can inspire the philosophy of history and historical thinking?

I came on Russian formalism in the late 1960s, I think. I was very taken by the precision, the clarity, the communicability of it. I still think that Propp's *Morphology of the Folktale* is one of the most beautiful works of criticism I have ever read. To me it was a brilliant insight that a narrative might have a grammar, like a sentence. Suddenly we were made to look closely at texts, at their internal structure. After decades of existentialism and phenomenology, it was like a breath of clean, fresh air. It appeals to the "positivist" in every British or French scholar—the sense that there is an object out there and that it is intelligible. But it was also linked in my mind with a whole movement in folklore studies, which emphasized the relation between *langue* and *parole*, or the framework of code and rule that is both the condition of and the constraint upon individual invention in the folk tradition.

I personally am less taken by Bakhtin. I was at first bowled over by his book on Rabelais (it coincided with the turmoil of the late 1960s, the work of Norman O. Brown, and others), but I am now considerably less enthusiastic. I find the opposition of popular and elite, the living and the institutional, etc. too schematic. I also think it was a pathological reaction to a pathological form of repression. I have expressed my misgivings in a review of Holquist's excellent biography of Bakhtin in *Comparative Literature*. Curiously, the Bakhtin I admire most—maybe it wasn't really Bakhtin!—is that of *The Formal Method in Literary Scholarship* (in fact a critique of formalism), which I reviewed earlier, in the same journal.

For the same reasons that I admire the clarity and logic of the formalists (incidentally, the Russian scholars always struck me as more lucid and elegant and a great deal less pretentious than the

194

I am very suspicious now of looking to history for a philosophical view of existence.

later French structuralists), I respect the work of Hempel and the "Anglo-Saxon" school—of which Ankersmit's already classic study seems to me to be a highpoint. I am very suspicious now, as I told you, of looking to history for a philosophical view of existence. Hayden White, I know, thinks that it always implies one. Although I do not deny that history is a practice that allows the articulation and refinement of values and understandings of the world (as does almost any cultural activity), I believe it is also a practice in which we exercise critical judgment. Above all, it is the practice of history, the discipline of researching specific historical questions and weighing evidence and arguments, that I think enriching and educative, rather than the study of history with a capital *H*. I also respect the kind of history practised by Malthus or Adam Smith or Montesquieu—who looked to history to support a better understanding of the way various aspects of social life, such as economics, politics, or demography, work and affect each other. That is probably not the kind of history I myself could ever do, but I think it is important that it be done. *Time on the Cross*, to which I refer in *Between History and Literature*, strikes me as an impressive recent example of that kind of history, despite (and in part because of) the interesting criticisms that it provoked. In other words, I am not dogmatic about the kind of history that can or should be done. The only kind I now have serious reservations about is the grand Hegelian to Spenglerian variety—though there, too, I have to admit that it is almost impossible for me to get rid of certain categories of thought that I have inherited from Hegel and Marx via Lukács. I need them. I question them and question the results they produce, but I acknowledge that I need them. I am not alone. Certain broad intellectual strategies have become the common inheritance of many scholars, and it is odd that the practical collapse of the only actual Marxist social experiment has not led to a more open discussion of the implications of that practical failure for theory.

You said that even if you cannot get rid of certain categories, you know that you need them. I think categories can play the role of a certain "point of view." They are like lenses through which one looks at reality or texts. Each epoch has some "master categories" and they are acceptable at a certain

time and in certain circumstances. There was a time when Marx was "on top." After the "linguistic turn" one of these master categories became metaphor. That was really a key word and it provided a completely new insight. Lastly, Franklin Ankersmit in an interview argued that the obsession with language and discourse is passé and we should change the subject. He himself opts for the category of experience. Isn't it fresh and inspiring? You yourself appreciate the role of categories in scientific research, but in your book *Between History and Literature* there is no such theoretical framework as White's tropology, for example.

Dear Ewa: I warned you I'm not a theorist and am not really happy discussing theoretical issues. I accept your understanding of "categories" as providing a point of view. I am less comfortable with the idea that these points of view simply change according to the age. As you say, Marx is now not "on top." Does that mean Marxian categories are unusable or unproductive? Why? I could see it if it was because people were genuinely no longer convinced of the heuristic value of Marxism, or if they felt that it had been disqualified by the practical failure of the Marxist experiment— though it is not clear, in my view, that the failure was *necessary*, that it would have happened had socialism been tried in a different context and had not had to get involved, in a relatively undeveloped country, in a ruinously expensive arms race. What does "on top" mean in intellectual and artistic matters? That "he who pays the piper calls the tune," as the English proverb has it?

Modern intellectuals are notoriously opportunistic. They love success—unlike poets, who cherish what is forgotten and no longer "on top." Formalism and structuralism are also no longer "on top" now, incidentally, but I find it hard to overlook the real insights that these "points of view" provided. I am not myself a strong enough philosophical "Kopf" to bring all the competing points of view together in a total, hierarchized system, but I am also not willing to give up points of view that seem to me to have value just because I cannot reconcile them with other points of view. That is a point I have probably made already. It is very important to me. I would rather live with loose ends, even contradiction, than sacrifice complexity to consistency, though I keep trying to achieve consistency and consider doing so an intellectual

I'm not a theorist.

Modern intellectuals are notoriously opportunistic.

I would rather live with loose ends, even contradiction, than sacrifice complexity to consistency.

196 obligation. I think I pointed out that one of the things that attracts me to the *historical* study of Basel (as distinct from any kind of *philosophical* study) is what I take to be the way in which that culture tried to accommodate opposing values and demands, constantly making fragile and transitory compromises and neither yielding to the demon of consistency at all costs (construction of a total theory or philosophy) nor sliding into complacent acceptance of multiple, uncommunicating "discourses" and spheres of knowledge and activity (complete renunciation of all synthetic ambition in favor of local empirical investigations). That is also why I am "between history and literature." If the book to which I gave that title formulates no consistent theoretical position, as you point out, that is not only because the essays in it were written at different times in my life when I had slightly different preoccupations (which I don't see as changing simply because fashions changed) but because I am more interested in the practice of criticism and the good life than in the theoretical definition of these. One needs theoretical reflection and theoretical categories, because a practice uninformed by them would not be a good practice. But one often has to carry out critical readings without having first elaborated a complete theory. Practical decisions (moral, financial, etc.) are made all the time in this way in everyday life. It doesn't often happen that the right decision is obvious in terms of some total, overarching theory. Usually there is a conflict of values and we have to negotiate that. I want to emphasize, however, that even though I am no theorist myself, I am not dogmatically opposed to theory. On the contrary, I admire work that I am incapable of myself and deplore the present tendency to denigrate theory. (Literary criticism and history alike would be immeasurably diminished without the self-consciousness that "practical" critics owe to those who think theoretically.) What I do not appreciate is what E. P. Thompson called "the tyranny of theory"—turning everything into a pretext for theory or an illustration of theory, and despising what is not theoretically interesting.

I am "between history and literature."

And what do you think of Ankersmit's proposed category of "experience"?

What Ankersmit calls "experience" corresponds *grosso modo* to what I call "literature" in the introduction to *Between History and*

Literature. It is obvious that I believe this category is essential, but I resist strongly its total penetration of history. The scholars I am presently studying (Bachofen and Burckhardt) are very close to the issues raised by Ankersmit: Bachofen's interest lies in pre-history, anthropology, myth; Burckhardt's in art. Both seem to want to arrest narrativity. I see this as closely related to their re-jection of Hegelian stories of historical progress—the core of "modernism." But I also believe their attempt to devise a kind of history that is not linear or narrative has an ideological basis in their own society and in their own position in that society. I cannot see it as "disinterested" or politically neutral. And, while I am sympa-thetic to their predicament, and not overly sanguine about some of the aspects of modernity that they disliked, I cannot share their undisguised hostility to the extension of culture and social bene-fits to wider strata of the population. Had Burckhardt and Bacho-fen had their way, we would not be having this interview. I, at least, would not be participating in it. I owe everything to the Scottish tradition of democratic education. I worry about what I see as the possible elitist implications of Frank's rejection of nar-rative in favor of "experience."

The search for a transcendence of shared linguistic or episte-mological categories and for some kind of unmediated "experi-ence" does seem to be a valuable and even indispensable correc-tive and criticism of established categories. It reminds us to be aware of the limitations of what passes for "knowledge." Dissatis-faction with established codes—seen not as facilitating but as ob-structing understanding—is as old as the romantics. Probably far older. At the colloquium at which Frank presented his paper here in Princeton, Natalie Davis recalled Svetlana Alpers's book and its argument that Dutch painting in its heyday had been an attempt to get beyond the pictorial rhetoric of the established Italian tra-dition to the "real." The history of the novel is also a history of re-peated attempts to transcend novelistic conventions. Every novel has been a "nouveau roman" in a way. Nietzsche's friend Franz Overbeck, professor of theology and church history at Basel, used to contrast religion and theology. Theology, he said, was "the Sa-tan of religion." Religion was the lived experience, theology the means by which that experience is institutionalized in categories borrowed from philosophy—and at the same time distorted and destroyed. Frank's category of historical "experience" seems to me

197

Hegelian stories of historical progress— the core of "modernism."

198

to be similar to Overbeck's category of religion. Of course, it is also a question whether there is such a thing as unmediated experience, whether even the Ur-experience is not already mediated by acquired categories. I seem to remember that Diderot has some very interesting ideas about this in his discussion of visual experience in the *Letter on the Blind*. Seeing, he argues (if I remember rightly), is a learned activity. One learns to see.

For myself, I am less despondent than Frank appears to be about the possibilities of historical knowing. I do not expect to have an "experience." I am not sure I even seek one. My own interest in history is primarily moral and political: I want to understand the nature of situations and choices better so that I can be a better human being and a better citizen. That sounds "corny," as we say in the United States (that is, trite and banal), but I believe it was essentially Burckhardt's objective, too. In any case, I accept rhetoric (and shared categories of thought and understanding) as still moderately effective. The simplest act of communication is a failure if one thinks that "my" unique meaning or experience has to pass via a common code in order to reach the other, because what the other receives via the common code would no longer be "my" meaning or experience, only what the common code could accommodate of it. But if one is willing to consider that the other already inhabits me, that "my" experience is not as autonomous and unmediated as is often believed but has already been shaped by the common and accumulated experience of society, maybe the chances of communication are a bit better (and likewise the chances of understanding the past). In other words, maybe the opposition of genius and routine, sublime insight and institutionalized understanding, is itself problematical. I, at least, am keenly sensitive to its possible ideological implications.

Moreover, the moment of communication with the past or of "experience" may itself depend on a massive amount of prior informational input. Audible language is unscrambled from an excess of audible information, but when we grasp what another person is saying, it seems to us that we do so immediately and we are hardly aware of the quite methodical sifting-through process that preceded that act of recognition. On the one hand, I realize that we can be "drowned" in chatter, as Overbeck complained—overwhelmed by information, by dead and sterile *Wissenschaft*. On the

I do not expect to have an "experience." I am not sure I even seek one.

My own interest in history is primarily moral and political.

other hand, it may also be through accumulation of information, 199
through "immersion" (to continue Overbeck's image), that we
achieve the kind of understanding of the other and of the past
that Frank now appears to favor. It isn't altogether clear what the
relation of acts of understanding or insight or decision is to the
information on which I believe they are necessarily based, but I
can't help thinking that we may not be right to make a big distinction between argument and experience. Moments of "experience" are probably not absent from the most erudite practice of
history, just as narrative and argument are probably indispensible
to "experience."

**Do you think that if such categories as "experience," the
"sublime," "memory," "consciousness," "to be between,"
etc. began to be considered as important concepts of our
understanding of the past, it means that we look to the
past because we cannot find ourselves in the present? Are
we faced with the destruction of values that were respected
in modern times?**

I am not convinced that we are faced with "the destruction of values" and that we are in a crisis of Western civilization. In certain
respects, the values of Western civilization (and we should be modest: some are values of not only Western civilization, but of other
civilizations, too) seem to me to be even more widely accepted
than ever. The current indignation over the ethnic cleansing and
the slaughter of civilians in Bosnia, or, to take a more trivial example, the shock and horror of the British in the face of the murder of a small boy by two other small boys, hardly much older—
these reactions indicate that people the world over still subscribe
to fairly traditional norms and share some basic common values.
In some cases—terrorists, for instance—it is partly an acute conflict of values that we are confronted with: that is why there are
always articles in our press trying to explain the position of Is-
lamic fundamentalists and so on. It is possible for us to understand the terrorists' position, even if we deplore it and think it
is wrong. More disturbing is the apparent breakdown of values
among fairly large segments of an alienated, culturally deprived,
and despairing population in many large cities in the West: the

200

random shooting (especially in the United States, where guns are readily available) and the general disregard for human life and suffering. This sort of breakdown is extremely disquieting. It may be more useful to think of it, however, not as a crisis of "Western civilization" but as a critical problem of our political economy and a consequence of our failure to acknowledge that free markets and consumer-oriented economics, with their emphasis on individual interest rather than the general welfare of the community, have undesirable results as well as desirable ones. As I believe it is possible to have values and to live humanly without ontological foundations or certainty, I am not inclined to look for the roots of problems in great philosophical or ideological changes—like desacralization, secularization, or relativism. Inevitably, one can always push the original crisis further back in history if one takes this view, from Nietzsche and Burckhardt to the Enlightenment, to the Renaissance itself (as Burckhardt himself did), to the waning of the Middle Ages and the realist-nominalist controversy, to the twelfth century, and so on and on back to the expulsion from the Garden of Eden. My own tendency is to try to situate these ideological changes and "crises" in specific social and economic conditions. These may produce extremely critical situations that people try to understand and respond to by conceptualizing them through categories elaborated by philosophy or theology. I do think there is an ideological vacuum right now, which has been provoked by the collapse of the only serious attempt we know of to realize socialism and by the simultaneous revelation that capitalism, too, has not resolved some basic problems concerning employment, community, work, ensuring that people are in a position to make responsible decisions, and so on. Neither the socialist success story nor the capitalist success story seems very convincing right now. A certain kind of nineteenth-century narrative, with which both capitalism and socialism are closely associated, now strikes us as unconvincing and unacceptable. That is what I understand by "postmodernism." I do not think all narrative is made redundant by this situation, but not all narrative—even in the nineteenth century—was progressivist and triumphalist. As I have tried to argue in various places, *history* is a word that covers many kinds of activities, carried out for many different purposes, and in widely differing institutional frameworks. Not all histories are histories of mankind or of nations and civilizations. Sometimes history is a

> I believe it is possible to have values and to live humanly without ontological foundations or certainty.

> There is an ideological vacuum right now.

way of approaching moral, political, legal, or economic—even demographic—problems and trying to improve our understanding of these. You might say that such works rest on the progressivist assumption that "we know better now." But that need not be the case. There seems to me no doubt that recent writing on the history of sexuality is largely inspired by a sense that our own thinking on this matter has not been so good and that we have much to learn from looking into what other societies and other times have thought and practiced. There is nothing progressivist or triumphalist about the work of Peter Brown on sexuality in the ancient world, for instance, or of Lawrence Stone on the history of the family.

To return to the issue of concreteness, when one says—as you do in a paper you e-mailed me—that the early nineteenth century was an epoch both of optimism and of despair and melancholy, it is important to me to define who exactly was optimistic and who was melancholic and who may not have been particularly one or the other. The epoch isn't anything (unless you believe in the *Zeitgeist* and such things). And to the degree that some people (Benjamin Constant, for instance) shared in both the optimism and the melancholy, one would have to try to account for that ambivalence, too, in some concrete way. Even the German propensity to construe the nineteenth century in terms of crisis—to which you rightly draw attention—needs to be explained. First, which groups precisely construed the age in this way, and were there contrary tendencies? Second, why was this crisis view of the world more widely shared in Germany (if indeed it was) than in England or France? You should take a look, on this topic, at a wonderful essay by Franco Moretti entitled "The Moment of Truth." In my own work on Burckhardt and Bachofen, I try to relate the "pessimism" of both, as you call it, to certain features of European culture and history and to specific features of the culture and history of Basel, as well as to Burckhardt's and Bachofen's place in that Basel culture and society.

What do you think postmodernism is (or was)?

I have a simple (probably oversimple) reply to that, but I have found that it clears the ground a good bit. I take modernism to be inseparable from the idea of progress and improvement. Not

I take modernism to be inseparable from the idea of progress and improvement.

202

necessarily in either artistic expression or moral conduct, but in understanding. The modern point of view, the most up-to-date point of view, embraces all those points of view that preceded it. Sometimes it is taken to be itself the end point of the process, sometimes as a point of view that will itself in time be embraced by a still more totalizing one. I take postmodernism to mark the end of all such narratives or myths of progress and of the belief that the universal or totality is either attainable or even desirable. The emphasis is on the fragmentary character of everything: history, society and the state, the work of art, the human individual. We cannot escape or deny our own experience or refuse to listen to the arguments of our fellows, and I personally have to concede that it is difficult to hold on to earlier beliefs about history and man (with capital H and capital M). But I continue to hope that a different kind of universality can be aimed at: a more modest one grounded on intersubjectivity rather than on objectivity. Richard Rorty, who has at times expressed a similar hope, has been accused of confining his vision of the world to the university, and even to the privileged universities of the East Coast of the United States, and of shutting his eyes to the harsher realities of the real world. I am vulnerable to the same sort of criticism (and considerably less capable of defending myself than Rorty). My belief, however, is intimately related to my professional life. As a teacher, a language teacher to boot, I am totally committed to creating conditions for mutual understanding and exchange of views. I cannot give that up and remain a teacher. Inevitably, my ideal bears some resemblance to the classroom as I try to make it.

> I take post-modernism to mark the end of all such narratives or myths of progress and of the belief that the universal or totality is either attainable or even desirable. The emphasis is on the fragmentary character of everything.

I think that postmodernism appeared in some way as a continuation of nineteenth-century pessimism and as an opposition to modernism. Modern culture was not able to respond in a satisfactory way to existential human needs. The process of "frustration" began in the middle of the nineteenth century. On the one hand, it was an epoch of progress, of industrialization. But on the other it was an epoch of despair, melancholy, and yearning for the sacral dimension of human existence. That frustration appeared in romanticism, in German idealism, and in the avant-garde. World wars and totalitarianism only postponed the "explosion" against the limitation of reason and science. Now this

pessimism, with the specific affirmation of man and "life," is back, under the mask of postmodernism.

When you say that "modern culture was not able to respond in a satisfactory way to existential human needs," I wonder what you are referring to. What "existential" human needs do you have in mind? And do you believe that these are universal? There has been a bewildering variety of social and cultural arrangements in the universe and none of them has been perfect. I feel I need to understand more specifically what the problem with "modern culture" is, as you see it, so that I can form a judgment as to whether it is more dire than the problems that have beset other cultures.

Just let me say right now that I don't see the emphasis on the universality of narrative as a return to myth, but almost as the opposite: it strikes me as a recognition of the necessity of a code for the production of a message. By making us conscious of the code, it also raises the question of its status, whether it can or should be modified, in what conditions, etc.

> I don't see the emphasis on the universality of narrative as a return to myth.

At the same time the philosophy of history took a "narrativist turn," historiography took an "anthropological turn." Could you please tell me what your opinion is of the most interesting trend in contemporary historical writing: anthropological history and *mentalité*. How do you find the works of such historians as Emmanuel Le Roy Ladurie, Carlo Ginzburg, Natalie Zemon Davis, and Simon Schama?

You ask me an embarrassing question. The truth is that I only occasionally read history books out of curiosity about the way history is written. Usually I turn to them when I want to know something specific or understand it better. In other words, I have a question, however vaguely defined. Right now, for instance, I am reading histories of Chinese studies in Germany because I am interested in the travel writings of an early-nineteenth-century Burckhardt who made the Hadj, or pilgrimage, to Mecca, and— more generally—in what happens to those individuals who immerse themselves in a foreign culture and act as go-betweens. I have read lots of histories of Near Eastern studies, books about Richard Burton, etc. But it happens that one of the more interesting examples of such persons is Richard Wilhelm—famous for

204

his translation and interpretation of the *I Ching*. So, to help me understand John Lewis Burckhardt I am reading up on Wilhelm and his work on China in the period just before and just after the First World War.

For myself, I do not have a great interest in simply knowing for its own sake how people in the past lived or thought or what their worldview or experience was. History isn't, for me, a form of aesthetic contemplation or exoticism. In some measure, my interest in history is political and ethical and I read history books in order to understand better the conditions in which other people at other times responded to ethical and cultural problems. I guess what I hope is that by finding out how such problems presented themselves in other times and situations, I will be able to deal with them myself more thoughtfully and with more understanding than I might if I remained confined to the ideas and categories of my own present. History, for me, is a way of freeing myself from the limitations (and the self-sufficiency) of the present. The situations in which problems present themselves are economic, social, and in some measure "anthropological" (*mentalités* and long-term social structures). Historians are rightly more aware nowadays of those "anthropological" contexts, of *longue durée*, if you like, than they used to be, but recognizing the importance of structures need not and should not mean disregarding the significance of particular acts, events, and decisions. Acts, events, decisions take place within a structure, but the structure itself evolves, in some measure at least, in response to those acts, events, and decisions as well as in response to outside influences. *Parole* (in the terminology of Saussure) is as intrinsically worthy of study, in my view, as *langue* and isn't adequately understood merely as a manifestation or actualization of *langue*.

But it's true that I sometimes expect other things from the reading of history. Goethe observed in the *Materialen zur Geschichte der Farbenlehre* that "[e]very good book is understandable and enjoyable only by the reader who can supplement it. He who already has knowledge will find infinitely more than he who goes only to learn." Goethe's own translation of Diderot's *Essay on Painting* is an example of what he means. The translation is interspersed with comments, arguments, questions. It is a real dialogue. Historians engage with other historians in such a dialogue when they read each other's books and articles. But it's possible

I read history books in order to understand better the conditions in which other people at other times responded to ethical and cultural problems.

History, for me, is a way of freeing myself from the limitations of the present.

to engage with certain works of history not so much in a scientific or scholarly manner as in the way one engages with works of general literature, including fictions; that is, in order to have our moral values and our views of the world challenged, enriched, and refined. Often the historical works that we engage with in this way are old, no longer up-to-date in terms of contemporary practices of history, and not likely therefore to provoke and challenge a professional historian, but of course even books that do challenge the professional historian in a scholarly way can be read for their more general value as literary works. My own reading of Gibbon and Burckhardt has been directed much more toward general wisdom and understanding than toward specifically historical understanding or knowledge. It wasn't as histories of the late Empire that the *Decline and Fall* and the *Age of Constantine the Great* engaged my attention, but for the sake of the vision of life they offer.

There is another way of reading. Historians sometimes read literary texts, not to engage with them on their own terms, but for what they can extract from them that is relevant to historical arguments. And literary readers like myself tend to read historical works not to engage with them in the investigation of a historical problem, but for the light they can shed on literary or philosophical texts. To achieve a fuller understanding of such texts, we often feel we have to contextualize them — and to do that we address ourselves to historians. For my work on Bachofen, Burckhardt, and Overbeck, I read all kinds of wonderful historical works that are hardly known outside of Basel. One is a company history of the Geigy chemical company. It is one of the most exciting social and economic history books I've ever read, but it strikes me that way chiefly because it provided answers to many of my questions and helped me situate contextually the texts I was really interested in. My reading of the history of sinology — to which I already referred — is similarly oriented toward the elucidation of texts that I am presently working on.

To some extent, the historians you mention are "writers" as much as historians — as, in fact, most historians in the past also were. They want to communicate a worldview and an ethical stance at least as much as an argument about a specific historical problem. (In that sense they are, perhaps consciously, historians in Hayden White's sense.) Most people read Foucault in this way,

My own reading of Gibbon and Burckhardt has been directed much more toward general wisdom and understanding than toward specifically historical understanding or knowledge.

206

I don't know
whether readers
really trust Fou-
cault as a historian.

for instance. I don't know whether readers really trust him as a historian; chiefly, I think they read him as a thinker who writes about
problems with an acute awareness of how they have emerged or
been constructed and framed—as someone who proposes large
hypotheses that historians then work empirically to support, re-
fute, or reformulate.

What all this reveals, I'm afraid, is that I am not properly a
historian. I do not pursue historical knowledge for itself; I want it
either as a guide to reflection about political and ethical problems
or as a help in reading texts from which I can derive something
that is more important to me than knowledge of historical objects.
I don't think one should dichotomize *Wissenschaft* and *Bildung*,
but I have no doubt that what counts most for me is *Bildung*.

What counts most
for me is *Bildung*.

Is there a crisis in historical thought?

History seems to be especially implicated in the move from modernism to postmodernism, as described above. To a large extent,
history, as defined by the great bourgeois historians of the nineteenth century, institutionalized in academies and universities, and
integrated into the curriculum of schools and colleges, reflected
the view that the present time has an advantage over the past in
that it can embrace it in a totalizing vision. There seems not much
doubt that this view and use of history is closely related to the
ideological justification of the post-Revolutionary regimes, as well
as of European imperialism. Is a "postmodern" history possible?
Why not? History was not always triumphalist and progressivist.
But perhaps a postmodern history cannot expect to occupy the
central place that history occupied in the thinking and the school
curricula of the nineteenth century. On the other hand, history is
not likely to be displaced as a means of questioning the existent
or, more modestly, of investigating and getting a better understanding of political, economic, and social behavior.

Is a "postmodern"
history possible?
Why not?

What is the difference between history and literature
(if there is any)?

Again I've addressed this question in "Toward a Rational Historiography" in *Between History and Literature*. I think there is a
difference. At one time history was a genre within the vast field of

literature. Marc Fumaroli's magnificent study of rhetoric in the Renaissance and classical periods, *L'Age de l'eloquence*, makes abundantly clear how much the notion of literature has been narrowed since the romantics. Still, we need to recognize that a good deal of the old connection survives. Every piece of writing is "literary" if we allow the "literary" to cover rhetoric as well as poetics: philosophy and politics and even science, no less perhaps than history. But once we do that, we have to begin discriminating among rhetorics. I take rhetoric in its broad sense, as a mode of argumentation, rather than in its narrow sense, as mere ornament or a set of devices to win over or even delude the reader. It is possible and useful to distinguish between the different kinds and levels of argumentation appropriate to different kinds of subject matter and rhetorical situation, as Stephen Toulmin has done in a remarkably fine college textbook entitled *An Introduction to Reasoning*. Historians are, in my view, subject to the constraints of the rhetoric (that is, the laws of argumentation) that has evolved over time and been generally accepted for historical discourse. Writers of fiction are not. A clever literary mystification, like Hildesheimer's *Marbot* (which presents itself as the biography of a "real" historical figure) can highlight the conventional character of our rhetorics, and it is important to be reminded of that, but it does not do away with the need for them or lessen their value.

> I take rhetoric in its broad sense, as a mode of argumentation.

What about truth in history?

I feel like responding with another question. What about truth in biology or astronomy or physics? Perhaps the natural sciences are less affected by ideology than history, but they are affected. Yet they do not renounce and we do not expect them to renounce the elaborate codes of investigation and verification they have evolved to establish "truth." The "truth" of history rests on codes, and it is not, any more than the natural sciences, a mirror image or simple representation of what is "really" out there. But that does not mean that "truth" in history is a meaningless or useless concept.

> The "truth" of history rests on codes.

History teaches us that only heretics can become classic authors. Who among contemporary "heretics" are going to be classics?

Who are the
heretics?

Who are the heretics? It's the same problem, I suspect, as that of the avant-garde in art and literature. The "heretics" are pretty established, if you mean historians like Carlo Ginzburg and Michel Foucault. So, at the risk of being wide of the mark, and not having understood your intention, here are some works that strike me as likely to endure and become classics of historiography: Ginzburg's *The Cheese and the Worms*, Braudel's *The Mediterranean*, Foucault's *Discipline and Punish*, E. P. Thompson's *The Making of the English Working Class*, Eugene Genovese's *Roll, Jordan, Roll*, perhaps Ariès's *Centuries of Childhood* and Peter Laslett's *The World We Have Lost*. One could easily add more titles to that list. All these works are well written, usually with some literary flair, not just a pleasant style; they have all left a mark and are all much referred to, and they all present a large vision of society and culture. None, you will note, is particularly technical. My hunch is that the essential contribution of those works that are chiefly technical will have been simply absorbed into the general knowledge of the historical profession. That is why I have not listed a truly major work such as Labrousse's *La Crise de l'économie française à la fin de l'ancien régime*. In fact, a lot of history writing is being done these days in the manner of Ginzburg and Foucault. But that in itself will not guarantee classic status.

A lot of history
writing is being
done these days in
the manner of
Ginzburg and
Foucault.

What is your conception of history?

I take it that you mean historical works. I move between two conceptions of history: the one contributes to practical knowledge and is a narrative explanation of how specific things came to be as they are; that knowledge may strive for "scientific" formulation in the form of laws of the social world, as in Adam Smith or Malthus. The other conception of history that I have is closer to literature. Inasmuch as historical texts invite further research, they are sooner or later superseded by texts that provide a more comprehensive or satisfactory explanation of the situation under investigation. But many historical texts may be used like literary texts—to arouse our imagination and sympathy, to make us think of things in different ways, to revise our perceptions of the world and of human relations. Conceivably, historical texts could function in both ways at the same time—i.e., as both *Wissenschaft* and *Bildung*. I suspect that the best ones regularly do.

Many historical
texts may be used
like literary texts—
to arouse our
imagination and
sympathy.

LIONEL GOSSMAN

How can one predict the future of humanistic disciplines?

This is the hardest question of any you have asked so far. I have
very little sense of how things will move now. A lot will depend on
the future of our cultural and educational institutions (universities, academies, etc.) because institutional frameworks radically
affect the character of reflection in my view. To me, the essential
question will remain the relation of *Bildung* and *Wissenschaft* in
the various studies we call humanistic. I do not believe it is a matter of choosing between them, but of relative weight. The bottom
line for me has always been *Bildung*. *Wissenschaft* is necessary for
Bildung. The goal is not knowledge but the good life, not theory
but practice.

> The goal is not knowledge but the good life, not theory but practice.

There is a constant danger, especially nowadays, that *Wissenschaft* will become an end in itself, or that *Bildung* (in the sense
now simply of forming or indoctrinating) will become detached
from *Wissenschaft*. I am not a scientist and I don't know how or
whether such problems arise in the sciences, but in the humanities I believe it is crucial that we neither lose sight of the ultimate
goal and justification of our research (the improvement of each individual's life and of the life of the community) nor hold that goal
so close to our face that we become narrow and didactic. As usual,
then, I find myself having to reconcile different objectives, each of
which must, in my view, enjoy a considerable autonomy. I think
of Goethe's descriptions in the *Italienische Reise*—at once totally
respectful of the object and directly related to the subject. I am
an unreconstructed humanist, I guess. My goals are still those of
the German classical writers. They provide the framework in which
I see the future of the humanistic disciplines—as I would like it
to be, at least.

> My goals are still those of the German classical writers. They provide the framework in which I see the future of the humanistic disciplines— as I would like it to be, at least.

The problem is how to make that vision compatible with democracy, popular education, and the great variety of human pop-
ulations, cultures, and traditions. For in the age of German classicism it was an elitist vision. I do not feel optimistic about how
that is to be achieved.

E-Mailed interview,
30 December 1993 to 13 May 1994

SELECTED WRITINGS

The Empire Unpossessed: An Essay on Gibbon's Decline and Fall. New York: Cambridge Univ. Press, 1981.

Orpheus Philologus: Bachofen versus Mommsen on the Study of Antiquity. Philadelphia: American Philosophical Society, 1983. Transactions of the American Philosophical Society, part 5, 73.

Between History and Literature. Cambridge: Harvard Univ. Press, 1990.

Geneva-Zurich-Basel: History, Culture, and National Identity, co-editor with Nicolas Bouvier and Gordon Craig. Introduction by Carl Schorske. Princeton: Princeton Univ. Press, 1994.

"Basle, Bachofen and the Critique of Modernity in the Second Half of the Nineteenth Century." *Journal of the Warburg and Courtauld Institutes* 67 (1984): 136–85.

"Burckhardt as Art Historian." *Oxford Art Journal* 11 (1988): 25–32.

"Overbeck, Bachofen und die Kritik der Moderne." In *Franz Overbecks unerledigte Anfragen an das Christentum*, ed. Rudolf Brandle and Ekkehaed W. Stegemann, 17–46. München: Chr. Kaiser, 1988.

"Antimodernism in Nineteenth-Century Basle: Franz Overbeck's Antitheology and J. J. Bachofen's Antiphilology." *Interpretation: A Journal of Political Thought* 16 (1989): 358–89.

"The Two Cultures in Nineteenth-Century Basle: Between the French Encyclopédie and German Neohumanism." *Journal of European Studies* 20 (1990): 95–133.

"Cultural History and Crisis: Burckhardt's *Civilization of the Renaissance in Italy*." In *Rediscovering History: Culture, Politics, and the Psyche*, ed. Michael S. Roth, 404–27. Stanford: Stanford Univ. Press, 1994.

"History and the Study of Literature." *Profession* (MLA) 94 (1994): 26–33.

Peter Burke

*From time to time historians
need to be shocked.*

How did you become interested in history?

■ When I was a small child I already thought I was going to be a
professor of history. I was a child in the Second World War. I played
soldiers. When the war was over and I couldn't have English fighting Germans, I started to fight historical battles. So, in fact—this
sounds very funny—I came into history through military history
as a hobby and then I read history at university and discovered
more kinds of history. Maybe the most exciting moment, when I
was a student at Oxford, was looking to see the options available
for special subjects. Every student of history at Oxford must take a
special subject in greater depth. Most of them were political, and
I suddenly realized I didn't want to do this. Politics was not the
activity I was most interested in. I wanted to write the history of
activities that I would like to participate in myself. The only special subject where you could write about art was the Italian Renaissance. So, I learned Italian, went to Italy, and studied that
special subject. Thus I got into cultural history and in some sense
I've stayed there.

I came into history
through military
history as a hobby.

Which historian could you describe as a model for you?

I'm a little suspicious of taking any one historian as a model. I
could easily name six or a dozen historians who have been very

212   important for me. And they would be very different. They would
include Burckhardt and Braudel, Warburg, Huizinga, also Ginzburg and Le Roy Ladurie. So, it would be a funny mixture of historians from whom I've taken maybe different things, which I'm
trying to combine to make my own synthesis.

**Which of the contemporary philosophers has most influ-
enced you?**

Wittgenstein is definitely the philosopher that influenced me most.
But if you mean someone still alive, I think, yes . . . Paul Ricoeur.

**Foucault in one of his interviews said that each of his works
has a biographical background. Do you think that events
from your life influenced your writing?**

I don't think that my books are as autobiographical as Foucault's
books. Maybe that's a weakness. I have often envied people who
are so passionately involved with the subject: so that there is only
one book they could write at a particular moment. Berlin's distinction between hedgehogs and foxes is very nice. I'm a fox, definitely, who at any one point could write maybe ten different books.
I just have to decide which research I will do because all these
things are equally interesting to me.

I think every work of history has got some autobiographical
background. If you don't feel at all involved in something, how
could you write about it? You don't have to love it—you can hate
it. One of my teachers—Hugh Trevor-Roper—has a very curious
capacity. He only writes well about what he hates. He started with
Archbishop Laud, then Hitler, then the Scots. He writes brilliantly
and savagely from outside about these people, but penetratingly.

**Cultural history, which appeals to you most, is not a new
mode of historical writing but at present it seems to have a
new spirit under the influence of anthropology. What kind
of features can you mention as characteristic of this new
cultural history?**

My general picture is that people began to think of cultural history as a separate kind of history in the late eighteenth century.
Then for the whole of the nineteenth century and the early twentieth century we had this classic cultural history of Burckhardt and

Huizinga and so on. Then in the 1960s and 1970s, there is the first change, the shift toward popular culture. So, instead of culture being viewed as something that belongs to elites, now everyone is seen to have a culture. And to put it geographically—it isn't only Western civilization that has culture, but everywhere else, too—they have cultures in the plural.

Maybe even more interesting is a later shift. This is more in the 1980s, when cultural history expanded not only to include more social groups, but also more kinds of activity, so that a cultural historian—or maybe one would say a sociocultural historian, because that's another common phrase now—is concerned with everyday life. And then of course, the problem arises: is this different from social history? But I think it can be, if one is interested in the rules of everyday life, the unspoken rules in a particular place and time; how to behave. What used to be the history of arts and literature has expanded in this fascinating and sometimes frightening way. I said frightening or bewildering, because it's raising all sorts of new problems that we collectively, the new historians interested in the new cultural history, are only just beginning to deal with.

In a review of two books, *The New Cultural History*, edited by Lynn Hunt, and *Interpretation and Cultural History*, edited by Joan H. Pittock and Andrew Wear, Laurie Nussdorfer suggested that perhaps there is no field called cultural history, but perhaps what there actually is are historians working in a "cultural mode." What is your opinion?

I don't think that there is now a field called "cultural history" with a subject matter that is distinct from others. This was true for the classic cultural history of Burckhardt and Huizinga. And it became untrue with this wide meaning of the concept of culture to include practices, representations, and so on. So, then if it's useful to define a field of cultural history separate from and opposed to a field of social history, then I think one has to do it in terms of approach. If one is particularly interested in the symbolic, for example, when one is looking at social life, then one may call oneself a cultural historian. When one is looking at exactly the same sources but from a different perspective—social change—then one may call oneself a social historian. Maybe this is good. It means that the distinctions between these subdisciplines are much weaker

I don't think that there is now a field called "cultural history" with a subject matter that is distinct from others.

I don't like fields
with fences
around them.

What you have to
find are methods
appropriate to
problems.

now than they used to be. And of course it means it's easier to move across from one to the other. I don't like fields with fences around them.

I don't believe that so many disciplines have their own methods. I think what you have to find are methods appropriate to problems. So, one doesn't say: "Because I'm an art historian I'm not going to do this." If the problem is to understand the iconography of this painting, whoever one is, wherever one's training, then there are certain things one has to do.

How do you place these similar subdisciplines—cultural history, history from below, anthropological history, and intellectual history?

They are all different but they overlap. They overlap but they don't coincide.

I usually use the term *intellectual history* in a relatively precise sense to mean the history of ideas. Originally the history of ideas was the history of the ideas of important people. Then it widened into being the history of everyone's ideas. If one goes along that line, it begins to be more and more like cultural history except that cultural history is not only concerned with ideas but with forms, the way in which people eat, whether they exercise a great deal of self-control, so that one is writing much more the history of practices than the history of ideas. So, intellectual history and cultural history overlap, but the differences are still clear.

Historical anthropology—this I think goes very well with the second shift, to make so many more aspects of behavior than before part of cultural history. It turned out that this was what anthropologists have been doing, for generations. That is, they were looking for the principles behind the differences in customs that by coming from one culture and living in another they instantly saw. And so at some point, various historians, independently in France, in England, and in the United States, recognized the value to their work of some of the concepts that the anthropologists were using. The example I know best, because it's my local example, is the man who taught me at Oxford—Keith Thomas. Thomas had been in another Oxford college—All Souls—with Sir Edward Evans-Pritchard, who was—unusually for his generation—a British anthropologist who believed in history. Most of his generation were structural functionalists who said: "We don't need to know about the past." Evans-Pritchard communicated this sense of the interdependence of history and anthropology to Keith Thomas. Meanwhile in France, Le Goff and Le Roy Ladurie were discovering a different anthropology, French style, Lévi-Straussian-style, Maussian-style. At the same time in the United States, where we find another kind of anthropology—cultural anthropology—other historians were involved. The convergence suggests this is not just a passing fashion, but something that is really necessary.

Why do cultural historians mostly concentrate their research on the early modern period?

I think there is also some very interesting cultural history of the Middle Ages being written, and maybe also of ancient Rome, maybe Greece, too. Maybe not so much the nineteenth and twentieth centuries.

If one wishes to write this new kind of sociocultural history, it's much easier if you take an age when the assumptions are very different from ours. The greater the cultural distance, the easier to recognize that cultural distance. And the problem with the nineteenth and twentieth centuries is that they are too near. Maybe then the great challenge for sociocultural historians is going to be to try to study less remote periods, using the same techniques.

Do you think that cultural history gives better insights into culture than traditional history?

Yes. And I also believe very much in learning from the social sciences. I go and study anthropology, sociology, and so on. But if possible I want to draw on those insights and express them without using the technical vocabulary that all these people themselves have used. One of the tests whether a theory is a good theory, is whether one can translate it out of the technical language and it still makes sense.

One of the tests whether a theory is a good theory, is whether one can translate it out of the technical language and it still makes sense.

Hayden White in *Metahistory* wrote about history's golden age in the nineteenth century, about the "reconstitution of history as a form of intellectual activity which is at once poetic, scientific, and philosophical in its concerns."

216   In the 1950s and 1960s, philosophy of history was marked by a "fetish of method" concerning historical explanation. The "narrative turn" in philosophy of history was partly a reaction against this dehumanization of history. However, during the last twenty years, the theory of history has shifted toward literary criticism, while historiography has focused on social history. So, historiography and its philosophy seem quite far from each other.

When I read the philosophy of history that one read in Oxford in the early 1960s—that is, one read Hempel, one read Dray, one read Gardiner, and so on—I found it very hard to understand why they were discussing what they were discussing, because it seems to me they had a picture of what historians were doing, which was what historians had been doing in 1900 or earlier, but had nothing to do with the historians I knew. It was not addressing the questions of economic history or social history. It was still philosophizing about history as if history was a narrative of political events and nothing else. Now, I'm not so sure. I think there are much clearer connections between philosophy of history and the practice of history. The existence of somebody like White, who is not easy to categorize—is he in philosophy; is he in literature; is he in history?—shows that the contacts are much stronger now.

What is your opinion about Hayden White's _Metahistory_ and about the narrativist philosophy of history?

I remember reading articles by Louis O. Mink about the way in which explanation is built into narrative. Not that telling any kind of story answers the big questions. But some big questions are most satisfactorily answered by writing a certain kind of narrative. Hayden White made much more impact. This is something to do with the way he writes, but he is also saying something a bit different from Mink, because he is more interested in the rhetoric of different kinds of narrative.

What I found most exciting when I read _Metahistory_—which I did with a totally open mind because I was sent the book to review at a time when I'd never heard of the author. So, I just picked this thing up, read it, and reacted to it. What I found most fascinating was this concern with the plots. Unfortunately, White never

What I found
most fascinating
was this concern
with the plots.

discusses the question of whether these plots are conscious or unconscious. Ranke, Burckhardt, and Michelet have these basic plots
in their heads, and they are looking for the period and the problem
that will enable them to reenact that plot that is their favorite. For
some historians, I found this tremendously convincing. I thought
the chapter on Ranke in particular was wonderful. But I also
thought that the book, as a whole, is too schematic. I am very interested in Burckhardt. I don't think that he can be reduced to the
aspects that White stressed. Burckhardt has a bit of all the techniques and a bit of all the attitudes. Maybe he is more ironic than
anything. I certainly wouldn't describe him as principally a satiric
kind of historian. But still, White saw some things that other
people hadn't seen very clearly and I think that maybe by exag-
gerating them he provoked people, and it was good because from
time to time historians need to be shocked, because only in that
case will they reexamine some of their assumptions.

From time to time
historians need to
be shocked.

**But do you think that the "narrative turn" can also be
observed in historiography, or is it just a philosophical
phenomenon?**

I think we can also observe this turn in historical writing. What I
am not so sure about is whether the philosophical movement and
the historical movement are deeply connected.

From maybe the mid-1970s, maybe a little earlier, the kind
of historian who had previously rejected narrative of events—
especially, but not exclusively, French historians associated with
Annales and the social historians of *Past and Present* as well—
they rediscovered narrative. And why did they rediscover narrative
at this time? That has something to do with the reaction against
determinism and the feeling that these big models, world systems, and so on, were leaving out too much of historical reality.
You used the term *narrative turn*, that's fine. Some people talk
of *revival of narrative*. I'm less happy with this, because I think
that the narrative they turned to was not exactly the same as the
kind of narrative against which they—or the generation before—
had reacted.

Maybe one of the most interesting features of historical writing in the last twenty years has been the search for new kinds of
narrative that will do a more complete explanatory job than the

218

old narratives of political events ever did. There could be a connection between the philosophical movement and the historical. I'm reluctant to commit myself because I'm wondering how many of the historians we think of when we think of this "narrative turn," how many of them were familiar with the philosophers at the time when they first experimented with the new methods. I'm sure that not all of them were; maybe some of them were. So, again as with the discovery of historical anthropology in different countries, I think we have different groups of people moving in the same direction without knowing one another. Maybe that shows how they are reacting to something in late-twentieth-century culture. Imagine how the cultural historians of the twenty-first century trying to write about the late-twentieth-century will see this.

We have different groups of people moving in the same direction without knowing one another.

Generally speaking, historians are very skeptical of this interest in narrative. They fear it may transform history into a myth or fiction.

I think we have three groups now. In England at least there are still plenty of really traditional historians who always wrote narrative and never thought of anything else. So, for them this idea of a "narrative turn" is totally meaningless and they don't know what's going on. They are not interested.

Then there is the second group that reacted against the first group and decided they would write economic and social history; they would write the history of structures; they would not bother with events. And some of them are still resisting, while others are tempted. I think the article by Lawrence Stone from the late 1970s, "Revival of Narrative," is a fascinating study in ambivalence, because in some ways he likes what he sees and in the other ways he hates what he sees. He has got this mixture of attitudes. He was never happy with Marxist determinism. His friends were Marxists. He wasn't a Marxist. So, he likes that liberation from determinism but he feels too much has been thrown out. He is still interested in the structures and he feels that some of these narrative historians lost interest. They just want to tell stories about individuals, which I think can be a cop-out from studying the historical process in which we are all involved. I think that this is very clear in the case of microhistory. For some people, microhistory is an easy way out. It's an easy way out technically. You just

For some people microhistory is an easy way out.

find the story in the archives, you serve it up, you comment, and it's easy to sell. Easier to sell than if you'd written a study of family structure or whatever. But for a few microhistorians—for Giovanni Levi, for Hans Medick—microhistory is much more ambitious and much more difficult because it raises the philosophical question of whether historical explanations need to be different when you are working on different scales—the microscopic level or the macroscopic level. I don't think they have solved these problems, but it's fascinating to see them working through them. I think this is one of the most important and exciting intellectual shifts in historical writing in the last few years.

Do you think that the new cultural history—I am thinking here especially of anthropological history—can be regarded as a manifestation or symptom of postmodernism in historical writing?

I have to think about this, because I have to decide whether I really believe in postmodernism.

As an intellectual historian I've been interested in the concept of modernity and I know that it has been in existence from the late classical period onward. But in every century, people have meant something different by it. One of the strategies of using the word *modernity* is to say that the generation we are living in is the really important one and that we are making a big break from the past. So, from my point of view as a cultural historian of the sixteenth and seventeenth centuries, postmodernism is simply a version of the modernity debate, using the same strategy in a more exaggerated form. Now people say we are postmodern and I begin to wonder who will be the post-postmoderns!

If we consider the strong thesis—that is, that we are entering a major new period of history since, maybe, 1980—then I'm very skeptical. But if we are talking about a trend in the history of ideas, among lots of other interesting trends, this is certainly an interesting trend of the late twentieth century. Lyotard illustrates this very nicely with his reaction against grand narrative. Derrida illustrates it very nicely with the desire to deconstruct all fixed categories. There is this sense of fluidity. I am less sure whether that kind of change would justify our saying that we are living in a totally new period—a cultural historian simply feels we've been through this so many times before.

I have to decide whether I really believe in postmodernism.

Postmodernism is simply a version of the modernity debate, using the same strategy in a more exaggerated form.

Leaving the big claim on one side, there are still interesting changes in attitude now, of which maybe I would single out, because it is terribly important for cultural history, this movement with various names like constructionism, constructivism. That is, we no longer think of society as something fixed and something outside us, but we think of it to some degree as something people invent. It used to be part of social history. It's become part of cultural history, and this all goes with a reaction against determinism. So, an intellectual trend of maybe post-1968, a rejection of Marxism, a rejection of structuralism, a rejection of functionalism, all because these were thought of as too deterministic.

Personally, I think this reaction has gone too far, and that people talk about, let's say the invention of Scotland or whatever, without thinking about the problem: are people free to invent any nation, any social group, they want? Are there no external constraints? I think this is a question that we have to think about very seriously in the next ten years.

I think that it was good to have this movement because the determinism was exaggerated. But we have to find some way of talking about both imaginative freedom and social constraints.

Postmodernism did not seduce you . . . ?

I'm fascinated by it, but I still feel somewhat detached from it. I think that there is a claim being made that the last twenty or thirty years is a totally new historical age, and I'm still not convinced that this is the case. I do agree that there have been some important new intellectual trends, but this is true in most generations for the last two hundred years or longer. So, in that sense I remain a bit skeptical of the larger claims that the postmodernists make. I am very interested in the lesser claims—the claims about the fluidity of all categories and constructions. I find that part more convincing. But it is not something that is being said absolutely for the first time. It's just that more emphasis is put on it now. One could also find thinkers of other periods who have been impressed by the way in which we construct the world.

I agree that there is nothing new in postmodernism.
Generally I consider postmodernism a continuation of

nineteenth-century philosophy through its connection with German idealism and the nineteenth-century way of writing about history. These ideas are used in a different way: they are put in a new context that makes them fresh. But postmodernism reflects a change of mentality. A shift toward ordinariness, commonness, and provincialism that has a completely new sense. History is probably the discipline best placed to legitimize this "transfiguration of the commonplace."

It might be, but there is always the possibility that it will subvert it. It's very interesting in England. There has been this debate on Victorian values because Mrs. Thatcher launched this phrase. Then the historians of the nineteenth century started to examine Victorian values, but they didn't find exactly what Mrs. Thatcher would have liked them to find. An appeal was made to history to legitimate a certain kind of return to tradition, but in fact the historians subverted it.

My sense is that there have been three epochs in the West, at least in a sense of three kinds of attitudes to the past. First the idea that the past was like the present; it goes back a long way but it's fundamentally the same. Then, from the Renaissance on, the past is viewed as different from us in important ways. If you like, the past is a foreign country, though not so far away that we can't understand it. Now, in the last few generations, especially with younger people, there is the view that the past is utterly remote. Anything before their own birth is as remote as the planet Mars. This generation is not impressed by your kind of argument.

Now in the last few generations there is the view that the past is utterly remote.

Anyway, I still think it's possible to learn from history, although someone said that we learn from history that people don't learn from history.

Someone said that we learn from history that people don't learn from history.

What is the task of history at present? Is there a new one?

I don't think there is "a new task," but there is an increasingly urgent task, which is to make sense of our rapidly changing culture. It's not just the economy or society that's changing. It's our culture that's changing. Maybe it cannot be summed up in a sentence but one of the most important changes is this globalization of culture that goes with awareness of different subcultures in each

An increasingly urgent task of history—to make sense of our rapidly changing culture.

222 place. So, there is an interest in cultural contact, cultural exchange, or, to use more negative terms, cultural invasion or cultural clash. And this is so pressing in our present world and it's going to be extremely important in the immediate future. I cannot see any other way of comprehending it than by cooperation with cultural historians.

You said that our culture is changing. Will you please say more about it.

Well, I think that the national cultures and the class cultures inside which people used to manage to live are dissolving. Some people like this; some people are frightened by it. Whatever they think, it's going to continue to happen. The physical migration of so many groups within Europe or outside Europe to other places brings with it this kind of cultural contact, encounter, clash, and so on. It's very clear of course in my country, where people have only recently become conscious of what they should have become conscious of twenty or thirty years ago: the cultural effects of the immigration of Asians and Africans in the 1950s. Whether we accept it or not, we are a multicultural society. We have to spend much more time to understand English culture now. You need the Koran as well as the Bible. In that kind of world, the cultural historian really does have a lot to do.

You need the Koran as well as the Bible. In that kind of world, the cultural historian really does have a lot to do.

But this change reflects a changing mentality. Already in the 1970s, many scholars, for example Daniel Bell, wrote about returning to the mythical base of culture. It is manifested in a special interest in magic, astrology, natural medicines, and so on.

I think there is an increasing disillusionment with a certain intellectual model, a kind of rational scientific model, which promised to bring certain social changes with it, which it didn't altogether. And so, rightly or wrongly, or for better or worse, many people are reacting against this. How serious this revival of magic is, I find it hard to decide, and it may be very different if one is talking about London or if one is taking about Los Angeles. I think that in England, people are playing with these ideas more than taking them a hundred percent seriously. You meet people who like to say: "I'm a witch, I'm a wizard, I'm a believer in paganism."

That doesn't mean much more than they are dissatisfied with atheism and Christianity.

Tell me what you think of the new history written by, for example, Le Roy Ladurie, Ginzburg, Darnton? How do you explain the interest in this kind of history?

There are two questions here. How am I reacting to this work and how am I reacting to the reactions to this work. First of all there is the post-1968 or whatever reaction against determinism, the discovery of the people, and so on. That was the first of the two characteristics I was talking about in the case of the new cultural history. My guess would be that this is what has really appealed to the readers, besides the fact that all three men write very well, they are brilliant historical writers—it's a different point from doing original research, which they also do, but they communicate wonderfully. Beyond that, it's the history-from-below attitude. So, ordinary readers can identify with ordinary people and at last somebody is talking about history that is like their own lives. The history of a village, the history of a miller, the history of some apprentices in a printing workshop in Paris. It's so much more immediate than what was going on in the cabinet or the tactics at the battle of Waterloo. What I think I'm suggesting is that it is not so much its location in a new cultural history but its location in history from below that makes people so enthusiastic for those three books.

> Ordinary readers can identify with ordinary people and at last somebody is talking about history which is like their own lives.

Are they popular because they show a counterimage of our own culture and society?

I think every change in the history of historical writing needs to be looked at from two points of view, internalist and externalist. I think that no important change would take place if there was not both an internal and an external explanation. I have already said a little about why the reading public, that is the people who are not professional historians, find microhistory more accessible and fascinating.

Usually the microhistorians have their place on the Left, at least in the sense that they are populists; they want ordinary people to read them. They are positive about ordinary people. If one were very conservative or elitist one wouldn't be wanting to do it. But I want also to emphasize that microhistory was something that was needed by the whole discipline at that particular point. That is, it arose out of a dissatisfaction with some dominant models of explanation of a macrohistorical kind. By the late 1960s, early '70s lots of us were seeing weaknesses in structural history. Microhistory, therefore, has got this technical aspect. In the case of Ginzburg, the two sides come together very neatly. He is passionately interested in the recent past of his subject and he was, if not a Marxist, at least sympathetic to Gramsci, and he really wanted to communicate to ordinary people. So, for him the choice was simple—he satisfied all these needs in one book. Of course he was lucky enough, or clever enough, to find a wonderful source in the archives.

Well, they also convince us that—as Barbara Hanawalt and Luise White in their review of Simon Schama's *Dead Certainties* put it—"history is a damn hard way to write fiction."

It's a nice phrase. Yes, history is the most difficult way of writing fiction, because there are all the problems of narrative that the novelist has but in addition there is the problem of relating what one is writing to the evidence of the sources. But there are several parts to your question. Another part of your question might to be whether historians can find the truth or whether they can reconstruct it, or whether they are only constructing.

What do you think of historians like Natalie Zemon Davis and Simon Schama?

I think that Natalie belongs very much to the group that you mentioned before; she goes with Ginzburg and Darnton and Le Roy Ladurie. In her case, she has an interest in women's history. But again, this means she writes the history of people who had been left out of conventional history and so she has to look at the whole of history from a different point of view. It's quite a close parallel to history from below.

Simon Schama is a somewhat different case. I never think of him as an American, because he was in Cambridge before he emigrated. He has some characteristics in common with the group

you mentioned. Of course, he is a brilliant communicator; he   225
writes beautifully. He is interested in social history. He claims—
at least in one book, that is *The Embarrassment of Riches*—to be
doing a kind of historical anthropology. But his interest in anthropology is much more superficial than that of the other people
in the group. He has taken over a certain Durkheimian idea of
community, which underpins a great deal in *The Embarrassment
of Riches*. He has not gone further. He is not interested in the debates between anthropologists and the refinement of concepts.
Then he went on to write *Citizens*, where he more or less threw
social history out of the window. It's a very interesting book. It
pretends to be a very oldfashioned narrative—he calls it a "chronicle." It's not quite that because there is a great deal of new cultural history in it. The attention to language, for example, the
kinds of speeches that people were making in the assembly, the
changing rhetoric or, parallel to Lynn Hunt, slightly after her, he
is interested in the symbolism of the changes in clothes, of calling
people "citizen," and so on. So, it is an interesting mix of new history with a traditional political narrative because he goes to the
extreme of saying that all the so-called economical and social
sources of revolution are rubbish, have nothing to do with what
happened. In that sense he is an extreme voluntarist. But it's all
combined with insights from the new cultural history. That puts
him, I think, in a separate group from the other people. You can't
say that he is an oldfashioned historian, nor can you say he belongs to this international group like Natalie Zemon Davis and
Carlo Ginzburg. He has this rather interesting, I think, maybe not
altogether consistent, position. I think there is self-contradiction
there.

**Which book offers the best image of the past, in your
opinion?**

I think it's maybe easier to answer when I look at a period in which
I don't specialize; then I would say instantly well, three, four, five
great medievalists, each of whom has written a book of this kind.
Maybe the least well known, but I think he is as good as others,
is the English medievalist Sir Richard Southern, who once wrote
a book *The Making of the Middle Ages* that for giving an outsider
some sense of how people thought and felt in another period, to
me was even more successful than Marc Bloch's famous *Feudal*

Society, though that's also a book I admire very much. I think some works of Le Goff and Duby have the same effect for me.

The book by Natalie Zemon Davis, *Fiction in the Archives*, is also interesting but is much less ambitious than the books I have just mentioned. It does one job well and very interestingly; the implications of this book for historical method are very great and have only begun to be felt because the conventional distinction was that historical facts are what you get by going to the archives and historical fiction is what is invented outside. Another way of putting it is that, like some of the new historicist literary critics, she is sensitive to the rhetoric of the nonliterary. I think *Fiction in the Archives* belongs with a group of recent studies. Sometimes they analyze letters, sometimes autobiographies, sometimes trials. In each case, something that officially is not written for literary effect but then you show that there are literary techniques in it. And in a sense that's the most devastating blow against the positivist that can be struck, because she has invaded the territory of the positivists to show that even there you cannot work without the linguistic, rhetorical turn. I think she left some very interesting questions really unsolved like: Did the people who were asking for pardon compose these letters or did professional scribes compose the letters?—at the level of the physical writing of them and also at the level of how the incidents should be presented. Maybe we can never answer these questions. I thought in a sense she was a little oldfashioned in giving the impression that it was always a person who had committed homicide that is telling his or her story. Of course, if there were mediators it makes her central argument still stronger. The documents are even further away from the event than we used to think.

I think one of the characteristic features of new historians is the different types of questions that they ask of their historical sources.

Yes. Either you find an interesting new source—it's always been the case—or you use the source for a new purpose. I think people knew, for example, about the letters of pardon, but they were interested in questions like: Did one king of France pardon more people then somebody else? Or the people who asked for pardon—had they committed murder or had they committed something else? And she is looking at the documents in a more literary way, with a different question. Either you find a new source or you find a new question that involves using the sources from a new angle.

You think that historians should be good writers.

Absolutely. I admit there are historians, that is a class of scholar, and I admire their work very much without wanting to imitate it, who are very technical, very professional, and they can make very big innovations in the subject. They find a different way to do source criticism and so on. I respect this. But I have always wanted to write in a more accessible way for a larger public—to give more of a total vision of a period in the past. I don't like, myself, to be writing technical monographs. That doesn't mean I think they should not be written. I am sure they should be written. But my own choice, which involves not being completely intellectually respectable in Cambridge, is to write about big subjects. Again, my kind of history involves learning from these new movements. But then the people who are important in these new movements, they don't approve of you if you write in plain language. Maybe they look down on you a little bit if you don't write in the jargon of *Representations*, for example, which is a journal I admire very much, but I wish the contributors would express themselves in something closer to ordinary language. I think they could make all the points they want to make in this way. So, again my decision is as far as possible to keep close to ordinary language.

> My decision is as far as possible to keep close to ordinary language.

What is your favorite book?

I don't think I have a favorite book. I have some books I constantly return to. They can be nonfiction, like Montaigne's essays, they can be novels like George Eliot's *Middlemarch*. Maybe I could think of ten or twenty such books but I can't, I'm afraid, think of one. So if you ask me this question, if I have only one book to take to a desert island, I'm afraid I would spend so long thinking about it, I'd probably miss the boat to the island.

I would like to ask you about the relation between history and literature. How can we mark out borders between history and literature?

228

Some history is closer to fiction and some fiction is closer to history.

I am fascinated by the parallels between the late seventeenth century and the late twentieth century.

I don't think there is a sharp border, but maybe one could say there is a frontier area, that some history is closer to fiction and some fiction is closer to history. This happens to be an area in which a great deal of work is going on at the moment—just as it was three hundred years ago. I am fascinated by the parallels between the late seventeenth century and the late twentieth century. In the late seventeenth century there was this movement of historical skepticism. At the time it was being debated, you have the rise of the historical novel—in England Daniel Defoe and in France the abbé de St. Réal, and people could not decide at the time whether they were reading history or fiction. And now we have the debate of postmodernism and at the same time we have this whole range of works. Let's just cite one example since it has just been made into the film *Schindler's List*. Here is a novelist who says he is going to write a piece of nonfiction that then gets a prize for fiction. He tells a story that, I believe, concerns a set of events that actually happened. He does historical research; that is, when one is working on that period, one does oral history, and Keneally did oral history—he interviewed people and so on. I don't know how far he did source criticism. I don't know how far he has that kind of critical training, to compare testimonies from different people that contradict one another and to decide between them. What he then did without warning the reader that he does it, is to invent some things; that is, he invents dialogue and he invents thoughts. It may well be plausible to suggest that a conversation of this or that kind took place or that Schindler, at that point, had the following plan, but there is no direct evidence for that. What situates him for me on the fiction side, despite his claims, is the fact that he does all this without ever discussing the problem. I would say that a historian studying the same episodes would both do the source criticism and refuse to invent dialogue, or would simply say, "I have reasons for thinking that something of this kind took place." But of course these are all very much late-twentieth-century criteria for historical writing. Thucydides is closer to Keneally than he is to me, because he invents all the speeches that have a terribly important explanatory function in his history. But still there has been a kind of collective decision by historians that that convention is more dangerous than it is useful and that we have to find a different way of giving explanations.

How can we solve the problem of historical truth where some researchers claim that there is no truth in history?

I'm a relatively simple English empiricist, but not quite. That is, I do believe there was a past that included events but also structures. I don't believe that we can have direct contact with that past. The past is always mediated through the "traces"—I prefer that word to "the evidence." This is partly just new language to describe something that historians have been aware of for quite a long time. Only, although they were aware of these problems of source criticism, they still used to employ the language of facts and objectivity so that they gave the impression that they thought they had a more direct access than they did.

I'm a relatively simple English empiricist, but not quite.

I think a way of coming back to this problem of truth is to reflect on what English people say when they bear witness in the law court. They swear to tell the truth, the whole truth, and nothing but the truth. It seems clear that historians never can tell the whole truth. To write the history of the Thirty Years War would of course take much more than thirty years because it would be thirty years in the lives of so many people. In any case, the evidence has not all survived. Who was it said that history is like a Swiss cheese—it's full of holes? There are things we will never know about, as well as things we can know. We can't tell the whole truth. Can we tell nothing but the truth? Well, that's more difficult. We can make a big effort to say only what we have evidence for, or, when we speculate, to make it clear to the reader that we *are* speculating. Maybe one could say that that is nothing but the truth. It would still be an individual's selection of what that individual thought interesting or important. And clearly that varies with the individual, with the generation, with the culture. In that sense one can't, as a historian, arrive at "the truth" in the sense of making a series of statements that would be equally meaningful to, and equally acceptable to, people in different periods and different cultures. So, in that sense—no, we can't arrive at the truth. Maybe it is better to say— we can arrive at some truths, and we can avoid telling falsehoods.

Is there a crisis in historical writing?

I like to use the word crisis in a relatively precise way. I like to use it to mean a relatively short period of turmoil that is followed by

230 a long-term change in the structure. It would follow from using the word so precisely that you can never know that you are in a crisis while you are in a crisis, because there are periods of turmoil that are not followed by the long-term shift. So, one could of course ask the question: Have we passed through a crisis? I certainly have the impression that this is the case in the sense that the model of historical writing I learned as a student in Oxford in the 1950s, and the model of historical writing I'm trying to follow now—the difference between the two is so great, it seems to me almost as great as the difference between history written in the Middle Ages and history in the Renaissance. So, in that sense I would agree that there has been a crisis. For some people the turmoil is still going on. Other people might feel that they have come out the other side.

Do you think that history written in a cultural anthropological mode—the history of *mentalité*—will be the main trend in historiography in the future?

Well, in the first place it seems that historical writing has an appeal now, a public appeal, that it was hard to imagine it was going to have thirty years ago. Of course, it is always possible that it will lose this appeal—that it's a short-term trend, a fashion. I happen not to think this is the case. The reason I don't think so is that I think that social change is still accelerating. The effect of accelerating social change is this unpleasant sense of being torn away from one's roots. And so there is a psychological need for most people to reestablish contact with the past. So, they need to read history, maybe not so much the kind of history I write but the history of the recent past, in order to reestablish these links. So that as long as the world continues to be changing in the ways and at the speed it is now changing, history is going to be something that many people are interested in. I think the new socio-cultural history and history from below, and microhistory, are flourishing precisely because they respond to these needs more than the traditional history did. I have to say that in my own country, maybe the most popular sector of history is a very old-fashioned one—it's the history of the Second World War, the history of battles. Of course, one should distinguish male readers of history and female readers of history, I think that a reason for the

> The new socio-cultural history and history from below, and micro-history, are flourishing precisely because they respond to these needs more than the traditional history did.

invention of social history in the eighteenth century was that it 231
uses something that the rising, female reading public was particularly interested in. But still, it is incredible the way in which traditional histories of the Second World War continue to sell. I don't know if this is a purely local thing or whether outside Great Britain there is also that trend.

An obsession with language marked the philosophy of the twentieth century. Frank Ankersmit, in his interview, told me that we should now change the subject and change the categories of analysis. He himself is interested in the category of "experience." What is your opinion?

In the nineteenth and early twentieth centuries the category of experience was something that was tremendously important for historians and also philosophers of history. Dilthey, Croce, and Collingwood are almost obsessed with historical experience. I would personally want to continue to try to write a kind of history that is concerned both with structures and with experience. Perhaps best of all would be the changing experience of changing structures. I don't think one should write only the history of what people are conscious of, just as I don't think one can or should try to write a history only of impersonal trends. What's really interesting is the interaction between the two.

Could you tell me what you imagine for the future of humanistic disciplines?

I think it is very important that they stop fragmenting and specializing. Or, at the very least, that the tendency to specialize and fragment is offset or counterbalanced by a deliberate effort to see things as a whole, to collaborate between the disciplines. This is something I have been trying to do all my intellectual life. I know a group of people who are trying to do it. I don't know whether we are strong enough to reverse the trend or not, because clearly there is a logic to this fragmentation. I think there is some chance that specialization can be combined with attempts to see things as a whole. That is, more and more in humanities courses in universities, teachers are becoming dissatisfied with making the students study just one discipline for three years or whatever.

232   Wouldn't it be better to have some kind of combined humanities
       course and let them specialize at the postgraduate level? Let them
       first of all try to see things as a whole. This is, at least where I live,
       a new trend. It is nice to see that things are moving a bit in this
       direction.

Prato, Italy
18 April 1994

SELECTED WRITINGS

Culture and Society in Renaissance Italy, 1420–1540. London: Batsford,
    1972.
Popular Culture in Early Modern Europe. New York: Harper & Row,
    1978.
*The Historical Anthropology of Early Modern Italy: Essays on Perception
    and Communication*. Cambridge: Cambridge Univ. Press, 1987.
The French Historical Revolution: The Annales School, 1929–1989. Cam-
    bridge: Cambridge Univ. Press, 1990.
Language, Self and Society: A Social History of Language, co-editor with
    Roy Porter, with an afterword by Dell Hymes. London: Polity Press,
    1991.
Editor, *New Perspectives on Historical Writing*. Cambridge: Polity Press,
    1991.
The Fabrication of Louis XIV. New Haven: Yale Univ. Press, 1992.
History and Social Theory. Cambridge: Polity Press, 1992.
Antwerp, a Metropolis in Comparative Perspective. Antwerpen: Snoeck-
    Ducaju, 1993.
The Art of Conversation. Ithaca: Cornell Univ. Press, 1993.
*The Fortunes of the Courier: The European Reception of Castiglione's "Cor-
    tegiano."* Cambridge: Polity Press, 1995.

"Historiography." In *The New Oxford Companion to Literature in French*,
    ed. Peter France, 382–384. Oxford: Oxford Univ. Press, 1995.
"The Invention of Leisure in Early Modern Europe." *Past and Present*
    146 (1995): 136–50.
"Reflections on the History of Encyclopaedias." In *The Social Philosophy
    of Ernest Gellner*, ed. John A. Hall and Ian Jarvie, 193–206. "Poz-
    nań Studies in the Philosophy of the Sciences and the Humanities,"
    vol. 48, 1996.

"Fables of the Bees." In *Nature and Society in Historical Context*, ed.   233
    Mikulas Teich, Roy Porter, and Bo Gustafsson, 112–23. Cambridge:
    Cambridge Univ. Press, 1997.
"The Self from Petrarch to Descartes." In *Rewriting the Self: Histories
    from the Renaissance to the Present*, ed. Roy Porter, 17–28. London:
    Routledge, 1997.

*Ricorso is not only a very important
historiographic phenomenon but
also a guide to our contemporary experience
of the world.*

Who or what is your main source of inspiration?

I get my inspiration from places and from people.

■ I think in many ways I get my inspiration—if I can put it like that—although I don't really use the term in the romantic way— from places and from people. By that I mean at the same time people and places in the contemporary world and people and places in the past. At one point I discovered, and it was rather a curious discovery, that a lot of my work had been dominated by figures whose names began with the letters *B A*. My major critical influence was Roland Barthes. I realized that my original interest as a research student was in the French historian Prosper de Barante and that the most recent figure whom I have become fascinated by was a canon of Canterbury in the seventeenth century called John Bargrave. My name also begins with *B A*, of course, and if one looks in an index to find one's own name, as one sometimes does out of vanity, one inevitably tends to find those people beginning with *B A*. I would also suggest that there is a kind of personal investment with me in the concrete milieu of different periods, which relates to my own living circumstances. For example, I live in a house built in the 1830s, which is very close to the period of my original research. I also live in a city, Canterbury, that has dominated my recent writing in one way or another.

And what about Ian Hamilton Finlay, for whom you seem to have a special affection?

That is a rather different story. I have written on him constantly and I have corresponded with him. We have an enormous correspondence from about 1964 onward. In this case, I think what matters most is that, at Cambridge in the early 1960s, history was a very ossified and a slightly puzzling discipline to study. I suppose this was true of other disciplines as well. But some of my closest friends at Cambridge were not actually historians. They were, for instance, people studying architecture and history of art. Right from my schooldays I'd painted and edited magazines and so on, and at Cambridge I came to be involved with the contemporary avant-garde. I visited Finlay with some friends for the first time in 1964. From about 1967 onwards I have visited him regularly almost every year, and together, in collaboration, we have been involved in a kind of creative recoil from modernism. I say that because I remember, for example, introducing him to some essays by Panofsky, which helped to stimulate his study of emblems. That was a kind of dialogue. I contributed a running commentary to his book *Heroic Emblems* in 1977. In a certain sense I wouldn't myself make a close connection between my interest in the avant-garde and my interest in history, except that at certain points they overlapped, they existed in a kind of counterpoint. But I suppose it is also true to say that what happened in the 1970s was a kind of return of neoclassicism. Modernism, as Ian Hamilton Finlay saw very clearly at the time, was collapsing. The area of reference for contemporary artists suddenly became vastly expanded in time, and that was not only true with Hamilton Finlay but also with a number of younger English artists whom I have come to know later—the generation of Stephen Cox, Antony Gormley, and Christopher Le Brun.

I came to be involved with the contemporary avant-garde.

Modernism was collapsing.

Kinetic art, which is also an object of interest for you, is related to the crisis of representation. Do you see such a crisis of representation in historical writing? What is the relation between art and history from the point of view of representation?

I think I would see that in a particular way. I mean, the question, in relation to history and historical writing, I think has been precisely: What is historical representation? And that's why in my book *The Clothing of Clio* I use the concept of the representation

236

of history as my subtitle. In effect, all the essays in that book have to do with representation. It is true to say that in historical terms (although obviously Hayden White's work drew attention to the way in which written history, historiography, is coded in rhetorical terms) very little attention was paid, until quite recently, to the different forms of historical representation, within which I would include not only historical painting, historical novels, but also, for example, the museum, which is a form of historical representation, or can be treated as a form of historical representation.

In the case of the arts, the crisis of representation implies, at least to some extent, a return to the concepts and, in a way, the governing principles of Western art in its original stages. Let's say, the ancient Greek period. I find it very interesting that the art historians whom I find congenial—someone like Georges Didi-Huberman in France, for example—are going back to anthologies of writings about Greek art, invoking the paintings that have disappeared, which are no longer extant, if they ever existed. (Norman Bryson also in his book *Looking at the Overlooked* on Dutch still life starts in the classical period.) So, to me, art and history exist in a kind of relationship that is close, but what is happening in the two domains is not identical. In historiography we are rediscovering the fact of representation, whereas in contemporary art we are rediscovering the historical basis that underlies it. It's not only representation in general but also generic structure that is being reinvestigated: the fact that the pop artist Richard Hamilton, for example, works in still life, landscape, and so on, shows that genre has an important determining influence within the context of contemporary art.

Thanks to the "narrative turn" in the philosophy of history and the "anthropological turn" in historical writing, history is placed closer to literature. Some books written by professional historians—for example *Dead Certainties* by Simon Schama—are in fact historical novels. In this new situation of "shaking" the borders between history and literature, how can we distinguish history from literature?

That was quite easy to do in the eighteenth century, when history was a subsidiary branch of literature. And it was also fairly easy in the nineteenth century, when history had decided that it was not literature and, therefore, that it would ignore its own signifying

dimension. But the problem is that *we* have the history of the
eighteenth century, and the nineteenth century, and finally of the
twentieth century to take into account, so it's not as simple for
us. What I think is important is a strategy that draws attention to
what I would call the wider historiographic field, or a field of historical representation that also includes concepts like conserva-
tion, and "museology," as it is often now called. To make historians aware, as far as one can, that their particular province which
is (in Geoffrey Elton's phrase) the rational reconstruction of the
past, is, in social terms, one of quite a number of uses, many of
them, in fact most of them, not capable of being safeguarded by
the same standards. In other words, I suppose, the difference that
I am talking about could be related basically to Nietzsche's strategy, in *The Use and Abuse of History for Life*. Obviously, I am not
recommending Nietzsche unreservedly, but I do agree with him
that one constantly has to ask not so much how far the professional standards of a discipline are to be sustained and what are
its links with other disciplines, but also the crucial question: How
is that particular discipline socially validated and are there not important social issues that are "bypassed" to the extent that the
historians remain inward-looking and concentrate an enormous
amount of effort on the exclusion of this kind of question.

**In one of your books you wrote about Natalie Zemon
Davis—how she prepared the script for the film *The Return
of Martin Guerre*. What do you think of "new history"?**

I think what interested me particularly with Natalie Zemon Davis,
whose work I genuinely admire, was that she became very much
involved with the making of the film *The Return of Martin Guerre*.
She was obliged to consider, and very clearly set out in her book,
the different factors actually governing representation in film
from those in the ordinary historical account: the way in which
plot structure, for example, was not an arbitrary decision, but
something integrally linked to the perceptions of the audience,
which therefore couldn't be dismissed as merely ornament or
style. Le Roy Ladurie was the "new historian" who most interested me, at least when I was writing in the 1980s, and I think
this leads to quite an interesting point. The French historians, in
the tradition of Michelet, seemed to find it quite natural to assert
themselves as authors. In the example of the French cinema, the

238

author (auteur) theory is developed to explain how it is that certain cinema directors are actually in control not only of the technical aspects of the work, but also of visual style, lighting, camera work, and so on. In other words—it becomes a total work of art. And in a certain way, I think, the French historian is able to be an author in a way that English historians find very difficult. The French historian will assert his or her subjectivity and will make, as in the case of Le Roy Ladurie, very conscious anachronisms. These are not inaccuracies, however, as the historians are consciously staging their own position as contemporary authors and not making a secret of it. In the case of Simon Schama, what is interesting about his works is precisely that he is taking that kind of risk, but taking it from a perspective that is rather different: I mean, against the whole weight of traditional historical writing, in the English and American tradition. One of the historians I most admire, I must say, is the Anglo-American historian Jonathan Spence, who wrote *The Memory Palace of Matteo Ricci*. This is a book about a seventeenth-century Jesuit who went to China, and each of the chapters is conceived as a kind of a "memory palace," the stocking of memory with a series of different appropriate objects, each one of which leads to another. Each of the chapters has a particular ideogram, a group of Chinese characters, placed at the start, in order to identify it. It is a book whose organization is determined by a succession of single images, each of them a particular kind of condensation, one might say in the Freudian sense, that will dominate the textual material of that particular section.

The thing I don't like about some of the new history (and I will not necessarily name any names) is that it often seems to be actually compiled straight out of the card index. In other words, you can see that a person has established a number of categories and then gone out to collect an enormous number of sources and found things relating to all the different categories; then he or she has simply gone through the index tying together the different kinds of information. That sort of strategy I think produces a very inadequate formal structure—more a kind of repertoire or encyclopedia than a historical work as I would classify it.

Don't you think that that kind of historical work could only appear in a "postmodern atmosphere"?

> The French historian is able to be an author in a way that English historians find very difficult.

I suppose it could, yes. I mean, I suppose one looks for postmodernism in a whole lot of different contexts and one manages to find it. The first work that I did that was related to postmodernism would be the essay that I did on the French new novel in the late 1960s and early '70s. In fact, one of my longest contacts over my whole life as a scholar, as a researcher, has been with the French new novelist Robert Pinget, who is still publishing, and now is well into his eighties. That kind of reorientation of the novel, which Fredric Jameson later pointed to as one of the signs of postmodernism in the 1960s, was obviously something I was aware of at the time. I think it is also true that I was aware in the 1960s of the shift from modernism to the kind of revived neoclassicism, or whatever one would call it, associated with poets and artists like Finlay. In historical terms, the problem perhaps is that for me the ideology of history is not specifically modernist; the normative history, the traditional history, is in a real sense still romantic. I agree with Lord Acton, who says that history issues from the romantic school; in other words, it is concerned with the myth of transparency, the notion of the dimension of representation being unimportant, the notion of the professional, scientific attitude that is the other side to romantic mythmaking, and, therefore, has to be differentiated from it. So the break in historical terms doesn't seem to me to be as clearly postmodernist, precisely because I don't really quite see what a modernist historiography could be like. I mean, modernist historiography presumably would be a kind of self-contradictory enterprise because modernism aspires, after all, toward the normative and the general and the utopian rather than toward any kind of objective, particularizing or scientific view of the past.

I was at a conference last weekend about the legacy of Michel Foucault, and one of the issues that came up there was the state of "new historicism." I am much more happy with the idea of new historicism, which seems to me to be an interesting development because it is basically an accession of historical sources, of documents, by people primarily concerned with literature, or with what Stephen Greenblatt calls "cultural poetics." And therefore, it could be seen as a kind of anthropological and literary recuperation of history. I suppose that could be regarded as a postmodern development, too, because former modernists can now reach back into history and take out what they wish without having to

239

The ideology of history is not specifically modernist.

The traditional history is in a real sense still Romantic.

I don't really quite see what a modernist historiography could be like.

New Historicism could be seen as a kind of anthropological and literary recuperation of history.

240   worry too much! So, new historicism can look as if it were just putting on the trappings of history. But I think that nevertheless it can result in a very important new synthesis.

Do you think that the characteristic of postmodernism as a shift from macro to micro, from outside to inside, can have a special importance for the future?

I could take, for an example, the essay that I contributed to an anthology on *Interpreting Contemporary Art* with my co-editor William Allen. This is on the Greek-Italian artist Jannis Kounellis. What I think is interesting in relation to Jannis Kounellis is that he doesn't have a traditional, classical position that is centered on one geographical and cultural place, New York, London, or Paris. But what he does have is a kind of topology in which Athens and then also the Byzantine Empire, the West, all of these strongly loaded cultural historical concepts, all these zones, come into play. And my feeling would be that the postmodern experience is not one of actually being released from cultural barriers, but it means that, instead of having fixed points, one has what I would call a topology. That is to say different structural points that are rooted in the past and that in combination influence how a work turns out. For the other case, I would take an artist whom I have written about recently, in a volume published by Stanford, *Material-ities of Communication*. This is the American artist Cy Twombly. Twombly is an extraordinarily important artist because he was a part of the New York school, and then, in the 1950s and again in the 1960s, he more and more went to Italy. He started to live there on a continuous basis. His work has since been concerned with a kind of mythic opposition of West and East. I have also written about this aspect to a certain extent in my book *The True Vine*.

When you speak about macro to micro, on that kind of shift, I would see it still as a situation in which postmodernism is certainly not global, in the sense that we lose any sense of specific culture. That would be a utopia. But it is a matter of reprocessing, recycling certain forms of mythic opposition that are still characteristically our experience. I mean, who would after all deny that the East and the West European division, which is no longer in the strict sense a political division, is still a crucially important cultural division? I have just finished editing a series of essays on

Frankenstein that also involves Dracula. And there is a wonderful   **241**
essay by the contemporary French writer Jean-Louis Schefer on
the way in which the Byzantine doctrine of the Eucharist as opposed to the Western notion of the Eucharist, of the real presence, is fundamental to the construction of the Dracula myth. And
that seems to me to be exactly the sort of point that is utterly determined in relation to our cultural position, at least in Europe; I
suspect, also for certain Americans as well, and certainly those
who come to live in Europe.

**By the way . . . what do you think of the romantic image of
Dracula? I have the movie by Coppola in mind.**

Unfortunately, I haven't seen it, the Coppola one, but I do know
that it's the first film that actually takes seriously the fact that
Dracula was a crusader. In other words, it has the historical background, which is very crucial to Bram Stoker. You couldn't find
that in *Nosferatu* or the other earlier Dracula films, where he was
taken as being somebody who came out of nowhere, or at least
from the dark doorway of the castle.

How would you rate the cinema of Peter Greenaway?

In the case of Greenaway, there are, I think, slightly different issues at stake. But Greenaway, I think, is important, and indeed
the reason why he is devalued in England, on the whole, is because he actually conceives of the issue of representation as being
not exclusive to film. Whereas narrative has been absolutely pri-
oritized in the well-made films in the Hollywood tradition, Peter
Greenaway, on the other hand, is interested in drawing up inven-
tories, constructing symmetries. One of his most entertaining
films that I know is the one that shows a series of bathrooms
(from *A* to *Z*). Peter Greenaway's exhibition in Rotterdam, which
I saw, redistributed a large part of the collection in terms of parts
of the body and lit them in quite different ways, so that you had
light flooding across a painting by Rubens in one part of the gallery and naked models in glass cases in another. What is interesting about Greenaway is that he has expanded the field of representation. Film is his medium, of course, but it is one aspect of an
overall view within which painting and film are not so far apart. I

242

am also interested, for example, in film directors like Jean-Marie Straub—his recent film on Cézanne, which I haven't had a chance to see yet but which I've read about. That kind of intrusion of the plastic arts, the history of the plastic arts, into the contemporary cinema—I find very fascinating.

What does postmodernism mean for you?

Quite frankly, I don't very often use the term postmodernism. So, it is very difficult to answer that question because I really haven't thought about it. I don't find it very useful as a concept. Modernism I find very important and useful, and a lot of my work is concerned with positions for and against or within and without modernism.

The idea of postmodernism seems to me to be more or less a kind of "catch-all" term, which means something, a little, in relation to architecture. For example, Charles Jencks's work, which I follow, is quite close, quite parallel to some aspects of Ian Hamilton Finlay. A lot of the artists whom I know and am interested in would be classed as postmodernists by Jencks. But I think that an area like architecture, which has a very clear series of positions through from the modernist to postmodernist, gives a precise content to the notion of postmodernism, whereas the more diffuse sense that applies to the visual arts or historiography is, I think, not so useful.

What I like better is the term that Vico uses—the term *ricorso*. I find it a very useful term because it doesn't mean simply going back. It means actually returning to and taking up again positions that were potentially there in the first place but of course mean something different the second time round. It presumes a kind of cyclical motion rather than a linear motion. Modernism is predicated upon the notion of linearity, notions of progress, notions of Enlightenment, and so on. As regards *ricorso*, for example, what I'll be working on in relation to John Bargrave is the notion of "curiosity." Now in this area it's a Polish scholar, Krzysztof Pomian, who has written in the most illuminating way, and I find him a very useful source. But what interests me is not only that around the 1980s people suddenly started to be interested in curiosity, but also the fact that contemporary artists now see curiosity as an important paradigm. For example, I went a

I don't find postmodernism very useful as a concept.

The idea of post-modernism seems to me to be more or less a kind of "catch-all" term.

Around the 1980s people suddenly started to be interested in curiosity.

couple of weeks ago to the Chateau d'Oiron not far from Poitiers, which is a wonderful sixteenth- and seventeenth-century chateau where there are emblems on the walls. There are also examples of fresco paintings and all kinds of other visual iconography from that period. And contemporary present-day artists, like the Swiss artist Daniel Spoerri, have introduced their own curiosities: strange and wonderful animals, and a particular collection of objects assembled in the nineteenth century, including a ball from the battlefield of Waterloo, that kind of thing. Now, I could imagine this being thought of as purely frivolous, as if the contemporary artist didn't know what to do. But I see the important point that curiosity is above all the validation of the single object, the individual object. The scientific revolution, as represented by Descartes and Bacon, was opposed to curiosity because curiosity would not allow general laws to be formulated. There's a preference always for the individual object over the general law. You can find this issue coming up also in a sense in Walter Benjamin, when Adorno talks about him being fascinated by plush and all sorts of inferior objects in relation to his Arcades project. And my feeling is that this kind of *ricorso*, which is a return to elements that were previously obliterated by the dominant ideology of modernism, is not only a very important historiographic phenomenon, because we suddenly see things in a new fashion, but also a guide to our contemporary experience of the world.

Ricorso, a return to elements that were previously obliterated by the dominant ideology of modernism, is not only a very important historiographic phenomenon, because we suddenly see things in a new fashion, but also a guide to our contemporary experience of the world.

Looking at contemporary historiography and philosophy of history, I observe common points of development with philosophy. Nicholas Rescher describes this movement in an article "American Philosophy Today." He points to "the widespread assault by a disaffected avant-garde against the discipline as normally practised" and a special interest in ethics and feminism, among other things. Maybe Frank Ankersmit, who is going to concentrate in the future on the concept of historical experience, can be seen as a symptom of the new "post-postmodernist" philosophy of history? What do you think?

It's interesting that you say that. Obviously I agree with Frank Ankersmit in that connection and in fact I've got two papers relevant to that issue to give at conferences on historiography in the next few months. One of them is in Bielefeld, a conference organized by Jörn Rüsen, where I'm going to be talking about the notion of "living the past." This is one of the main subjects of *Romanticism and the Rise of History*, a book that I am going to be bringing out soon in the United States. I am interested in the actual phenomenon of the experience of history, not of course as something that is inaccessible to reason, but the experience of history insofar as it can be explained and represented. For example, one of the figures I've been looking at is the French nineteenth-century writer Pierre Loti, who created in his house, on the French coast at Rochefort-sur-mer, a series of very elaborate and beautiful rooms, one after another; that is, a Renaissance room, a little medieval "Gothic" room, and then also a Middle Eastern room with Arab artefacts, and a Chinese room. All of these things, in other words, respond to a kind of experiential need both to revisit exotic places like the Far East, which he had visited, and to recreate what he hadn't visited at all, such as the Middle Ages. At the opening of the medieval room, Loti had an elaborate and fascinating banquet, with people dressing in different costumes, singing minstrel songs. So the whole thing became a kind of working experiment in the restoration of a certain kind of historical milieu.

So, you think that we can experience the past?

I don't really doubt that we can experience certain forms of intuition that refer to the historical past, but what particularly interests me is the way in which people try to materialize what they consider to be their experience of the past. The other paper that I plan to do early next year is about what I call "the furnishing of the past." It has to do with the stage in the early nineteenth century when people suddenly began to realize that in order to see what the past was like you had to think of homely things like furniture. What chairs did they sit on? And there is a very clear tendency, which is found both in literature with people like Prosper Merimée, and in museums, like the Musée de Cluny, not to mention painters like Bonington, to try to reconstitute the scene as something independent of the actors. Certain forms of chairs particularly, but also beds, become very important. The furniture works as a kind of shifter between the human presence and the idea of the environment, or a milieu. You will see, for example, in

American museums, and to some extent in English museums, how at a certain stage in the nineteenth century people began to constitute period rooms. That's to say, they take the entire set of furniture out of a French chateau (including the wall and floor), and put it in Philadelphia in a new room of identical dimensions. Now, that again seems to me a very fascinating development. I mean, there is nobody there, except the museum visitors, but the phenomenon testifies to a need for a certain kind of recreation that was inconceivable before the nineteenth century. Before about 1820, nobody would have understood that need to reconstitute a milieu comprehensively.

So, is it possible to say that contemporary historical writing is more interested in experience than in representation?

I wouldn't agree with that because I think the only evidence we have of experience is in representation. That is the only evidence I would address myself to. But I think it may well be that there is a possibility of talking about such experience in the same way as in ethics one obviously talks about considerations of choice and conscience. Perhaps historical consciousness could be investigated in a similar way.

> The only evidence we have of experience is in representation.

Memory . . .

Yes, memory, of course. And that is something that on the whole has been much better dealt with by novelists or by philosophers, probably, at least since Plato. But I'm interested in the experience as mediated by representation, at least at the moment.

New historians ask new questions of the sources and receive answers that are required by readers living in an age of uncertainty and hesitancy . . .

Well, no. Not historians alone. Questions were also asked by historical novelists. They were asked by Sir Walter Scott; they were asked by Prosper Merimée. In other words, it's partly a matter of historians continually trying to disavow that separation between fiction and history that was so crucial to the establishment of the discipline in professional terms in the nineteenth century.

246   **Maybe we can find a new common point for historians and novelists—they are beginning to ask the same questions.**

I think that they may ask very similar questions, and yet the form that their answers take is, at the same time, very different because there are various codes and usages in a historical novel that we would not expect to find in history; like, for example, the use of direct speech, of dialogue. That reminds me of Sir Walter Scott's case: his famous scene in *Ivanhoe*, where he has two Saxons talking to one another about the contemporary situation. All sorts of historians from Augustin Thierry to Karl Marx recognized how important this was, because for the first time in accounts of the history of the Norman conquest it was apparent that the Saxons were still there—they were still talking. But, of course, when Thierry writes a history of the Norman conquest he doesn't have Saxons talking. He simply tries, as he puts it, to "construct" the Saxon point of view. So, there are still important markers of difference. Even Le Roy Ladurie doesn't actually have the inhabitants of Montaillou talking to each other, except through the medium of the transcript that they provided for the ecclesiastical inquisitor. But I would agree that there are certain markers linguistically that virtually anybody interested in or accustomed to historical writing would take as being not proper to a historian. And one of those would be direct speech.

Except dialogues included in sources.

Yes. This is a paradox, really. I mean, on the one hand the source exists, particularly when there are tape recordings, or other oral sources. But I think the point is, you can't simply transcribe direct speech; you have to stage it. You have to have certain devices: not only what so-and-so said but also how they said it. Do they say it loudly or softly, kindly or violently? I analyzed some sources from the First World War, in an essay called "Analyzing the Discourse of History," basically a manuscript source and several different variants, and I took two examples of how they had been used, one from A. J. P. Taylor's *History of World War I* and the other one from Correlli Barnett's *The Sword Bearers*. And one discovers that immediately the dialogue comes across as being staged. Although the basic materials are the same, the sources are the same, it comes out quite differently. And it does so precisely because when you try to speed it up or slow it down, emphasize a certain aspect or another, you are effectively enabling it to be dramatized or staged for the reader, usually with a particular ideological bias that is clearly detectable.

How did it happen that you turned from an interest in art to the theory of history?

That has not really been very difficult for me. I have realized recently or over the past few years that I probably don't work like other historians. I mean, I don't choose a subject and then shut myself in archives for five or six months, and then work on the material for a year and publish a book after three years. That's not usually been my practice. How I work is to have certain continuing concerns, usually related to particular figures, which are going on all the time, and these are partly (maybe very often) anchored in places or pictures that I have seen when I have been traveling. And they reoccur in different sorts of configurations. For example, I saw a wonderful painting in the museum at Nantes a few years ago by Paul Delaroche called *The Childhood of Pico della Mirandola*. I looked at and thought about it from different angles, and recently I did a paper about "Generating the Renaissance," which investigates how such an image could be said to "generate the Renaissance." We know that the Renaissance was created in the nineteenth century—that authors of the nineteenth century like Michelet effectively gave a new content to an idea that had previously been very schematic. So then we had *the* Renaissance. But what role did the image play in all this? What I try to argue is that there is a type of historical consciousness that can be created specifically by images.

It seems to me that always in your background was your own private experience.

Almost always, yes. The initial experience is almost always personal. But that is precisely because the pattern of my life has become one of traveling a great deal, traveling particularly to France, Italy, and other European countries, and to a certain extent to the United States. I very much enjoy, what might be called, the effects of transumption, when I talk about a very obscure Canterbury figure in Chicago or Lausanne or Cambridge. I have a very

247

There is a type of historical consciousness that can be created specifically by images.

The initial experience is almost always personal.

direct pleasure in not actually looking at the mainstream, but at the side issues, issues that are actually always deserving of being brought to prominence provided that one does it in a particular way. For example, Prosper de Barante, the person I worked on first of all—Barante's aim, in his writing, his historiography, was actually to leave no marks of his own authorship—to construct a source that would be as if it had come from the Middle Ages, from the fifteenth century. It's rather like what Roland Barthes calls the "zero degree of writing." Nobody of course ever reaches that objective. Writing is not capable of being reduced to the zero degree. But the particular historical circumstances in which this ambition can be developed, the way it's worked out in a specific cultural context, I've always found very interesting. I find the historical figures who are self-deprecating, and whose achievement lies deliberately on the sidelines, extremely engaging.

In the case of John Bargrave, for example, I've tried to set up a simple model where there are two kinds of historical figure, which we know all too well; there's the great man, and then we read about him as an agent, or alternatively (as with Braudel writing about Philip II) we read about him and we find that he wasn't, actually, in control of things. So it's a question of agency. Then, there is the artist: in this particular study I take the case of Vermeer, of whom we know virtually nothing. All we have is his pictures, and that's fine. He is absorbed in the product of representation. But in the middle of that, to take Pomian's term, there's what he calls the "semiophore" man—somebody who is creating sense, who's not a great man, who's not an artist, who is, as I would put it, living symbolically, leaving signs that are sometimes ambiguous, that have to be connected one to the other retrospectively to make sense. That kind of figure, I think, is crucially important, if one wishes to appreciate past cultures.

The "semiophore" man, somebody who is creating sense, is crucially important.

Don't you think that scholars have finally come to express their point of view openly in their work? Subjectivity is now legalized?

The French always have a term for everything. They call this *égo-histoire*. And that suggests that it could be a little bit overdone. But I think that's something that artists as well, but certainly historians who have not been used to that kind of self-revelation, have begun more and more to put to the forefront. It's certainly

The French always have a term for everything.

true in the case of art historians. And in some ways, I suppose, this is accelerated by the pressure of feminism, because obviously feminism requires that one acknowledge oneself as being gendered rather than, as it might be, an impersonal, nongendered authority. That is, at least, a kind of important preliminary move. Now obviously that's not the end of it. The fact that you are born in a particular class, in a particular culture, you have particular experiences, is also important.

Do you agree that there is a revival of interest in anthropological philosophy: philosophers like Ortega y Gasset, for instance.

Yes, unquestionably. And that relates to what I was saying in relation to new historicism and cultural poetics. I suppose that you could say that in most countries the conditions of work, of research and teaching in universities, have, on the whole, become more barbaric over the last few years. Clearly this depends not on a particular national culture but on a more diffused situation. In Britain, we depend a lot on judgments about teaching and research, funding decisions, and so on, that are made obviously without reference to the desires of individual teachers and scholars. There is a tendency toward quantification of results; how many articles you have written, what sort of grading your department has been given. All of these modes of control and regulation have arrived but I would suspect that that has already created its own kind of reaction. After all, there is still a difference between people in the exact sciences and people in the humanities. This resides not only in the fact that we are less methodical, or less scientific in the strict sense, but also in the fact that the personal investment is more to the fore. I don't mean that the great scientist isn't personally responsible for and engaged with his or her material. That would be nonsense. But it's certainly true that the historian, for example, can and must draw on aspects of individual memory, on individual experience, that are resistant to quantifying and perhaps even quite inappropriate for quantification.

> In most countries the conditions of work have become more barbaric over the last few years.

> There is a tendency towards quantification of results.

There is now a special interest in the problems of love, sexuality, death, childhood, friendship, and so on. Maybe we

are facing an age when the best histories will be written by amateurs. Look at Ariès, for example.

Yes. Ariès is a very interesting case because he does say that the strength of his own experience (as a child) led him to postulate that childhood must have been something quite different in the past, and not at all what he had experienced. And therefore he took as his first principle not that people have always loved children, but that if there was no evidence of loving children, then there was no reason to believe that this was the rule. Historians who object to Ariès that I've often come across say: "Oh, yes but it's quite clear that people in certain centuries did love their children, look here at these examples,"—which is perfectly fair, but the enterprise of Ariès is still fully justified because it creates a kind of estrangement effect. It puts the burden on the historian to find the evidence for certain kinds of view that would otherwise be naturalized within culture to such an extent that we would find it hard to envisage the possibility of anything else.

What about the obsession with death? Hans Kellner in his "Narrativity in History: Post-Structuralism and Since" quoted Paul Ricoeur's suggestion that recent work on the history of death may represent the farthest point reached by all history.

That reminds me of the book that I'm correcting the proofs for at the moment. It is focused on a number of inscriptions on gravestones, and the last image is an image of a gravestone, or marble slab, that is obliterated. People have walked over it so much that the inscription is no longer there, but that is the gravestone of the person who is the subject of the book.

In fact, if you are attentive to punning titles, you recognize the significance of the very name of the person I am writing about: Bar Grave. *Bar* means to cancel out, to stand in front of. *Grave*, of course, is the place where the body is buried. This is a book that is really about the body symbolically, and the traces it leaves behind. One interesting thing about Bargrave is that he preserved in his collection two bodies: one is a fractional body, with a "finger" of a "Frenchman," which is still there, the other a dry, desiccated chameleon that is also still there. The question remains, of course, how you carry out the work of history or use the forms that history offers to us. All of these myths about death and birth, and all the other aspects of human life, need to be capable of an adequate kind of transcription or commentary that takes the form of a historical account.

Is it possible to say—metaphorically speaking—that the narrativist or new historian is a person who can see the past through her or his own experience? She/he uses characters from the past as mediums in order to express feelings, beliefs, opinions?

That might be so, but I think that there is also another concern that is very important, and that is the formal area, the area of form. I can appreciate the arguments about narrative. But the problem for me is not always narrative. It's the problem of varying the form in such a way as to provide a kind of artistic congruence. For example, probably nobody notices this, but the book that I wrote called *The True Vine* is divided into three sections; each of these has three subsections. There is a kind of symmetry between them; each concentrates on a different aspect; and in combination I would see that formal element as having an important role in establishing the work as literature. The book that I have written recently on romanticism again has a three-by-three structure, in which each of the sections is longer than the previous one. So there are three very short pieces, three medium-sized pieces, and then three very long pieces at the end. And I suppose that (rather like Lévi-Strauss putting the word *Overture* at the beginning of his book *The Raw and the Cooked*), the sort of analogies one would find there would be with musical structure. Although, of course, it's narrative in the general sense, the hint of musical structure seems to me to be very important, as if one had something like sonata form, or a theme with variations. In the Bargrave book, each section is concerned with a different mode of history. One is a simple family history: another is an interrogation, an epistemology, of the concept of collecting and so on, and the interest to me lies in being able to dovetail those different sorts of approach within an overall unified structure.

Do you share Hayden White's dream about the "reconstitution of history as a form of intellectual activity

that is at once poetic, scientific, and philosophical in its concerns"?

Definitely, yes. That's one of the phrases in his book that has always struck me, and it's really what justifies the book as a whole. In many respects the method is not what one would use today as regards the mode of analysis, but what is so important about *Metahistory* is that it presumes that in this golden age there is a kind of a global field of historical consciousness or historical awareness that includes, of course, both historical narrative and historical philosophy or philosophy of history. All of that comes within one corpus, and can be thought out in a consistent way.

All I would say in addition is that this golden age was not only an age of philosophers and historians but also of many kinds of other people: poets and novelists, and painters, and museum collectors, and creators of waxworks and other forms of spectacle, and they are also important. On the whole, my own reference points are with them rather than with the philosophers of history.

How did you become interested in Russian formalism?

Russian Formalism was the title of a book of essays that developed when I was editing a magazine called *Twentieth-Century Studies*. In the 1960s I was already interested in structuralism before I was aware of Hayden White's work. My first article using the method was a structuralist investigation of historiography that I published in 1970, in which I used the new rhetorical modes of analyzing discourse (it was later incorporated in *The Clothing of Clio*). Russian formalism was at that stage not at all well known. It was a time when I was also investigating Russian art, editing a book on constructivism. And it seemed that in England very little was known, apart from those people who read Tzvetan Todorov's *Théorie de la littérature*. Therefore, the point was to simply bring together a group of texts that would actually be involved with the analysis of all the different forms of contemporary art and literature. One text I include is Shklovsky's "The Resurrection of the Word," that at my university is still used for teaching students in the Film Studies Department. Such critical writing was unusual at this period because it was essentially a revival of rhetorical criticism and cut

across all the native traditions of English criticism, which had become strongly entrenched in the universities in the 1950s and
1960s.

**Mikhail Bakhtin is also very important. He is not strictly
connected with the Russian formalist school but is considered an idol for postmodernists.**

Yes, absolutely. And I was made aware of this once again last year
when I translated and edited Julia Kristeva's work on Proust, compiled from lectures that she gave here at Kent. I was thinking that
the first piece of Kristeva's work that I published was on Bakhtin,
in 1972. Kristeva called this piece on Bakhtin "The Ruin of a Poetics." She was looking at how the initial assumptions of formalism
were at the same time being repudiated and developed further in
his work.

**I find his conception of dialogue and dialogism very inter-
esting and inspiring.**

It's certainly interesting. One of the most recent things I've written is a foreword for a collection of texts relating to Russian visual culture, or Soviet visual culture, that has been edited by two
Russian students who are now in the United States. Most of the
pieces were written in the 1950s, '60s and '70s. What these writers suggest is that the idea of Russian culture—and particularly
Russian avant-garde, modernist culture—that people in the West
developed in the 1960s and '70s was a kind of negative utopia because everybody saw what kind of activity had been going on in
the 1920s and idealized it, desperately trying to get the work out
of Russia in order to see it. But this meant that they neglected
what had happened in the 1930s, '40s, and '50s, and it was quite
a surprise to find that people were still active in Russia working
on quite different sorts of art: people like Kabakov, for example.
So now, I think, the thing has come full circle and formalism is
still crucial as a method. But at the same time the antiformalist
tendency, the attempts to reestablish some form of critical reference in those years, may not just be regarded as a kind of second
best to the Soviet avant-garde of the 1920s.

254 **Art in some way always reflects the condition of a given culture. Russian formalism was connected with the "flourishing Communist system" and now the antiformalist movement reflects the present situation in Russia. Artists are like litmus paper showing the changes in a culture.**

It's possible for one culture to generate a sort of myth about the other one, which is perfectly all right.

Absolutely. That's exactly right. The point is that it's possible for one culture to generate a sort of myth about the other one, which is perfectly all right. It's not surprising, but it can be a barrier to understanding, and therefore it's a good thing, I think, that we see that Russian antiformalism has its own sort of consequences. It seems to me that Kabakov provides a kind of postmodern version, or equivalent, of the fascination of the 1920s with modernist forms: with aerial flight, for example, as in the famous Kabakov installation about the man who flew out of his apartment. It is clearly a kind of ironic and contemporary commentary on the constructivist notion of flight as a metaphor for human liberty.

What do you predict will be the future for historiography and for philosophy of history?

It is a difficult question. But I suppose I would answer it in two ways. On the one hand, from the point of view of the university, in general I have always been committed to what was called in the 1960s "interdisciplinary" study—what Roland Barthes called the "tarte à la crème" of the contemporary university. What I see now is more than an interdisciplinary approach. It's a genuine confluence within the humanities of all sorts of areas of concern. For example, a large number of students that I teach, more and more of them from year to year, do more than one subject. It used to be the case that students were primarily historians, or studied English, or history of art. Now, a large number of really good students want to do film, they also want to do visual arts, they want to do poetry, and of course it's possible, even though obviously not everybody can do everything. This is the tendency in our graduate program. We have what we call the program in modern studies, where people can choose a whole spectrum of courses within the terms of, say, an M.A. in film and art theory. So on the one hand, I think, the disciplinary shift is changing the whole idea of university study. Wolfgang Iser has talked about how the study of literature will finally have to justify itself from the anthropological point of view. It could never really justify itself from the moral point of view. The idea of cultural poetics seems to me to be one of the integrating factors that would draw at least some of the humanities areas together.

I am also very conscious at the moment of the end-of-century perspective. I edited a collection of essays with a colleague on *Utopias and the Millennium* last year. I am preparing a conference on *Walter Pater and the Culture of the "fin de siècle"* in July. The ends of centuries, I think, are always interesting and fascinating times, precisely because there is a kind of cultural and poetic need to postulate some form of break or novelty and therefore all kinds of things come to the surface. There are sometimes rather painful transitions involved, but I see the challenge as being basically an exciting one, however much there are causes for cultural pessimism in other aspects of our situation.

255

The idea of cultural poetics seems to me to be one of the integrating factors that would draw at least some of the humanities areas together.

Canterbury, England
5 May 1994

SELECT WRITINGS

The Clothing of Clio: A Study of the Representation of History in Nineteenth-Century Britain and France. Cambridge: Cambridge Univ. Press, 1984.

Ian Hamilton Finlay: A Visual Primer, by Albrioux, Yves, author of introductory notes and commentaries. Edinburgh: Reaktion Books, 1985.

The True Vine: On Visual Representation and the Western Tradition. Cambridge: Cambridge Univ. Press, 1989.

The Inventions of History: Essays on the Representation of the Past. Manchester: Manchester Univ. Press, 1990.

Interpreting Contemporary Art, co-editor with William Allen. London: Reaktion Books, 1991.

Frankenstein, Creation and Monstrosity, editor. London: Reaktion Books, 1994.

Under the Sign: John Bargrave as Traveller, Collector, and Witness. Ann Arbor: Univ. of Michigan Press, 1994.

Romanticism and the Rise of History. New York: Twayne, 1995.

256   "Inscription and Identity in the Representation of the Past." *New Literary History* 22, no. 4 (1991): 937–60.

"Generating the Renaissance, or the Individualization of Culture." In *The Point of Theory: Practices of Cultural Analysis*, ed. Mieke Bal and Inge E. Boer. Amsterdam: Amsterdam Univ. Press, 1994.

" 'Wilder Shores of Love': Cy Twombly's Straying Signs." In *Materialities of Communication*, ed. Hans Ulrich Gumbrecht and K. Ludwig Pfeiffer. Stanford: Stanford Univ. Press, 1994.

"History as Competence and Performance: Notes on the Ironic Museum." In *A New Philosophy of History*, ed. Frank Ankersmit and Hans Kellner, 195–211. Chicago: Univ. of Chicago Press, 1995.

Ewa Domańska

(self-interview)

History is like life, life is history.

Why did I choose history?

■ I have always been interested in the human experience of the world. Every kind of human activity is essentially a way of searching for oneself and for self-realization. I read. Not about politics and facts. I read about people. Visiting places marked by history, I tried to touch things that "they" had touched—people who were staring at me from portraits: people whose spiritual presence I seemed to sense at those places. The passion of getting to know other people and other cultures is still with me. The endeavor to understand and experience. The passion of looking for people possessing the same metaphoric way of conceiving of the world.

I am recalling my secondary-school history teacher, a noble lady of the Polish eastern frontier, full of beauty and femininity. Keen intellect and feminine appeal were fused in her so-much-admired personality—the ideal I have always wanted to attain. Her fragility and delicacy were in real tension with her invincible resistance to the pressures of the Communist authorities that she was constantly subject to. I have inherited from her deep patriotism and, so undesired in these times, idealism. She recommended to us the classics of historiography: Burckhardt and Huizinga. Thus, I saw the past through their eyes—through the history of culture—when I decided to study history at the university.

My university studies coincided with the riveting but difficult

> The passion of looking for people possessing the same metaphoric way of conceiving of the world.

258 period of Poland's history: 1982–1987. We were more attracted by "the small conspiracy" than the classes. We were buying "banned" books and attending those classes where our lecturers sometimes smuggled in the "truth" about our past. Consequently, I belong to the last generation of "fighting idealists" who grew up with Solidarity and who have their roots in the Polish independence resurrections. "Wild capitalism" and the now-pervasive, particularly among the young, attitude of career-and-moneymaking (at any price) have come after us.

Our course lectures in history were mostly factography-ridden. Grand syntheses, histories of states, empires, and civilizations provided the factographic skeleton and knowledge of historic processes. But they lost the human being. It was not this dehumanized history that I desired to learn. Therefore, besides required readings, I was anxious to read biographies. I was interested in arts, music, in anything that was "human," emotional, and experiential. I studied conscientiously the history of philosophy. I was fascinated by Aristotle, the German idealists, and Kołakowski.

I was interested in arts, music, in anything that was "human," emotional, and experiential.

I was fascinated by Aristotle, the German idealists, and Kołakowski.

Alas, the influence of the analytic philosophy of history on the academic establishment was especially forceful. The so-called Poznań school of the philosophy of science had popularized a nonorthodox version of Marxism. The absorption of these sophisticated scientistic theories was eased to some extent by the pedagogical talent of Jerzy Topolski. He was then taking part in the debates over the issue of historical narratives and the role of truth in history. As for me, I was at that time busy with "removing the white spots" from the history of Poland. With the help of my friends, I was producing posters whose content was identified by the local Communist party as "nationalistic."

In general, students rebelled against a methodology that they unequivocally associated with the Marxism that tried to legitimize Communist totalitarianism, on the one hand, and, on the other hand, with a dehumanized theory of history obsessed by explanations invoking covering laws, models, and generalizations. We yearned for freedom, liberty, and tolerance. We did not want laws governing social development. We wanted philosophy that would enable us to find our way in the political turmoil.

Upon graduation, I began to work in the Department of History and Philosophy of Religion at Adam Mickiewicz University. I concentrated on the history of early Christianity and in

particular on its symbolism and heresies. I do not have good
memories from this period of my academic career but I learned
there two things: that people concerned with moral philosophy
are not always moral themselves and that there is no progress
without heresy. I was glad to return to the Institute of History,
where I have been working ever since.

I do not trust scientism. Science was not indifferent to the
tragedies of wars and totalitarianisms of our age—it supported
them. The faith in reason that replaced the faith in God has been
in crisis since the beginning of the nineteenth century. Man needed
a revelation.

Postmodernism was brought to my attention at the end of
the 1980s. It was the subject of discussions mainly among the
theorists of literature. Foreign publications were hardly available.
I was, however, in a convenient position: Jerzy Topolski and a seminar that he conducted were famous for their tolerance and openness. Moreover, the intellectual potential of the participants of
the seminar was widely known. I owe much to my friends and
colleagues, particularly to Wojciech Wrzosek, Gwidon Zalejko,
and Andrzej Zybertowicz, who stripped me of my personal and
intellectual naïveté. Fortunately not entirely. . . .

I learned about Hayden White from Topolski and Jan Pomorski. Pomorski handed to me, in 1989, a copy of *Metahistory* and
his article about White. I was surprised by the two planes in which
White's discussion took place: on the one hand, a structuralist
conception—an attempt at creating a model (and in that respect
White did not diverge from scientism); on the other hand, a completely new convention of looking at historical writing through
the prism of narratives, rhetoric. That was precisely what I was
looking for: a depiction of the literary and artistic face of history
and a yearning for nineteenth-century historiography. The thing
that attracted me most, however, was the legitimation of the historian's subjectivity as she strives to create her vision of the past.
Soon after that I read Ankersmit's *Narrative Logic* and I spotted
the discussions of postmodernism that were published in *Past and
Present* and in *History and Theory*. Everything in my mind began
to fall into its proper place, creating a comprehensive picture:
White, Ankersmit, Kellner, Gossman—the blurring of the line between history and literature, focusing upon the analysis of historical narratives, text seen as a whole, the rejection of the classical

260 definition of truth, figurative language, rhetoric, persuasion. I was sure that these conceptions would change the way we see the past.

How it started — that is, how I became, temporarily, a postmodernist.

It began with Richard Rorty's visits to Poland in the early 1990s. It was then that a specific Rortian version of pragmatism found its home in Polish philosophical awareness (especially among the young). And it was then that I met a person who greatly inspired me. In the same year, I was awarded a grant and left for Groningen, the Netherlands. There, under the kind supervision of Frank Ankersmit, I worked on a book about narrativist philosophy of history. My way of thinking about the world, life, and history changed. I became a postmodernist. I believe that if not for a fracture in my subconscious caused by deep personal experiences on the one hand and Ankersmit's tutorial on the other hand, postmodernism would not have become so close to my mind and heart. Postmodernism enchanted me and devoured me entirely. It was free, inscrutable, uncontrollable, unpredictable, decentralized, relative, deceptive, unstable, ironic — but inspiring, shocking, heretical, and perverse. It was the philosophical reflection of my personality at that transient time. It appealed to emotions and to the subconscious. It offered a radically new way of perceiving the world, the world seen through intuition and emotions; the world long lost, the world of *sacrum* . . . the paradise that the human being creates for herself and the hell that ensues after it. That was the world I lived in. That was the philosophy I craved. I thought then of one thing only: how to exploit such an intellectual resonance to the maximum, almost suck out the inspirations flowing out of it — fast, as fast as possible, before it burns away and disappears into a banal past. I may have made it.

I wonder if we should not begin disclosing, in what we write, our souls.

Why these confessions? Well, I wonder if we should not begin disclosing, in what we write, our souls — or even, if it is our obligation to do so.

Postmodernism is passé and it should be put to death to enable a careful postmortem.

Hunting for postmodernists — first interviews.

Postmodernism is passé, and it should be put to death to enable a careful postmortem. It goes away having fulfilled its task of offering the enlivening rain that fell on the field of culture dried out by reason and logic.

Postmodernism has played out the role of medieval heresies and of the modern avant-garde. It has reevaluated the ruling way of perceiving the world—shown us the world's new look. Postmodernism has placed the old categories in a new context. Thereby it seemed to be refreshing and it has refreshed the humanities. It has killed all that was traditional and conventional, bringing out what used to be associated with "apostasy." I am, nonetheless, afraid of its overwhelming popularity, of the disappearance of elites, masters, authorities: of the phenomenon that, following Arthur Danto, I would like to call the "transfiguration of the commonplace." In postmodernism, everything that had been considered "abnormal" was getting attention, and actually one might say that it was not "the abnormal" that was sick, due to a normal context, but "the normal," because of an abnormal context. That is why writing on the philosophy of history I shied away from the category of postmodernism. For it played the role of a "meta-creature" that was devouring all that was seen as new, nontraditional, and refined. It is for this reason that I began to use the expression "PASTmodernity" and "PASTmodernism" in order to denote the phenomena indicating that modernity and modernism had lived itself out since its potentialities had burned out. However, I did not regard PASTmodernity as a new epoch but as a messenger foretelling its coming; in other words, I thought of PASTmodernity as a transitory period. The thesis of such a transmission was apparently confirmed by the emergence of various philosophical orientations that were deliberately radicalizing their assumptions, noisily contesting the values that had been obligatory. This radicalism provoked an opposition and gave rise to a critical debate. As time flowed by, these trends were silencing its extremists, seeking some consensus with those of more moderate persuasions.

Living in the state of postmodern suspension, of intellectual weightlessness, I was looking for a master, for a heretic; I was hunting for a postmodernist. In February 1993, Hayden White arrived at Groningen. . . .

Invited by Ankersmit, he gave a talk, "Vico and the Eighteenth Century." The lecture hall was crowded. I expected a stormy discussion. Sitting in front of such a personality, of a man who made the "narrative turn" in the philosophy of history, directing it on

Marginal notes: "PASTmodernity" and "PASTmodernism"; I was hunting for a postmodernist.

wholly new tracks, I anticipated questions that would touch on the controversial issues of philosophical postmodernism, of textualism, deconstruction, and so forth. To my surprise, the questions that were raised dealt with minute details of White's theory—details that, by and large, were known only to White and the questioners. I believed that the opportunity opened by White's presence had been lost.

Since I was planning to devote a substantial part of my book to White's views, I asked him for an appointment. I took a tape recorder, realizing that I might be unable to note down everything I wanted to. Having in mind the impression of the unsatisfactory discussion, I started to ask the most general questions—questions that prevented the exchange from dissolving into mere details. I asked about his inspirations and interests, about his views on other philosophers, about postmodernism. I knew that in this kind of conversation, the interlocutor would often find himself in a somewhat awkward situation, being forced to admit or confess things that he would not say in writing, for text imposes a genre in which the author sloughs off a certain intimacy, privacy, and subjectivity. In a direct conversation, by contrast, facing a question that has just been posed, the interlocutor is inclined to answer it, at least by reason of etiquette. At that time, I did not think of the conversation as an interview. Neither was I going to publish it.

In February of the same year, Hans Kellner, invited by Ankersmit, came to Groningen. Encouraged by the successful conversation with White, I decided to try again. When I transcribed the talks from the recordings I found both of them to be gold mines of inspiration. I concluded that I could not keep them solely for myself. It appeared to me that I might arrange some excerpts into a written composition. This resulted in a text that was published in *Diacritics* (spring 1994).

In May 1992 I asked Franklin Ankersmit for an interview. I have preserved in my memory this wonderful evening. I exactly recall the moment when Ankersmit said: "This obsession with language and discourse has become boring. We've been talking about language for almost a hundred years. It's time to change the subject. Personally I am in favor of the category of *historical experience*." Afterwards, I asked him to elaborate on this point. It seemed to me particularly relevant. I see the point as fundamental for the future philosophy of history. It symbolizes the transgression of the border separating historiography and the philosophy of history. For *experience* can be a theoretical category as well as the plot of historical narratives. For those reasons I asked each of my subsequent interlocutors what he thought about the category of *experience*. There has always been an attempt in the theory of history to find a category that would be all-encompassing. In the analytic philosophy of history, this role was played by explanatory models. Under the rule of the philosophy of language, the function was performed by narrative, discourse, metaphor. Now, at the time of "the anthroplogization of history," the category of *experience*, along with other categories that accompany it—such as the *sublime, memory, consciousness*—may decisively renew the philosophy of history. This may happen through the return to its nineteenth-century tradition and by taking advantage of the inspirations offered by anthropological philosophy and by anthropological history. Life is made up by experiences. Can there be anything more encompassing than our being-in-the-world? History is, after all, also an experience. Perhaps, to paraphrase Roland Barthes, it is worth saying: History is like life, life is history. Isn't it true that a precious gem of contemporary historiography, Emmanuel Le Roy Ladurie's *Montaillou*, is an attempt at interpreting life on the basis of human experiences and an attempt at the interpretation of history by tracking life?

An enlivening blow.

By creeping into historical research, postmodernism exposed the schizophrenic relationship between historiography and the philosophy of history. The two seemed to develop independently of each other. Historiography was not much concerned with what was happening in the philosophy of history, and the latter (I mean here the narrativist philosophy of history) was focused mainly on eighteenth- and nineteenth-century historiography, considering those periods the peak of historiographical achievement.

The scent of Nietzsche's deconstructive thought and of the philosophy of life was discernible quite clearly in postmodernism. It was Nietzsche, after all, who criticized historicism, looking at

264

it from the vantage point of life. That was precisely—according to Herbert Schnädelbach—the origin of what later came to be called the philosophy of life. In fact, its roots stem from German romanticism, where life was placed in overt opposition to the rationalism of the Enlightenment. *Life*, as fundamental to history, became the norm and objective of historical concern, and history was now seen as the science of human life.

The affirmation of life and humanity, underlain, strangely enough, by a kind of pessimism, was interwoven with more and more voices proclaiming the cultural disintegration of the West. The symptoms of the disintegration were seen in the vanishing sacral experience of the world and in the resulting fall of the hierarchy of universal values. Pessimistic visions of the future emerged, warning of the destructive effects of technological progress. Crisis afflicted all the spheres of culture. Culture was "boiling," but the final explosion was delayed by the world wars and by totalitarianisms. These historical events are responsible for the fact that the crisis of thinking in terms of the Cartesian *ratio* returned not as a decadence characteristic of "the end of the century" but as all-embracing postmodernism now pervading every humanistic discipline. At the same time, postmodernism reflected the profound transformation of culture and mentality. Postmodernism was the culture of the frustrated postindustrial society that, remembering the tragedy of war and the rule of totalitarianisms, was experiencing the triviality of pop art, and that, with astonishment and fear, noticed the "empty heaven" above.

The advent, in the mid-1970s, of new historical literature, like *Montaillou* (the flourishing of anthropological history) and *Metahistory* (the flourishing of the narrativist philosophy of history), reaches with its roots to the second half of the nineteenth century, when, due to Nietzsche, the philosophy of life arose, and therefore it refurbishes some of the conceptions of that period. But this time it is done under the authority of history. All this is the outcome of the long crisis that began in the sixteenth century and consisted in the advancing laicization and desacralization of life, coupled with the longing for a new "enchantment of the world." Romanticism, the avant-garde of the turn of the century, and now postmodernity are the offspring of this crisis. Reason has been mystifying, but postmodernist philosophy has laid the mystification bare.

> Postmodernism was the culture of the frustrated postindustrial society that, remembering the tragedy of war and the rule of totalitarianisms, was experiencing the triviality of pop art, and that, with astonishment and fear, noticed the empty heaven above.

The anthropological turn in historiography.

The arcadian vision of the world that Le Roy Ladurie constructed in *Montaillou* is a countervision to the frustrated twentieth-century society. But this is not an idyllic or primitive arcadia. The arcadian myth of Montaillou is the proof of its moral wisdom.

The myth enables Le Roy Ladurie to gain knowledge alternative to that of science. For myth offers a journey to the depth of reality that becomes correlated with emotional states and that thereby exists in the way it is experienced. Such a myth elevates existence, even in its most banal configurations, to the sublime. A myth, so construed, has nothing to do with fantasy or fiction. It is a story of sacral dimensions. It manifests the truth in the deepest sense of the word. It allows us to touch the essence of reality, of life, of the human being. The arcadian character, Montaillou, is an embodiment of the fundamental myth of sublimation. But this myth is constructed not so much by Le Roy Ladurie, the historian, as by Le Roy Ladurie, the human being.

If more and more frequently we are talking of the recovery of the humanities under the auspices of history, it is because history is playing a more and more significant role. We are turning to the past because the present is not sufficient for us. The breakthrough that we have been experiencing for some twenty years has raised history to the rank of an intellectual enterprise that sustains the values of life philosophy. Only history is still normal, and that is why it is now one of the few havens of values. The "new" history becomes an anthropological story about human life, about the human experience of the world. "Anthropological stories" now being written by historians are assuming the role of compensatory myths, that are supposed to elevate reality to the sublime. As such they are countervisions to contemporary culture, displaying the drama that erupts between us and the world.

And truth?

Neither the "modern theoreticians of history" nor the "new historians" deny the existence of reality or of truth, as such. They only indicate that reality and truth are relative, emphasizing that our statements about the world are a sort of construct: they are the interpretations of the world. I believe, therefore, that there is

"Anthropological stories" now being written by historians are assuming the role of compensatory myths, that are supposed to elevate reality to the sublime. As such they are countervisions to contemporary culture, displaying the drama that erupts between us and the world.

266   no problem with truth: there are only problems with accuracy and adequacy of interpretations and, in the first place, problems with ourselves. At this point, it is ethics that we touch upon. For truth is a moral category (as is the gun).

The future

A new history that will not dominate historiography, even though it will be its main current, is a collection of separate biographies of individuals or small communities; hence, a collection of micro-histories. This history is a story about a world different from the one we happen to dwell in. The historian performs the role of a medium who speaks with the voices of ordinary people. These people have been sentenced by the grand syntheses (Lyotard's metanarratives) to sink into oblivion. In this way, a sacralized vision of past times emerges before the reader's eyes. This vision can then be experienced and let us touch the sublime.

It does not seem that departing postmodernism has helped us, even theoretically, to solve the vexing problems of today's culture. It has fulfilled its role, though; it has shocked us. It has showed researchers that history is essentially a life-story; it has reminded the philosophers of history that history is also literature and that truth is a moral concept. It has revealed that there is nothing more historical than a myth that manifests our unremitting desire to perceive the world as ordered, and whose axiology amounts to a two-value logic (the good and the evil). We should now wonder how to transform the commonplace into art, how to resacralize the profane, how to turn everyday life activities into a ritual, how to unearth the immutable patterns hidden deep within the layers of culture. In a word: how can we enchant the world this one more time?

We should now wonder how to transform the commonplace into art, how to re-sacralize the pro-fane, how to turn everyday life activ-ities into a ritual, how to unearth the immutable patterns hidden deep within the layers of culture.

And me?

Well, I love *Montaillou* because I am a bit like Béatrice de Planis-soles, who was a "young and pretty" woman who never forgot her great love—Pierre Clergue, and who was a heretic. . . .

Poznań, Poland
summer 1994
Translated from the Polish by Paweł Ozdowski

SELECTED WRITINGS   **267**

Historia: O jeden most za daleko? (History: one world too far?), editor.
Poznań: IH UAM, 1997.

"Metafora—Mit—Mimesis. Refleksje wokół koncepcji narracji historycznej Hayden White'a" (Metaphor—myth—mimesis: Reflections
on Hayden White's concept of historical narration). *Historyka* 22
(1992): 29–44.
"Historia feminizmu i feministyczna historia" (History of feminism and
feminist history). *Odra*, nos. 7/8 (1994): 22–28.
"The Image of Self-Presentation." *Diacritics* (spring 1994): 91–100.
"Kryzys tradycyjnego rozumienia historii w filozofii anglosaskiej" (The
crisis of the traditional understanding of history in Anglo-Saxon
philosophy). *Historyka* 24 (1994): 57–65.
"Współczesna filozofia sztuki a narratywistyczna filozofia historii (Przy-
padek Arthura C. Danto)" (Contemporary philosophy of art and
narrativist philosophy of history: The case of Arthur C. Danto). *Historyka* 25 (1995): 75–87.
"Historiografia czasu postmodernizmu po postmodernizmie. Retro-
spekcja" (The postmodern era's historiography after postmodernism: Retrospection). In *Wobec kultury. Problemy antropologa*, ed.
Ewa Karpińska, 111–29. Łódź: Wyd. UŁ, 1996.
"Montaillou—Arkadia "heretyckiego' historyka" (Montaillou—the arcadia of a "heretic" historian). In *Mit historyczny. Jego funkcje ideo-
logiczne i polityczne w XIX i XX wieku* (Historical myth: Its ideological and political functions in the nineteenth and twentieth
centuries), ed. Alina Barszczewska-Krupa, 89–110. Łódź: Wydawnictwo UŁ, 1996.
"Od postmodernistycznej narracji do po-postmodernistycznego doś-
wiadczenia. Propozycja Ankersmita" (From postmodern narrative to
post-postmodern experience: Ankersmit's proposal). *Teksty drugie*,
nos. 2/3 (1996): 190–209.
"Po-postmodernistyczny romantyzm. (Sensitivism—"nowa' filozofia
historii—Franklin R. Ankersmit)" (Post-postmodernist romanticism: Sensitivism—the "new" philosophy of history—Franklin R.
Ankersmit). *Kultura Współczesna*, nos. 1–2 (1996): 69–86.

Postscript

Lynn Hunt

■ The philosophy of history rarely sounds a personal note; since the days of Hegel, its practitioners have written in a highly abstract mode that gives few hints of the worries, uncertainties, expectations, or passions of those who have contributed to the genre. For all their differences, both the analytical philosophy of history and the newer postmodernist strains have maintained and even cultivated this tradition. Thus, it was with high hopes and even a certain sense of relief that I opened the collection organized by Ewa Domańska. Here at last might emerge a firsthand, informal, everyday account of some of the most pressing and difficult issues in our intellectual life.

Those expectations were not disappointed, especially since the particular turns and twists of the enterprise could not be foreseen even by the participants. Readers will not find here any systematic guide to the disputes over truth, postmodernism, the linguistic turn, or the narrativist approach, yet they will discover something more tantalizing: fascinating, wide-ranging, and sometimes contradictory *dialogues* on all those issues and more. The book speaks volumes, no doubt sometimes even more than was intended, about how some of the leading philosophers of history think about their practice; that is, how they construe it through their own interests, past experiences, ego-involvements, aesthetic preoccupations, and ambitions for the future.

This is a very personal book, then. But whose book is it? Just what does it represent? Does it reflect Ewa Domańska's views, since she picked

270   the interlocutors, posed the questions, and in a sense directed the conversation? She does not consign herself to the role of midwife; she does much more than help others give birth to their fledgling thoughts. She seems akin to a movie director, who daily revises an unfinished script and yet demonstrates a clear sense of where she wants to take the production, even if unsure of the eventual denouement of the story. Do the exchanges between the participants reveal, as one might reasonably assume, the opinions of those interviewed, who graciously allowed themselves to be drawn out, prodded, cajoled, and teased, but who set the agendas in the first place by their writings? These men (and they are all men, a point worth pondering) do not respond like actors in someone else's movie; they resemble the subjects of a documentary, who actively intervene in the accounts being constructed of them and their work. Do we not also detect here a more general zeitgeist, a kind of collective meditation about the meaning of history-writing, one built up patiently from individual dialogues about the questions and answers of our era? Certainly Domańska's own reflections on the endeavor seem to suggest as much, and even if the reader does not always agree with her construction of the issues, it is hard to resist the conclusion that the interviewer, the interviewees, and the implied readers share a larger set of worries, expectations, and aspirations about the meaning of the past. A kind of collective psychohistorico analysis has taken place without our knowing it.

Besides offering these different layers of significance within the rhetorical triangle of questioner, responder, and reading bystander, the book also forces us, by its very structure, to raise questions about the nature of scholarly communication more generally. The conversational, dialogic format resists all attempts to impose linear, systematic modes of thought; that is, precisely the modes most typical of the philosophy of history as a written genre. In other words, this collection about the philosophy of history tends to undermine the thought processes usually associated with that kind of reflection. Or does it more benignly supplement them, rounding out our understanding in more informal fashion? Even though the results of the conversations are written down, they still retain some of the hesitation, uncertainty, and unpredictability of their largely oral beginnings. As in all dialogue, the consequences of the interaction cannot be neatly confined; the back and forth between the interviewer and the authors soon raises other, unstated, and perhaps even unwanted, issues. Are the authors the best interpreters of their own work? Domańska's queries to them seem to imply that this might be so, and readers presumably take up the book with this conviction in mind, but the authors' answers do not always confirm this presupposition; words once published tend to take on a life of

their own, and the writers of those words do not always see all their implications, as they themselves recognize. Just how does the transcribed speech
of authors bear on their published written words? Should we read these
transcriptions as lesser, degraded versions of thought because they could
not be systematically organized or as something radically different and informative in other ways? Does transcription capture the original oral expression or is our reading inevitably distorted by the absence of gesture and
demeanor? Such questions go to the heart of the conventions of scholarly
interchange and raise problems that printed books often efface, to our loss.

In more than one way, this book, while still a book, presents scholarly
communication in a form much closer to our everyday experience: topics
change quickly and in unforeseen directions; answers come haltingly and
incompletely; responses change as the questions continue more insistently.
With its personalizing, interactive, even confrontational mode, the book
compels us to remember that ideas do not emerge full-blown from the
heads of intellectuals. They arise from dialogues with teachers, students,
colleagues, and lovers; they float in the miasma of a certain period of time;
they often remain beneath the surface, only to leap out unexpectedly; and
they take strange, often peculiar, forms when articulated, whether orally
or in writing. Although Domańska does not comment upon it, some of
the conversations rendered here took place on the Internet. One can only
speculate as to how that form of communication, certainly not oral in the
usual sense but also not exactly written in the usual sense either, changed
the way the thinking proceeded.

Quite aside from the explicit philosophical and theoretical positions
taken by the interviewees, the form itself of their exchanges with Domańska offers an implicit commentary on the meaning of history as an experience and as a discipline. In recent years, the philosophy of history has
been much concerned with the nature of narrative, and postmodernism as
a theoretical stance has been identified by many with suspicion or in-
credulity about metanarratives. At times, the narrative mode of historical
writing has come very much under fire as inherently mythomanic, impe-
rialist, and incompatible with science and real criticism. But are not one
or more metanarratives germinating here (many have noted that postmodernism's critique of metanarrative itself rests on an implied metanarrative)? At the very least, one would have to say that narratives are sprout-
ing right and left in these conversations. In part, this must be attributed
to Domańska's directing voice. She clearly wants to place postmodernism
in a historical framework, appreciate its value, declare its termination, and
figure out the emerging new directions of historical thought; that is, construct her own, new metanarrative about life and thought after the much

proclaimed deaths of God and man. She aims to ascertain the flow of thinking about history and perhaps even channel it.

But she is certainly not alone in this quest. Every time she asks a question about the meaning of one of her interviewee's positions, he (the male patient of the female analyst?) in response to her question, invariably spins a narrative web: what I was thinking when I wrote that . . . who taught me . . . who inspired me . . . what I think now . . . where I think things are going for myself and for others interested in similar questions, and so on. Both their personal experiences and their stances on history as a discipline seem caught up in narrative netting. Another book remains to be written about the meanings of those narrativizing responses, whose form seems almost inevitable. No one here avoids it.

If the tangle of narrative proves inescapable, at least in this context, then what about its truth content? The "problem" of truth comes up again and again in these pages. As Domańska observes, the problem of truth remains the most thorny issue (at least in the West) today, and, she might have said, in discussions not only of the philosophy of history but in almost every domain of knowledge. In many respects, it is coterminous with the problem of reason. If we are now actively reimagining history, as Hayden White claims, what is the role of reason in this endeavor? Although he is surely right to emphasize that our relationship to our personal past (or our collective past) cannot be a purely conscious connection, that it includes imagination as well as reason, it still does include reason, but to what extent and in what form?

Almost every author queried here pleads for a more capacious understanding of historical reasoning and consequently of the motives for writing history. Hans Kellner insists that historians operate on the basis of a rarely self-conscious "tacit knowledge," which they transmit to their students in the form of vaguely specified anxieties. He introduces the recurring motif of history as a response to loss. This sense of loss sometimes takes the form of an almost melancholic longing for the past; Frank Ankersmit, for instance, confesses that he would like to live in the eighteenth century. Almost everyone cites the work of men now dead, often long dead, as their chief inspiration: Barthes, Foucault, Collingwood, Croce, Leibniz, Edmund Burke. The urge to identify always seems to be intensely retrospective.

The sense of loss and longing is obviously tied to a rather dark view of the present. The interviewees return again and again to the themes of disintegration, whether in the form of the death of metanarratives, the fragmentation of knowledge, or the loss of confidence in the linear progression of history. Even though they often applaud these developments, or at least regard them as salutary, they still paint them with tinges of lack, loss, and disappearance. Jörn Rüsen states it most starkly when he refers to the meaningless world of modern societies. Domańska clearly shares this view, and its overcoming may be her chief purpose in preparing this volume.

The association between a threateningly disintegrative present and longing for an irremediably lost past is a romantic, Nietzschean, antimodernist, fin de siècle trope. It no doubt enters into the enthusiastic reception for some of the most celebrated recent work in cultural and microhistory: Emmanuel Le Roy Ladurie's *Montaillou*, Natalie Davis's *The Return of Martin Guerre* and Carlo Ginzburg's *The Cheese and the Worms*, in particular. As Domańska observes, however, it is difficult to find examples of history written in the postmodernist spirit. She turns to these three as likely candidates, but in most respects they do not really fill the bill. These works may exemplify a loss of belief in metanarrative and reflect the fragmentation of knowledge, since they are so insistently local in focus. Yet they brim with confidence in the historian's power to evoke, recapture, and, yes, tell the truth about the past, even while raising questions about the way the sources work to distort and distract our vision of what happened. They reflect the best of the current interest in the seemingly insignificant and peripheral things of life, because they insistently use those tiny things to illuminate much broader questions about religion, scientific knowledge, family life, sexual relations, and lower-class aspirations in the past. They certainly do not represent a giving up on history or a loss of conviction about reason; in many respects, Le Roy Ladurie, Davis, and Ginzburg are among the most resolutely "modernist" of historians, because they push on the constraints of conventional forms, even while writing out of a deep sense of affirmation of the future.

That sense of affirmation is also present in these pages. As Kellner insists, historians write the kind of history that enables them to envision the future they hope for. Most (I would argue all) of the authors interviewed here still think about the future—and consequently the past—in terms that are indebted in large measure to classical scientific notions of reason and truth (despite various protests to the contrary). These notions have now been expanded and nuanced rather than completely jettisoned. Jerzy Topolski reminds us that postmodernism in the most extreme form—arguing for the complete destruction of classical notions of reason and truth— would only be another dogmatism. In practice historians will not and cannot renounce explanation—that is, refuse to ask why; an orientation to the future depends on it. We cannot say where we want to go from here without an at least implied narrative of why we came to where we are now; past, present, and future are linked through our causal language.

In Topolski's view, which I find convincing, the question of truth cannot be confined to limited statements about separate historical facts; it must also concern the working of a whole narrative, however much narrative is inherently caught up in aesthetic, ethical, and political concerns. The authors interviewed here first came to widespread notice by forcefully pointing out the various unspoken, supposedly extraneous elements implicated in narrative structures. They showed, in short, that history-writing was not objective in the positivist sense. We may want to conclude from their work, as Lionel Gossman does, that truth in history works more successfully with a conception of intersubjectivity than with old-fashioned notions of objectivity. Yet as he suggests, we need not conclude that truth in history is a meaningless concept just because the writing of history draws on various codes of representation.

There appears to be an implied narrative flow in Domańska's presentation, for the most "radical" challengers to historical truth, Hayden White and Frank Ankersmit, come first and the collection ends on a more cautionary note with Arthur Danto and Peter Burke. Danto says that he has become a narrative realist, and he offers an interesting psychological and perhaps aesthetic argument for his position: unless we feel that the stories are true, our propensity to listen to them will wither. Peter Burke grants that from time to time historians need to be shocked and that the new narrativist and postmodernist theories have succeeded in doing this. But he maintains that we can arrive at some truths and avoid telling falsehoods. Moreover, he hints that the fashion for micro- and cultural history may have run its course: without careful attention to larger structures of explanation, the local focus loses its edge. The tried and trusted techniques of historians do not seem so out-of-date after all.

Whatever Domańska's intentions in lining up her interlocutors in this fashion, we are ultimately left on our own to figure out the future. Do we, following Ankersmit, have to opt now either for language or for experience? He provocatively declares himself for the latter, associating experience with consciousness (and presumably claiming that language does not fully encompass consciousness). Historians might take some comfort from this, because should we shift from asking how we represent reality to how we experience it, then the historians might get their revenge on the philosophers by providing new and essential answers. Or must we, as Burke insists, devote our attention both to structures and experience, recognizing that experience can hardly constitute an unmediated category?

In thinking about future directions, I found myself most struck by two remarks made by Rüsen. In the first, he maintains that history combines aesthetics, politics, and cognition and that we need to appreciate the working of all three. In a sense, we might say that White and Ankersmit underline the aesthetic dimension, whereas Danto and Burke emphasize the cognitive. My point is not to place each historian or philosopher along a three-dimensional axis, but rather to agree with Rüsen that we need to devote more attention to examining the intertwining without downplaying any of the three elements. In a second remark, Rüsen reminds us of one of the most compelling reasons to hold to some notion of historical truth: it happens that the sources tell us something that we did not expect—even something that counters our own concept of meaning. This is a perfect example of Rüsen's insistence on the interconnections between the aesthetic, cognitive, and political dimensions of historical knowledge: aesthetically, we cannot be satisfied with the predictable; cognitively, the surprise reminds us that our knowing does not come just from within ourselves; and politically, the unexpected reminds us to be wary of our own preconceptions.

This brings me to a postscript of my postscript. Earlier I drew attention to the fact that all the interviewees were men; they are also all European or American (at least so I assume). Although they offer richly provocative accounts of themselves and their crafts, they do not address one of the great realms of the unexpected today: the history being inscribed by those previously excluded from the making of historical knowledge. Women, minorities, and non-Westerners now turn out their own historical accounts, sometimes of their own peoples, sometimes of others, sometimes following canonical forms, sometimes not. This explosion of historical consciousness calls out for attention. But that is a postscript to a postscript—a plea to follow the unanticipated wherever it takes us. Heresies, as Domańska calls them, are rarely found in the places you expect.

SELECTED WRITINGS

Politics, Culture and Class in the French Revolution. Berkeley: Univ. of California Press, 1984.
The New Cultural History, editor. Berkeley: Univ. of California Press, 1989.

276   *The Family Romance of the French Revolution.* Berkeley: Univ. of California Press, 1992.

The Invention of Pornography: Obscenity and the Origins of Modernity, 1500–1800, editor. New York: Zone Books, 1993.

Telling the Truth about History, co-author with Joyce Appleby and Margaret Jacob. New York: Norton, 1994.

Histories: French Constructions of the Past, co-editor with Jacques Revel. New York: New Press, 1995.

The French Revolution and Human Rights, editor. Boston: Bedford Books, 1996.

"The Revenge of the Subject / The Return of Experience." *Salmagundi,* no. 97 (1993): 45–53.

"The Virtues of Disciplinarity." *Eighteenth-Century Studies* 28 (1994): 1–7.

"Forgetting and Remembering: The French Revolution Then and Now." *American Historical Review* 100 (1995): 1119–35.

Works Cited

Ankersmit, Franklin R. "Historiography and Postmodernism." *History and Theory* 28, no. 2 (1989): 137–53. Discussion: Perez Zagorin. "Historiography and Postmodernism: Reconsiderations." *History and Theory* 29, no. 3 (1990): 265–74; and Franklin R. Ankersmit. "Reply to Professor Zagorin." *History and Theory* 29, no. 3 (1990): 275–96.

——. *Narrative Logic: A Semantic Analysis of the Historian's Language*. The Hague: Nijhoff, vol. 7, 1983.

——. "Tocqueville and the Sublimity of Democracy." *Tocqueville Review* (1993): 179–201; *Tocqueville Review* (1994): 193–218.

Ariès, Philippe. *Centuries of Childhood*. Trans. Robert Baldick. Harmondsworth UK: Penguin, 1979.

Aristotle. *De Anima*, edited and with introduction and commentary by David Ross. Oxford: Clarendon Press, 1961.

——. *De Sensu and De Memoria*. Text and translation with introduction and commentary by G. R. T. Ross. New York: Arno Press, 1973.

Auerbach, Erich. *Mimesis: The Representation of Reality in Western Literature*. Trans. Willard Trask. Princeton: Princeton Univ. Press, 1968.

Austen, Jane. *Persuasion*. London: Zodiac, 1949.

Bakhtin, Mikhail. *Rabelais and His World*. Trans. Hélène Iswolsky. Bloomington: Indiana Univ. Press, 1984.

——, and P. N. Medvedev. *The Formal Method in Literary Scholarship: A Critical Introduction to Sociological Poetics*. Baltimore: Johns Hopkins Univ. Press, 1978.

Bann, Stephen. "Analysing the Discourse of History." In his *The Inventions of History: Essays on the Representation of the Past*. Manchester: Manchester Univ. Press, 1990.

278   ——. *The Clothing of Clio: A Study of the Representation of History in Nineteenth-Century Britain and France*. Cambridge: Cambridge Univ. Press, 1984.

——. "Generating the Renaissance or the Individualization of Culture. In *The Point of Theory*," ed. Mieke Bal and Inge E. Boer. Amsterdam: Amsterdam Univ. Press, 1994.

——. "'Wilder Shores of Love': Cy Twombly's Straying Signs." In *Materialities of Communication*, ed. Hans Ulrich Gumbrecht and K. Ludwig Pfeiffer. Stanford: Stanford Univ. Press, 1994.

——. *The True Vine: On Visual Representation and the Western Tradition*. Cambridge: Cambridge Univ. Press, 1989.

—— and William Allen, eds. *Interpreting Contemporary Art*. London: Reaktion Books, 1991.

—— and John E. Bowlt, eds. *Russian Formalism: A Collection of Articles and Texts in Translation*. Edinburgh: Scottish Academic Press, 1973.

—— and Krishan Kumar, eds. *Utopias and the Millennium*. London: Reaktion Books, 1993.

Barnett, Correlli. *The Swordbearers: Supreme Command in the First World War*. Harmondsworth UK: Penguin, 1966.

Barthes, Roland. "The Discourse of History." In *Structuralism: A Reader*, ed. and intro. Michael Lane. London: Jonathan Cape, 1970.

——. *Elements of Semiology*. Trans. Annette Lavers and Colin Smith. New York: Hill & Wang, 1968.

——. *Mythologies*. Paris: Seuil, 1957.

——. *A Lover's Discourse: Fragments*. Trans. Richard Howard. New York, 1978. French edn.: *Fragments d'un discours amoureux*. Paris: Seuil, 1977.

——. *S/Z*. Trans. Richard Miller. New York, 1974.

Bell, Daniel. *The Coming of Post-Industrial Society: A Venture in Social Forecasting*. Harmondsworth UK: Penguin, 1976.

Bernstein, Richard J. *Beyond Objectivism and Relativism: Science, Hermeneutics, and Praxis*. Oxford: Basil Blackwell, 1983.

Bloch, Marc. *Feudal Society*. Trans. L. A. Manyon. London: Routledge & Kegan Paul, 1989.

Borkenau, Franz. *Der Ubergang vom feudalen zum bürgerlichen Weltbild: Studien zur Geschichte der Philosophie der Manufakturperiode*. Paris: Félix Alcan, 1934.

Braudel, Fernand. *L'Identite de la France*. Paris: Arthaud-Flammarion, 1986.

——. *The Mediterranean and the Mediterranean World in the Age of Philip II*. Trans. Siân Reynolds. London: Collins, 1972–73.

Brown, Norman O. *Life against Death: The Psychoanalytical Meaning of History*. London: Routledge & Kegan Paul, 1959.

——. *Love's Body*. New York: Random House, 1966.

Bryson, Norman. *Looking at the Overlooked: Four Essays on Still Life Painting*. Cambridge: Harvard Univ. Press, 1990.

Burckhardt, Jacob. *The Age of Constantine the Great*. Trans. Moses Hadas. New   **279**
York: Pantheon, 1949.

Bürgin, Alfred. *Geschichte des Geigy-Unternehmens von 1758 bis 1939: Ein Beitrag
zur Basler Unternehmer- und Wirtschaftsgeschichte*. Basel: Birkhäuser, 1958.

Carnap, Rudolf. *Logische Aufbau der Welt*. Hamburg: Meiner, 1966.

Collingwood, R. G. *The Idea of History*. New York: Oxford Univ. Press, 1946.

Danto, Arthur C. *Analytical Philosophy of History*. Cambridge: Cambridge Univ.
Press, 1965.

——. "The Artistic Enfranchisement of Real Objects: The Artworld." In *Aesthetics: A Critical Anthology*, ed. George Dickie and R. J. Sclafani. New York:
St. Martin's Press, 1977.

——. "Beautiful Science and the Future of Criticism." In *The Future of Literary
Theory*, ed. Ralph Cohen. New York: Routledge, 1989.

——. "A Future for Aesthetics." *The Journal of Aesthetics and Art Criticism* 51,
no. 2 (1993): 271–77.

——. *The Transfiguration of the Commonplace: A Philosophy of Art*. Cambridge:
Harvard Univ. Press, 1983.

Davis, Natalie Zemon. *Fiction in the Archives: Pardon Tales and Their Tellers in
Sixteenth-Century France*. Stanford, California: Stanford Univ. Press, 1987.

——. *The Return of Martin Guerre*. Cambridge: Harvard Univ. Press, 1983.

Derrida, Jacques. *Glas*. Paris: Galileé, 1974.

——. *La Vérité en peinture. Lire Condillac*. Paris: Flammarion, 1978.

Descartes, René. *Méditations métaphysiques*. Texte, trad., objections et réponses
présentés par Florence Khodoss. Paris: PUF, 1986.

Dewey, John. *Art as Experience*. New York: Capricorn Books, 1959.

Diderot, Denis. "Essai sur la peinture." In *Oeuvres esthétiques*, ed. P. Vernière. Paris:
Garnier, 1968.

——. "Lettre sur les aveugles." In *Ouvres philosophiques*, ed. P. Vernière. Paris: Garnier, 1964.

Dray, William. *Laws and Explanation in History*. Oxford: Clarendon Press, 1957.

Droysen, Johann Gustav. *Historik, historisch-kritische Ausgabe*, ed. Peter Leyh,
vol. 1, Stuttgart–Bad Cannstatt: Frommann-Holzboog, 1977.

Eco, Umberto. *Foucault's Pendulum*. Trans. William Weaver. San Diego: Har-
court Brace Jovanovich, 1989.

——. *The Name of the Rose*. Trans. William Weaver. London: Secker & Warburg,
1983.

Eliot, George. *Middlemarch*, ed. W. J. Harvey. Harmondsworth UK: Penguin,
1985.

Ermarth, Elizabeth Deeds. *Sequel to History: Postmodernism and the Crisis of Rep-
resentational Time*. Princeton: Princeton Univ. Press, 1992.

Finlay, Ian Hamilton, Ron Costley, and Stephen Bann. *Heroic Emblems*. Calais
VT: Z Press, 1977.

280   Flores, Marcello. *L'Immagine dell'USSR: l'Occidente e la Russia di Stalin (1927–1956)*. Milano: Il Saggatiore, 1990.

Fogel, Robert W. *New Sources and New Techniques for the Study of Secular Trends in Nutritional Status, Health, Mortality, and the Process of Aging*. Cambridge: National Bureau of Economic Research, 1991.

—— and Stanley L. Engerman. *Time on the Cross: The Economics of American Negro Slavery*. Boston: Little, Brown, 1974.

Forster, E. M. *A Passage to India*. London: Arnold, 1978.

Foucault, Michel. *The Archeology of Knowledge and the Discourse on Language*. Trans. A. M. Sheridan Smith. New York: Pantheon, 1972 (Originally *L'Archaeology du Savoir*, 1969, and *L'Ordre du Discours*, 1971, Paris: Gallimard).

——. *Discipline and Punish: The Birth of the Prison*. Trans. Alan Sheridan. Harmondsworth UK: Penguin, 1979.

——. *Histoire de la folie à l'âge classique*. Reprint Paris: Gallimard, 1985.

——. *The Order of Things: An Archeology of the Human Sciences* (*Les Mots et Les Choses*, 1966). New York: Random House, 1970.

Freud, Sigmund. *The Interpretation of Dreams*. Trans. James Strachey. Reprint New York: Avon, 1965.

Friedlander, Saul. *Reflections on Nazism: An Essay on Kitsch and Death*. Trans. Thomas Weyr. Bloomington: Indiana Univ. Press, 1993.

Fumaroli, Marc. *L'Âge de l'éloquence: Rhétorique et "res literaria," de la Renaissance au seuil de l'époque classique*. Geneva: Droz, 1980.

Genovese, Eugene. *Roll, Jordan, Roll: The World the Slaves Made*. London: Deutsch, 1975.

Gibbon, Edward. *The Decline and Fall of the Roman Empire*. Intro. Christopher Dawson. London 1957–60.

Ginzburg, Carlo. *The Cheese and the Worms: The Cosmos of a Sixteenth-Century Miller*. Trans. John Tedeschi and Ann Tedeschi. London: Routledge & Kegan Paul, 1980.

Goethe, Johann Wolfgang von. "Italienische Reise." In Goethe, *Poetische Werke*, vol. 14. Berlin, 1961.

——. *Die Schriften Zur Naturwissenschaft*, vol. 4, *Zur Farbenlehre: Widmung, Vorwort, und Didaktischer Teil*. Weimar: Böhlau, 1955.

Goldmann, Lucien. *Le Dieu caché*. Paris: Gallimard, 1956.

Gombrich, Ernst. *Meditations on a Hobby Horse and Other Essays on the Theory of Art*. London: Phaidon, 1963.

Goodman, Nelson. *Languages of Art: An Approach to a Theory of Symbols*. Indianapolis: Bobbs-Merrill, 1968.

Gossman, Lionel. *Between History and Literature*. Cambridge: Harvard Univ. Press, 1990.

——, ed. with Mihai Spariosu. *Building a Profession: Autobiographical Perspectives on the Beginnings of Comparative Literature in the United States*. Albany: State Univ. of New York Press, 1994.

———. "Toward a Rational Historiography." In Gossman, *Between History and Literature*. Cambridge: Harvard Univ. Press, 1990.

———. Review of Michael Holquist and Katerina Clark, *Mikhail Bakhtin*, in *Comparative Literature* 38 (1986): 337–49.

———. Review of Mikhail Bakhtin, *The Formal Method in Literary Scholarship*, in *Comparative Literature* 31 (1979): 403–12.

Habermas, Jürgen. *The Philosophical Discourse of Modernity: Twelve Lectures*. Trans. Frederick Lawrence. Cambridge: MIT Press, 1987.

Hanawalt, Barbara, and Luise White. Review of Simon Schama, *Dead Certainties: Unwarranted Speculations*, in *American Historical Review* 98 no. 1 (1993): 121–23.

Hegel, Georg Wilhelm Friedrich. *Aesthetik*. Ed. Friedrich Basseng. Berlin, 1955.

Heidegger, Martin. *Being and Time* (*Sein und Zeit*, 1927). Trans. John Macquarrie and Edward Robinson. New York: Harper & Row, 1962.

Hempel, Carl. G. "The Function of General Laws in History." *Journal of Philosophy* 39 (1942): 35–48.

Hildesheimer, Wolfgang. *Marbot: A Biography*. Trans. Patricia Crampton. New York: G. Braziller, 1983.

Himmelfarb, Gertrude. *The New History and the Old*. Cambridge: Belknap Press of Harvard Univ. Press, 1987.

———. "Telling It as You Like It." *Times Literary Supplement*, 16 Oct. 1992: 12–15.

Hofmannsthal, Hugo von. "Ein Brief." In Hofmannsthal, *Sämtliche Werke*, vol. 30. München, 1991: 45–56.

Ingarden, Roman. *Untersuchungen zur Ontologie der Kunst*. Tübingen: M. Niemeyer, 1962.

James, Henry. *The Golden Bowl*. Intro. R. P. Blackmur. New York, 1952.

Jones, Gareth Stedman. *Languages of Class: Studies in English Working Class History, 1832–1982*. New York: Cambridge Univ. Press, 1983.

Kammen, Michael, ed. *The Past before Us: Contemporary Historical Writing in the United States*. Ithaca: Cornell Univ. Press, 1980.

Kant, Immanuel. "Idea for a Universal History with a Cosmopolitan Purpose." In Kant, *Political Writings*. Ed. Hans Reiss, trans. H. B. Nisbet. 2d enlarged ed. Cambridge: Cambridge Univ. Press, 1991: 41–53.

———. *Kritik der Urteilskraft*. In Kant, *Werke*, vol. 8. Ed. Wilhelm Weischdel. Darmstadt, 1968.

———. "An Old Question Raised Again: Is the Human Race Constantly Progressing?" In Kant, *On History*. Ed. L. W. Beck. Indianapolis: Bobbs-Merrill, 1985.

Kellner, Hans. "A Bedrock of Order: Hayden White's Linguistic Humanism." *History and Theory* (1980) Beiheft 19: Metahistory: Six Critiques: 2–28.

———. "Hayden White and the Kantian Discourse: Freedom, Narrative, History." In *The Philosophy of Discourse. The Rhetorical Turn in Twentieth-Century Thought*, vol. I, ed. Chip Sills and George H. Jensen. Boynton/Cook: Portsmouth NH, 1992.

282 ——. *Language and Historical Representation: Getting the Story Crooked*. Madison: Univ. of Wisconsin Press, 1989.

——. "Narrativity in History: Post-Structuralism and Since." *History and Theory* (1987). Beiheft 26: The Representation of Historical Events.

Keneally, Thomas. *Schindler's List*. London: Sceptre, 1994.

Kmita, Jerzy. *Elementy marksistowskiej metodologii humanistyki* (Elements of the Marxist methodology of the humanities, in Polish). Poznań, 1976.

Koselleck, Reinhart. *Historische Semantik und Begriffsgeschichte*. Stuttgart: Klett-Cotta, 1979.

——. *Kritik und Krise: Eine Studie zur Pathogenese der bürgerlichen Welt*. Frankfurt am Main: Suhrkamp, 1976.

Kowecka, Elzbieta. *Dwór "najrzadniejszego w Polszcze magnata"* (The court of "the most frugal magnate in Poland," in Polish). Warszawa: Instytut Kultury Materialnej PAN, 1991.

Krieger, Leonard. "The Horizons of History." *American Historical Review* 63 (1957): 62–74. Reprinted in Leonard Krieger, *Ideas and Events: Professing History*, ed. M. L. Brick, with an introduction by Michael Ermarth. Chicago: Univ. of Chicago Press, 1992.

Kristeva, Julia. *Proust and the Sense of Time*. Trans. Stephen Bann. London: Faber, 1993.

——. "The Ruin of a Poetics." In Stephen Bann and John E. Bowlt. *Russian Formalism: A Collection of Articles and Texts in Translation*. Edinburgh: Scottish Academic Press, 1973.

Kula, Witold. *Rozwazania o historii* (Reflections on history, in Polish). Warszawa: PWN, 1958.

Kuzminski, Adrian. "A New Science?" *Comparative Studies in Society and History* 18, no. 1 (1976): 129–43.

Labrousse, Ernest. *La Crise de l'économie française à la fin de l'ancien régime et au début de la révolution*. Paris: Presses Universitaires de France, 1944.

LaCapra, Dominick. "Is Everyone a *Mentalité* Case?" In his *History and Criticism*. Ithaca Cornell Univ. Press, 1985.

Laslett, Peter. *The World We Have Lost*. London: Methuen, 1965.

Leibniz, Gottfried Wilhelm. *Discourse on Metaphysics; and The Monadology*. Trans. George R. Montgomery. Buffalo: Prometheus Books, 1992.

Le Roy Ladurie, Emmanuel. *Montaillou, village occitan de 1294 a 1324*. Paris: Gallimard, 1975. English edn.: *Montaillou: Cathars and Catholics in a French Village, 1294–1324*. Trans. Barbara Bray. New York: Penguin, 1984.

Lévi-Strauss, Claude. *The Raw and the Cooked*. Trans. Doreen Weightman. Harmondsworth UK: Penguin, 1986.

Livius, Titus. *Titi Livi Ab urbe condita; Libri X*. Leipzig: Teubner, 1982.

Lord, Albert B. *The Singer of Tales*. Cambridge: Harvard Univ. Press, 1960.

Lotman, Iurii Mikhailovic. *Lektsii po struktural'noi poetike*. Introduced by Thomas G. Winner. Providence: Brown Univ. Press, 1968.

Lyotard, Jean-François. *The Postmodern Condition: A Report on Knowledge*. Trans.

Geoff Bennington and Brian Massumi, foreword by Fredric Jameson. Minneapolis: Univ. of Minnesota Press, 1984.

Malewski, Andrzej. "Empiryczny sens materializmu historycznego" (The empirical sense of historical materialism, in Polish). In *Studia z metodologii historii* (Studies in the methodology of history) ed. Andrzej Malewski and Jerzy Topolski. Warszawa: PWN, 1960.

Martin, Rux. "Truth, Power, Self: An Interview with Michel Foucault." In *Death and the Labyrinth: The World of Michel Foucault.* Trans. Charles Raus. London: Athlone Press, 1986.

Marx, Karl. *The Eighteenth Brumaire of Louis Bonaparte.* New York: International, 1972.

McCullagh, C. Behan. Review of *Narrative Logic. A Semantic Analysis of the Historian Language,* by Franklin R. Ankersmit. *History and Theory* 23, no. 3 (1984): 394–403.

Megill, Allan. "Recounting the Past: 'Description,' Explanation, and Narrative in Historiography." *American Historical Review* 94 (1989): 627–53.

Meinecke, Friedrich. *Die Entstehung des Historismus.* Hrsg. und eingel. von Carl Hinrichs. München: Oldenburg, 1959.

———. *Die Idee der Staatsräson in der neueren Geschichte.* Hrsg. und eingel. von Walther Hofer. 4. Aufl. München: Oldenburg, 1976.

Merleau-Ponty, Maurice. *Le Visible et l'invisible: Suivi des notes de travail.* Paris: Gallimard, 1971.

Mommsen, Theodor. *Römische Geschichte,* vols. 1–5. Berlin, 1912–1917.

Montaigne, Michel de. *Essais.* Paris: Librairie Generale Francaise, 1985. English edn.: *The Complete Essays.* Trans. M. A. Screech. London: Penguin, 1991.

Moretti, Franco. "The Moment of Truth." *New Left Review,* London, no. 159 (1986): 39–48. Republished in Franco Moretti, *Signs Taken for Wonders: Essays in the Sociology of Literary Forms.* Trans. Susan Fischer, David Forgacs and David Miller. London: Verso, 1988.

Nagel, Thomas. "What Is It Like to Be a Bat?" In Nagel, *Mortal Questions.* Cambridge: Cambridge Univ. Press, 1983: 165–81.

Negt, Oskar, and Alexander Kluge. *Geschichte und Eigensinn.* Frankfurt a.M.: Zweitausendeins, 1985.

Nelson, John S., Allan Megill, and Donald N. McCloskey. *The Rhetoric of the Human Sciences.* Madison: Univ. of Wisconsin Press, 1987.

Niethammer, Lutz. *Posthistoire. Ist die Geschichte zu Ende?* Reinbek bei Hamburg: Rowohlt, 1989. English edn.: *Posthistoire: Has History Come to an End?* Trans. Patrick Camiller. London: Verso, 1992.

Nietzsche, Friedrich. *The Genealogy of Morals: An Attack.* Trans. Francis Golffing. New York: Doubleday, 1956.

———. *The Use and Abuse of History.* Trans. Adrian Collins with an introduction by Julius Kraft. Indianapolis: Library of Liberal Arts Press, Bobbs-Merrill, 1957.

Novick, Peter. *That Noble Dream: The "Objectivity Question" and the American Historical Profession.* Cambridge: Cambridge Univ. Press, 1988.

284   Nussdorfer, Laurie. Review of *The New Cultural History*, edited with introduction by Lynn Hunt. Berkeley: Univ. of California Press, 1989; and *Interpretation and Cultural History*, ed. Joan H. Pittock and Andrew Wear. New York: St. Martin's Press, 1991. *History and Theory* 32, no. 1 (1993): 74–83.

Perelman, Chaim. *Raisonnement et démarches de l'historien*. Brussels: Éditions de l'Institut de Sociologie de l'Université Libre de Bruxelles, 1963.

——. *Le Champ de l'argumentation*. Brussels: Presses universitaires, 1970.

Pocock, John Greville Agard. *The Machiavellian Moment: Florentine Political Thought and the Atlantic Tradition*. Princeton: Princeton Univ. Press, 1975.

Propp, Vladimir. *Morphology of the Folktale*, edited and with an introduction by Svatava Pirkova-Jakobson. Trans. Laurence Scott. Bloomington: Indiana Univ. Press, 1958.

Proust, Marcel. *A la recherche du temps perdu*. Etablie par Nathalie Mauriac et Etienne Wolff. Paris: Grasset, 1987.

Rescher, Nicholas. "American Philosophy Today." *Review of Metaphysics* 46, no. 184 (1993): 717–45.

Ricoeur, Paul. *Time and Narrative*. vol. I. Trans. Kathleen McLaughlin and David Pellauer. Chicago: Univ. of Chicago Press, 1984.

Rigney, Ann. *The Rhetoric of Historical Representation: Three Narrative Histories of the French Revolution*. Cambridge: Cambridge Univ. Press, 1991.

Rorty, Richard. *Consequences of Pragmatism (Essays: 1972–1980)*. Minneapolis: Univ. of Minnesota Press, 1982.

——. *Philosophy and the Mirror of Nature*. Princeton: Princeton Univ. Press, 1980.

——. ed. *The Linguistic Turn: Recent Essays in Philosophical Method*. Chicago: Univ. of Chicago Press, 1967.

Rüsen, Jörn. *Studies in Metahistory*, edited and introduced by Pieter Duvenage. Pretoria: Human Sciences Research Council, 1993.

Schama, Simon. *Citizens. A Chronicle of the French Revolution*. New York: Knopf, 1989.

——. *Dead Certainties: Unwarranted Speculations*. New York: Knopf, 1991.

——. *The Embarrassment of Riches: An Interpretation of Dutch Culture in the Golden Age*. New York: Knopf, 1987.

Schefer, Jean-Louis. "The Bread and the Blood." In *Frankenstein, Creation and Monstrosity*, ed. Stephen Bann. London: Reaktion Books, 1994.

Schier, Flint. *Deeper into Pictures: An Essay on Pictorial Representation*. Cambridge: Cambridge Univ. Press, 1986.

Schiller, Friedrich. *Letters on the Aesthetic Education of Man*. Translated and edited by Elizabeth M. Witkinson and L. A. Willoughby. Oxford: Clarendon Press, 1967.

——. "Was heisst und zu welchem Ende studiert man Universalgeschichte." In *Werke*. Nationalausgabe, Weimar, 1970, XVII.

Scott, James C. *Weapons of the Weak: Everyday Forms of Peasant Resistance*. New Haven: Yale Univ. Press, 1985.

Scott, Joan Wallach. *Gender and the Politics of History*. New York: Columbia Univ. **285**
Press, 1988.

Sewell, William. *Work and Revolution in France: The Language of Labor from the Old Regime to 1848*. Cambridge: Cambridge Univ. Press, 1980.

Shusterman, Richard. *Pragmatist Aesthetics: Living Beauty, Rethinking Art*. Cambridge MA: Blackwell, 1992.

Southern, Richard. *The Making of the Middle Ages*. London: Hutchinson, 1953.

Spence, Jonathan D. *The Memory Palace of Matteo Ricci*. New York: Viking, 1984.

Spengler, Oswald. *The Decline of the West*. Trans. with notes by Charles Francis Atkinson. New York: Knopf, 1926–28.

Stanford, Michael. *The Nature of Historical Knowledge*. Oxford: Basil Blackwell, 1986.

Stone, Lawrence. *The Family, Sex and Marriage in England, 1500–1800*. New York: Harper & Row, 1977.

———. "The Revival of Narrative: Reflections on a New Old History." *Past and Present* 85 (1979): 3–24.

Taylor, A. J. P. *History of World War I*. London: Octopus Books, 1974.

Thompson, E. P. *The Making of the English Working Class*. Harmondsworth UK: Penguin, 1968.

Todorov, Tzvetan. *Théorie de la Litterature*. Paris: Seuil, 1965.

Topolski, Jerzy. *Wolnosc i przymus w tworzeniu historii* (Freedom and coercion in the making of history). Warszawa: PIW, 1990.

———. "Załozenia metodologiczne Kapitalu Marksa." In *Załozenia metodologiczne "Kapitalu" Marksa* (Methodological assumptions of Marx's "Capital"). Warszawa, 1970.

———. *Methodology of History*. Trans. Olgierd Wojtasiewicz. Warszawa: PWN, 1976.)

———. "A Non-Postmodernist Analysis of Historical Narratives." In *Historiography between Modernism and Postmodernism*.

———. Teoria wiedzy historycznej (Theory of historical knowledge). Poznań: Wydawnictwo Poznańskie, 1983.

———, ed. *Historiography between Modernism and Postmodernism: Contributions to the Methodology of the Historical Research*. "Poznań Studies in the Philosophy of the Sciences and the Humanities." Amsterdam: Radopi, 1994.

Toulmin, Stephen, Richard Rieke, and Allan Janik. *An Introduction to Reasoning*. New York: Macmillan; London: Collier-Macmillan, 1979.

Toynbee, Arnold. A *Study of History*, vols. 1–12. London. Oxford Univ. Press, 1935–61.

Vico, Giambattista. *The New Science*. Trans. of 3d. edn. (1744) by Thomas Goddard Bergin and Max Harold Fisch. Ithaca: Cornell Univ. Press, 1968.

Vries, P. H. H. *Vertellers op drift: een Verhandeling over de niuewe verhalende geschiedenis*. Hilversum: Verloren, 1990.

White, Hayden. "The Burden of History." *History and Theory* 5, no. 2 (1966): 3–34.

286 ——. *The Content of the Form: Narrative Discourse and Historical Representation.* Baltimore: Johns Hopkins Univ. Press, 1987.

——. "Foucault Decoded: Notes from Underground." *History and Theory* 12, no. 1 (1973): 23–54. Also in White, *Tropics of Discourse.*

——. *Metahistory: The Historical Imagination in Nineteenth-Century Europe.* Baltimore: Johns Hopkins Univ. Press, 1973.

—— and Willson H. Coates. *The Ordeal of Liberal Humanism*, vol. 2 of An Intellectual History of Western Europe. New York: McGraw-Hill, 1969.

——. *Tropics of Discourse: Essays in Cultural Criticism.* Baltimore: Johns Hopkins Univ. Press, 1978.

——, ed. *The Uses of History: Essays in Intellectual and Social History.* Detroit: Wayne State Univ. Press, 1968.

Wilhelm, Richard. *Botschafter zweier Welten.* Selections, with an introduction by Wolfgang Bauer. Düsseldorf: Eugen Diederichs, 1973.

Index